PHILOSOPHY OF EDUCATION

S. S. Chandra
Rajendra K. Sharma

PUBLISHERS & DISTRIBUTORS (P) LTD

PUBLISHERS & DISTRIBUTORS (P) LTD
7/22, Ansari Road, Darya Ganj, New Delhi
Tel.: +91-11-4077 5252, 2327 3880
E-mail: orders@atlanticbooks.com
Web: www.atlanticbooks.com

Published by Atlantic Publishers & Distributors (P) Ltd., 2004
Reprint 2006, 2020, 2022, 2023, 2024

Disclaimer

- The author and the publisher have taken every effort to the maximum of their skill, expertise and knowledge to provide correct material in the book. Even then if some mistakes persist in the content of the book, the publisher does not take responsibility for the same. The publisher shall have no liability to any person or entity with respect to any loss or damage caused, or alleged to have been caused directly or indirectly, by the information contained in this book.
- The author has fully tried to follow the copyright law. However, if any work is found to be similar, it is unintentional and the same should not be used as defamatory or to file legal suit against the author.
- If the readers find any mistakes, we shall be grateful to them for pointing out those to us so that these can be corrected in the next edition.
- All disputes are subject to the jurisdiction of Delhi courts only.

Printed & bound in India by Atlantic Print Services

PREFACE

Philosophy of Education includes discussions on Western 'isms' of Philosophy and Indian Philosophy of education from the Vedas to Contemporary Indian Philosophies. Besides clarification of the philosophical issues emphasis has been laid on drawing the philosophical implications of every 'ism'. All the eminent Great educators, Western and Indian, have been included in this book. Subject matter has been arranged according to problems of Philosophy of Education.

Philosophy is the criticism and clarification of concepts. Thus, clarification and criticism have been the twin objectives of discussion in this book. Question Bank has been given at the end of the book for preparation for examination. Thus, the book is expected to serve as an ideal textbook on the subject.

However suggestions for improvement are most welcome.

SOTI SHIVENDRA CHANDRA
RAJENDRA K. SHARMA

CONTENTS

1

Philosophy: Nature, Problems, Scope and Value

Aristotle devised metaphysics to be studied after physics. Thus etymologically speaking, metaphysics means "after-physics". It is the last science, the science of sciences. It is also the first science, the mother of all sciences. He also calls it the science of being though such a science is impossible since science deals only with processes of phenomena. Philosophy deals with Being as much as with Becoming. Thus, it includes sciences within its ken. Man experiences eternity as well as change. Philosophy as an explanation of the total experience of man seeks the integral truth.

The rationalists, in the early dawn of modern philosophy, defined metaphysics as a knowledge deduced from self-evident principles. This attempt at rationalisation or mathematisation of philosophy sought to make it more exact. But metaphysics with thought as its instrument should never dream of being exact like mathematics since thought, though real, cannot be identified with Reality. To be inexact is both a weakness as well as the strength of metaphysics. The philosopher is a lover of knowledge and never a sole possessor of it. The complete comprehension of Infinite by finite, is a logical impossibility and yet the destiny of man lies in progressing for an ever near approximation to it. Human thought which always bifurcates Reality into form and essence, subject and object, "that" and "what", can never truly represent the Reality which is an all inclusive spiritual unity. Philosophy is not a matter of logico-mathematical deduction or induction.[1] The

1. "It is subtle even than chemical subtlety and therefore not to be deduced, induced, inferred or discovered by a reasoning which proceeds from a consideration of the elements of name and form and makes that its standard."
— Sri Aurobindo, *The Advent*, Vol. X, No. 2, p. 95.

laws of geometry are not applicable to Metaphysics any more than they are applicable to chemistry or physiology. Every new field of experience has its own laws. Philosophy, the moment it loses touch with immediate experience of Reality, forgets its way in the wilderness of human ratiocinations which lead us nowhere.

The necessity of basing philosophy on experience was loudly proclaimed by the opposite school of empiricists represented by Locke. Berkeley and Hume. Locke pointed out that for its content the form and instrument of metaphysics is dependent on experience. This was a great corrective to rationalistic extreme and yet by confining metaphysics to mere sense experience, the empiricists shifted the balance in the opposite direction which led to the negation of all metaphysics. This is obvious, since if sense experience is the only experience, philosophy is a mere wild goose chase. To be itself, philosophy should widen its field to include all types of experience, religious, moral, scientific, spiritual, etc. Hume denied the supremacy of Reason. But if reason is a slave to passion, the refutation of reason, being itself ratiocination, stands self-condemned. All refutations of reason are subject to *hysteron—proteron*. Hume's "criticism of rationalism and *reductio ad absurdum* of empiricism, however, gives a lesson which philosophy should not forget. Reason is its surest instrument but to get its data, it should rely on experience."

Kant combines the Baconian idea of the extension of knowledge with the Cartesian idea of certainty. But he also fights shy of all metaphysics in the ultimate sense. Only the metaphysics of Nature and metaphysics of knowledge is possible. Thus, it was left to Hegel to revive in full vigour the ultimate status of philosophy. The object of philosophy, according to him, is to search out the concept, the purpose, the significance of phenomena and to assign to these their corresponding positions in the world and in the system of knowledge. It systematises the values in a unified whole. Here, for the first time, we find a true view of Philosophy as a systematisation of values and facts. But, by the identification of Nature with Logic,[1] Hegel arrives at an intellectualism which led Bradley to assert with a vengeance, "Metaphysics is the finding of bad reasons for what we believe on instinct."[2]

1. Hegel, Preface to *The Philosophy of Right*.
2. Bradley, F. H., *Appearance and Reality* (Preface).

This curt remark is a timely warning to all who attempt at reduction of Reality to mere thought but its rejection of all metaphysical speculation as bad reasons appears to be too sweeping. The intellect is not rejected in Spirit but transformed into a better instrument to receive the truth.

Bergson's approach here seems to be more balanced than that of Bradley. Philosophy, according to him, must take into account not only sensory but also mental and intuitive experiences. It must be based on real experience.[1] Bergson shows a true insight into the problem when he points out that the difference between various schools of philosophy is because of their fragmentary glimpse of Reality, supplemented by different kinds of intellectual interpretation and elaboration. He suggests that by mutual comparison and elimination of peculiarities, philosophers may grasp the universal character of basic Reality.[2]

Again, philosophy according to Bergson, "does not only facilitate speculation, it gives us also more power to act and live. For with it we feel ourselves no longer isolated in humanity," humanity no longer seems isolated in the Nature that it dominates.'[3] Finally, Bergson is an anti-intellectualist only when by intellect he means the faculty in its usual capacity in practical life, intellect working on data supplied by sense-perception. Otherwise, the intellect may co-operate with intuition by assembling the data of intuition and forming fluid concepts.[4] Intuition and Reason are equally necessary in philosophy.

Contemporary thought witnesses a chaos in the field of metaphysics. All sorts of arguments have been advanced to support widely divergent views of Reality. All kinds of reactions are raising head under high sounding names of 'isms'. All types

---

1. "Philosophy can only be an effort to dissolve again into the whole, the ocean of life in which we are immersed, whence we draw the very force to labour and to live and from which both matter and intellect originate."

— Bergson, *Creative Evolution*, p. 202.

2. "The object of Philosophy would be realised if this intuition could be sustained, generalised and above all, assured of external points of reference in order not to go astray."

— Bergson, *Ibid*, p. 252.

3. Bergson, *Creative Evolution*, p. 285.
4. *Ibid*, p. 251.

of methods have been put to test. The purpose of Nature beneath all this burning cauldron of ideologies, however, seems to be the manifestation of an integral philosophy which may reconcile all and transcend all and rouse itself from its dogmatic slumber. A true philosophy is an '*esprite de ensemble*', a synoptic vision of Reality. It is the intellectual search for the fundamental truth of things.

It is generally agreed by all that philosophy must be based on experience but as we have already seen, often the term experience has been limited to certain specific regions. The root fallacy underlying all the conflicting schools of philosophy is a shift from the centre to periphery, an exaltation of part as whole, a dogmatic denial of everything beyond the limited ken of intellect and finally, an unwarranted application of the logic of finite to the matters of the Infinite. 'The work of philosophy" as Sri Aurobindo rightly points out, "is to arrange the data given by the various means of knowledge, excluding none, and put them into synthetic relation to the one truth the one supreme and universal Reality."[1] Philosophy should be all comprehensive, affirmative, synthetic and spiritual. Philosophy, meaning love of wisdom (Philo=love, Sophia=wisdom) should be distinguished from mere opinion. Knowledge, as the Indians conceived it, is the knowledge of that by knowing which everything else can be known.[2] Thus, philosophy is the knowledge of Ultimate Reality. But Ultimate Reality, as Indian philosophy truly maintains, is not only Existence but also Consciousness and Bliss. Hence, philosophy, as the quest after ultimate truth, is science of value *par excellence*.[3] It should not only criticise facts but also satisfy human aspirations. It should synthesise value and existence, religion and science. To quote Sri Aurobindo, "It should be a discovery of the real reality of things by which human existence can learn its law and aim and the principle of its perfection".[4]

1. Sri Aurobindo, *The Renaissance in India*, p. 72.
2. कस्मिन्न् खलु भगवो विज्ञाने सर्व मिदं भवति।

—Mundakopanisad, I, i. 3.
3. Maitra, S. K., *Sri Aurobindo Mandir Annual*, Vol. II, p. 61.
4. Sri Aurobindo, *The Human* Cycle, p. 93.

DEFINITION OF PHILOSOPHY

A beginner in philosophy is perturbed to find that different philosophers have given different definitions of philosophy. While some philosophers have laid emphasis on psychological facts, others have given more importance to values. According to John Dewey, "Whenever philosophy has been taken seriously, it has always been assumed that it signified achieving a wisdom that would influence the conduct of life".[1] On the other hand, according to Windelband, philosophy is "...the critical science of universal values". While there is much difference in Indian and Western definitions of philosophy, one finds widely different definitions presented by Western philosophers also. Of these definitions some emphasize the critical aspect of philosophy while others lay emphasis upon its synthetic aspect. Some examples of these two types of definitions of philosophy are as follows:

(*a*) *Philosophy is a critical method of approaching experience.* Examples of this type of definitions are as follows:

1. "Philosophy is essentially a spirit or method of approaching experience rather than a body of conclusions about experience."[2]

—*Edgar S. Brightman.*

2. "It is not the specific content of these conclusions, but the spirit and method by which they are reached, which entitles them to be described as philosophical..."[3] —*Clifford Barrat.*

3. "Were I limited to one line for my answer to it, I should say that philosophy is general theory of criticism."[4] —*C.J. Ducasse*

(*b*) *Philosophy is comprehensive synthetic science.* The following definitions of philosophy emphasize its synthetic aspect:

1. "Philosophy like science, consists of theories of insights arrived at as a result of systematic reflection."[5] —*Joseph A. Leighton*

2. "Philosophy is concerned with everything as a universal science." — *Herbert Spencer*

---

1. John Dewey, *Democracy and Education*, p. 378.
2. Brightman E.S., *Introduction to Philosophy*, Henry Holt & Co., New York (1925), p. 9.
3. Barret, C., *Philosophy*, The MacMillan Co. (1935), p. 5.
4. Ducasse, C.J., *Philosophy of Art*, Dial Press, New York (1929), p. 3.
5. Leighton, J.A., *The Field: of Philosophy*, Appleton Century Crofts, New York (1910), p. 4.

3. "Our subject is a collection of sciences, such as theory of knowledge, logic, cosmology, ethics and aesthetics, as well as a unified survey".[1] — *Roy Wood Sellars*

The above mentioned definitions of philosophy show that while some philosophers have mainly emphasized critical philosophy, others have defined it as a synthetic discipline. In fact, both these viewpoints are one-sided because philosophy is both critical as well as synthetic. Literally speaking, the word 'philosophy' involves two Greek words—*Philo* meaning love and *Sophia* meaning knowledge. Thus literally speaking, philosophy means love of wisdom. It should be noted here that this definition of philosophy is different from the sense in which the word "Darshan" has been taken in India. The literal meaning of philosophy show's that the philosopher is constantly and everywhere engaged in the search for truth. He does not bother so much to arrive at final conclusions and continues with his search for truth throughout life. His aim is the pursuit of truth rather than its possession. Those who enjoy journey do not care so much about the destination, neither are they perturbed when the destination is lost in sight in spite of continued long journey.

In an effort to define philosophy, one arrives at the difficulty that there is no genus in this case and also no differentia. In defining a science one points out to the genus science and also to the particular area of the particular science which differentiates it from others. This is, however, not possible in the case of philosophy because philosophy is one and not many. Hence, in order to arrive at the meaning of philosophy you will have to discuss its problems, attitude, method, process, conclusions and results. In brief, *philosophy is a philosophical process of solving some characteristic problems through characteristic methods from a characteristic attitude and arriving at characteristic conclusions and results.*[2] Some might find this definition very vague and inadequate. But while defining science, do we not say that science is scienteing or that it is method? And can we understand this definition of science without understanding scientific method? When science cannot be understood without knowing scientific method, how can we hope to understand philosophy without knowing philosophical

1. Sellars, R.W., *The Principles and Problems of Philosophy,* The MacMillan Co., New York (1926), p. 3 .
2. Sharma, R.N., *Problems of Philosophy,* Kedarnath Ramnath (1982), p. 6.

method? Again, in understanding the definition of science we are required to understand not only scientific method but also scientific attitude, scientific process, scientific problems and scientific conclusions because all these together form a science. Therefore, what is vague and inadequate if we say that in order to understand philosophy one must understand the attitude, problems, activity, conclusions and results peculiar to it? This will also clarify the distinction between philosophy and science which has been forgotten by many philosophers.

1. Philosophical problems: Each branch of knowledge gives rise to certain peculiar problems. In the early human life on this planet when man was struck with wonder at the natural phenomena or when he found complex and conflicting phenomena in life and was filled with discontentment at the existing order of things, it was the beginning of philosophy. While the philosophy of Vedas began in wonder, the philosophy of Gautam Buddha began in discontentment with the miserable world. In the West the early beginning of philosophy was in wonder while the modern Western philosophy had its origin in doubt. In the words of Patrick, "Although philosophy among the ancients began in wonder, in modern times it usually begins in doubt"[1]

This wonder and doubt gave rise to several types of problems. A general characteristic of these problems was that they were concerned with general and universal questions and not with the questions of particular nature. In this sense the philosophical problems are different from scientific problems which have their origin in particular questions. Some examples of philosophical problems are: What is knowledge? What is world? Who has created the world? Is there a God? Who am I? What is the aim of my life? Why should I live? What is the purpose of the world? etc. In fact, a description of all the philosophical problems will almost form a book. Hence for our present purpose it is sufficient to say that philosophical problems are those which arise in the field of philosophy. Now, what is the field of philosophy? The philosophical field includes epistemology, logic, philosophy of science, sementics, metaphysics, axiology, philosophy of religion, social philosophy, political philosophy, philosophy of history, philosophy of education, etc. In brief the field of philosophy includes all knowledge but the philosopher raises questions of

1. Patrick, G.T.W., *Introduction to Philosophy*, Houghton Mifflin, p 3.

general nature only. For example, about the beautiful things his question will be what is beauty? Some philosophers have divided philosophical problems into the following three classes:[1]

(*a*) *Concerning knowledge and experience*: These include problems of epistemology, philosophy of science, sementics, etc.

(*b*) *Concerning reality or existence*: This class includes problems of metaphysics, ontology, cosmology and theology, etc.

(*c*) *Concerning values*: These include problems of axiology, aesthetics, ethics, social philosophy, philosophy of religion, political philosophy, philosophy of education, economic philosophy, philosophy of history, etc.

In the above mentioned classification of philosophical problems it should be noted that problems of different fields of philosophy cannot be absolutely isolated from each other because in fact philosophical problems are not so much problems of a particular field as problems of a particular type. In other words, as opposed to the particular problems of science, these are general problems.

Philosophical problems may be viewed from two aspects—critical and synthetic. In the critical aspect the problem of philosophy is to critically examine the postulates and conclusions of different sciences. In the synthetic aspect, its problem is to present a complete world-view based on the conclusions of sciences. Thus, in brief, philosophy is a totality of some peculiar problems of which some are problems of philosophical sciences while others are problems of criticism and synthesis of the postulates and conclusions of different sciences.

2. Philosophical attitude: Philosophical attitude begins in wonder or doubt. It is critical, reflective, tolerant, detached, continually progressive, directed by experience and reasoning and devoid of hurry in arriving at conclusions.

3. Philosophical method: The philosophical method is not exclusively employed by philosophers only. Every man, some time or the other, utilizes philosophical method in his thinking on philosophical problems. However, the philosophical method is mainly utilized by the philosopher. Secondly, the philosophical method is not absolutely different from scientific method. As has been already pointed out, philosophical problems have much

1. Bahm, A.J. *Philosophy, An Introduction*, Asia, Bombay, (1964), p. 7.

in common with the scientific problems. It goes without saying that in solving its problems concerning science, the philosopher utilizes the same methods of induction and deduction as used by a scientist. Thus, in the understanding of the philosophical method, these two methods must be discussed.

(*i*) *Induction*: The principles of different sciences are arrived at by means of inductive process. For example, in psychiatry, some general principles concerning mental diseases are discovered by observation of the behaviour of mental patients, its recording, its analysis, classification and finally generalisation to arrive at certain common principles. This is the method of induction. The philosopher does not act on the facts like the scientist. He has no laboratory work to do. He utilizes concepts and propounds new theories, *e.g.*, materialism, idealism, etc. And then he tries to explain his experiences satisfactorily on the basis of these theories. As in science so in philosophy a theory is acknowledged to the extent it satisfactorily explains experience, otherwise it is substituted by another theory which is more successful for this purpose. The cure of bad philosophy is not the negation of all philosophy but the affirmation of a better philosophy. The failure of a particular philosophical theory does not mean the failure of philosophy itself because very soon a better philosophical theory substitutes the earlier and this process goes on *ad infinitum.* The process to arrive at a general proposition by means of several particular propositions is known as the inductive process and it is equally found in philosophical as well as scientific thinking.

(*ii*) *Deduction*: Deduction is the process to arrive at certain particular propositions from a general proposition. For example, All men are mortal. Socrates is a man. Therefore, Socrates is mortal. Deductions like this are occasionally made in philosophical thinking.

Besides the two above mentioned methods, philosophical thinking involves another method peculiar to it, known as dialectical method.

(iii) Dialectical method: This is a natural method of philosophical thinking. It is a commonplace experience that when we think, over a problem we arrive at certain positive facts. This is thesis. Now, after some time we come to know some facts which are contradictory to the thesis: this is anti-thesis. Thesis and anti-thesis cannot live together for long hence they are synthesised into

a synthesis. This synthesis, arrived through anti-thesis is more comprehensive than the original thesis. Thus, knowledge grows in a dialectical process through thesis, anti-thesis and synthesis To illustrate, in the beginning a philosopher takes the world to be real as it is. As he progresses in the knowledge and experience he finds that the world is unreal. When he proceeds further in the realm of knowledge and experience he finds that the world is neither real nor unreal but both. Thus, philosophical thinking proceeds from thesis, anti-thesis to synthesis. In fact, the dialectical process is the thinking of thought. In it the man re-thinks over his earlier thought and discovers hitherto unknown facts.

While searching for the solution of his problems the philosopher utilizes two methods with regards to his experience, analysis and synthesis. While some philosophers have exclusively emphasized the value of philosophical thinking, others have absolutely denied its value. It goes without saying that these two extremist views are equally one-sided.

(*iv*) *Analysis*: Analysis means the process of distinction between different elements involved in a particular state of experience so that they might be more clear. Realist philosophers have emphasised this procedure while absolutists have advanced arguments against it.

(*v*) *Synthesis*: This process involves connecting together the scattered elements in a particular experience which brings into light new patterns and facts. The Idealist philosophers have laid emphasis on synthesis. But, as has been already pointed out, philosophical thinking requires both analysis and synthesis. Analysis, therefore, cannot be banished from the field of philosophy, though it might be useless in certain conditions.[1] The contemporary school of Logical Positivism has taken analysis as the sole method in philosophy. Though the method of logical analysis solves many intricate problems in philosophy it does not negate the value of synthesis.

Thus philosophical method is multi-sided. Though the philosophers have sometimes emphasized this or that method exclusively, yet all the above mentioned methods have been found to be useful in philosophical thinking.

---

1. See Spaulding, E.G., *The New Realism*, p. 155.

4. Philosophical activity: Once an eminent psychologist was asked what is psychology? To this, he replied: psychology is what the psychologists do. Similarly, we can say, philosophy is what the philosophers do. The activity of philosophers is philosophising. Philosophising involves thinking, criticism and the process of solving the philosophical problems through different philosophical methods. Philosophical activity begins in a state of wonder, discontentment and doubt. In it the philosopher thinks over his own experience. This thinking is critical and the attitude is philosophical. In brief, philosophical thinking has the following characteristics.

(*i*) Philosophical thinking is gradually matured with the increase in knowledge and experience.

(*ii*) Philosophical thinking is concerned with philosophical problems.

(*iii*) Philosophical thinking utilizes philosophical methods and philosophical attitude.

(*iv*) Philosophical thinking is done in individual and group situation, alone and together with others.

(*v*) Philosophical thinking is comprehensive while non-philosophical thinking is one-sided.

In the end, the real nature of philosophical thinking can be known only after one himself takes recourse to it. The above mentioned discussion only points out its chief characteristics.

5. Philosophical effects: Different types of knowledge affect the individual and group differently. This effect of philosophy is as follows:

(*i*) *Effect on the philosopher*: The effect of philosophy can be seen in the life of the philosopher, in his expectations and aspirations, in his aim of life, in his bent of mind, and in his different activities.

(*ii*) *Effect on group-life*: The effect of philosophy is seen not only in the life of the individual but also in group-life. The influence of democratic philosophy can be seen in the democratic societies of the world

(*iii*) *Effect on civilization and culture*: In any time and place contemporary philosophical trends express the process of thinking in contemporary culture Philosophical changes are the expressions of cultural changes. A comparison of the history of philosophy with the history of culture will prove this fact.

6. Philosophical conclusions: It has been said regarding philosophical conclusions that while a philosopher raises questions he does not answer them. Ordinarily, philosophical conclusions are the conclusions arrived at by the philosophers regarding philosophical problems where a question arises as to who is the philosopher. In answer to this question one may point out to the names of hundreds of thinkers who have presented widely different and mutually contradictory conclusions. A beginner in philosophy is very much perturbed to see this difference of opinion. He fails to understand as to which are the philosophical conclusions and which are non-philosophical. Another definition of philosophical conclusions may be given by calling them the conclusions of philosophical problems. Here it is difficult to prepare a final list of philosophical problems and even those which are quite well-known have been solved in so many different ways that no definite conclusions can be derived.

A non-philosophical person may raise a question as to why philosophers so much disagree regarding the conclusions of philosophical problems. Will the philosophical thinking always be unconcluded? Can all the philosophical conclusions not arrive at any final truths? Now, while we find differences in the views of different philosophers we also notice that the same philosopher presents widely different views at different times. But this is not the case with the philosophers alone. As William E. Hocking has said, "Everybody has a philosophy and the differences between man and man are chiefly philosophical differences. I will say more than that; the difference between a man and himself is a philosophical difference by which I mean that people frequently fall into a philosophy which does not belong to them and leads them away from themselves because they borrow a philosophy from somebody else".[1] The truths of this statement can be ascertained by any one who looks to his own experience and thinking.

In fact, the diversity of philosophical conclusions is not a weakness of philosophy. Different philosophers have thought over philosophical problems from different perspectives and

---

1. Hocking, V. E., Philosophy—The Business of Everyone, *Journal of American Association of University Women,* June 1937, p. 212.

however wide, integral and comprehensive a perspective might be, it always remains one-sided. The philosophical conclusions, therefore, are workable and limited. As the philosopher develops in his thinking, his philosophical conclusions are also modified and even changed. This does not mean that he is changing his position but only that he is visualizing new truths, which show the one-sidedness and limitations of the truths known earlier. In fact, the philosophical aim is never completely achieved nor is the philosophical curiosity ever completely satisfied because if this is done then philosophical thinking will stop. Actually speaking, the aim of the philosopher is not so much to arrive at certain final conclusions regarding the philosophical problems as to sustain philosophical thinking. His efforts should not be evaluated on the basis of definite conclusions but by his philosophical insight, maturity and constant thinking. To Glaucon who asked, "Who are the true philosophers?" Socrates replied, "Those who are lovers of the vision of truth.[1]

The above discussion regarding philosophical conclusions shows that the main function of the philosopher is to raise philosophical questions and constantly think over them through philosophical methods and from philosophical standpoint. Hence it cannot be said that philosophy raises certain questions and leaves them unanswered. If by leaving a question unanswered we mean the absence of any final answer to it then this is the case with the philosopher and this has been already discussed. But if leaving a question unanswered means absence of any efforts to solve it, it does not apply in the case of the philosopher. Thus, it goes without saying that the philosopher raises certain questions, meditates upon them through philosophical methods and tries to arrive at certain conclusions but does not take them as final and therefore continues with his philosophical reflections.

NATURE OF PHILOSOPHY

Whenever it is asked regarding a science as to what is its nature, it is said that it is scientific. Thus the nature of psychology, sociology, economics, political science and other social sciences is scientific. Similarly, if it is asked that what is the nature of philosophy a natural answer will be that it is philosophical. In order to understand the scientific nature of a science we have

1. Plato, *The Republic,* Book VI, p. 485

to understand scientific method, scientific attitude, scientific problems and scientific activities. Similarly, in order to explain that the nature of philosophy is philosophical, we will have to explain the philosophical problems, philosophical attitude and philosophical activities, etc. Philosophical problems are the general problems of different philosophical sciences. In its critical and synthetic aspects, the problems of philosophy are the examination and synthesis of the postulates and conclusions of different sciences. Philosophical attitude is reflective, curious, tolerant, guided by experience and reasoning and a persistent effort to reach the truth though never in a hurry to arrive at final conclusions. Philosophical methods include induction, deduction, analysis, synthesis and dialectical method. Philosophical activity begins in wonder, curiosity and discontentment at the existing order of things. This activity may be individual as well as social, alone as well as in group. The aim of this activity is to present a total world-view. Different philosophers arrive at different conclusions through philosophical methods. However different these conclusions might be, they are different from scientific conclusions as a class by the very virtue of the fact that they are philosophical. The philosophical nature of philosophy shows the effect on the individual, group and community. In brief, the philosophical problems, philosophical attitude, philosophical method, philosophical activity, philosophical conclusions and their effect on the individual and society show that the nature of philosophy is philosophical. It follows that when we say that the nature of philosophy is philosophical we mean all these problems, methods, attitude, activity, conclusions and effects characteristic of philosophy.

PROBLEMS OF PHILOSOPHY

Philosophical Problems are General Problems

Different types of questions give rise to the problems of different sciences. For example, if it is asked whether two and two make four, it is a problem for mathematics. If it is asked that in which year Akbar the Great ruled India, it is a problem for the historian. If it is asked as to what different types of climate are found in India, it is a question for geography. Similarly, the political, economic and social problems fall within the scope of political science, economics and sociology, respectively. The philosopher is not concerned with these particular problems. But does it mean that his problems are entirely unconnected with the problems of different sciences? No. In the different problems mentioned above, the questions of general nature will fall within the scope of philosophy. For example, questions like: What is space? What is time? What is beauty? What is right? What is good? What is knowledge? are philosophical problems. Thus, it is clear that philosophical problems are concerned with general questions rather than with questions of particular nature.

Types of Philosophical Problems

Philosophical problems are mainly of two types. On the one hand, there are problems of those studies which are known as philosophical sciences. These include Epistemology, Logic, Philosophy of Science, Metaphysics, Axiology, Aesthetics, Philosophy of Religion, etc. On the other hand are the problems which fall within the field of philosophy as a universal science. Both these types of philosophical problems will now be discussed in sequence.

Problems of Philosophical Sciences

As has been already pointed out, philosophical problems include problems of the sciences which are different from physical sciences in spite of bearing the name science. The main distinction between philosophical sciences and the physical sciences is that the former raise more fundamental and basic questions as compared to the latter. For example, Aesthetics is not so much concerned with the distinctions between beautiful and ugly objects as with the fundamental question about the nature of beauty and art. What is beauty? What is art? Does art lie in the artist or in his artistic expression? Similarly, other philosophical sciences raise fundamental problems in their own field. Broadly, the main problems of philosophical sciences are as follows:

(1) *Metaphysical problems*: Metaphysics is the science of existence or Reality. Its main problems are: What is Reality? Is the world one or many? What are the fundamental characteristics of creation? What is space? What is time? What is matter? What is relation? What is cause and effect? What is the purpose of creation? Is the world progressing? Is there a God? Is change real or unreal? In brief, metaphysics discusses the three aspects of Reality, *viz.,* the world, the self, and the God. Some thinkers fail to distinguish

between metaphysics and philosophy. Metaphysics is the main branch of philosophy. Thus, philosophy includes many other branches covering widely different fields than metaphysics. When a student of philosophy studies the philosophical thought of any philosopher, he has to study not only his thoughts about metaphysical problems but also about the problems falling within the field of logic, ethics, religion and epistemology, etc. However, it can be said that metaphysical problems constitute the central problems of philosophy.

(2) *Epistemological problems*: Epistemology is the science of knowledge and truth. Its problems are the fundamental problems of the process of knowledge. Is it not strange that though so many thinkers are busy in the acquisition of knowledge, not many think over the general questions concerning the nature of knowledge, its limits and the relation of knower with the known? These questions are raised in epistemology. Therefore, epistemology provides the basic foundation of knowledge. For example, an epistemological problem is concerning the question whether one knows the object outside him or only the content of his mind. Epistemology critically examines different methods to achieve different types of knowledge. Philosophers have discussed such problems since time immemorial and conclusions of philosophers like Immanual Kant of Germany have proved to be epoch-making.

(3) *Logical problems*: Logic is the science of methods of thought and the implication of judgement. It studies the structure of thought, its laws and fallacies. What is thought? What is its relation with Nature? How does mind solve a problem? What are the natural methods of thinking? What is definition, hypothesis, division, explanation, etc.? How can we arrive at the meanings of a proposition? All these are the problems falling within the scope logic. Thus, like epistemology, logic also provides fundamental basis to knowledge because every science requires thinking and logic is the science of correct or valid thinking.

(4) *Problems of semantics*: Sementics is the science of the meaning of words. It is concerned with the question about the relation of words and objects. In other words, it is a science of meaning of language. In it the different words, symbols, signs, etc., are analysed and their meanings fixed. It goes without saying that like pistemology and logic, sementics is also a basic science in the achievement of knowledge. Logical positivism, a contemporary

school of philosophy, admits sementical problems as constituting the basic problems of philosophy.

(5) *Philosophy of science*: As has been already pointed out, philosophy is intimately connected with science and discusses their problems of general nature. For example, all the sciences believe in the postulate of causality. The philosophy of science critically discusses the concept of causality and finds out its truth and limitations. The philosophy of science also critically examines different scientific methods used in different sciences and finds out conditions in which they are valid. The philosophy of science is mainly concerned with developing a world-view based on the conclusions of different sciences. Hence, in the modern times, the problems of the philosophy of science are considered to be very important. Even the philosophers who do not admit any value of philosophy in modern times, consider the function of philosophy of science to be very much valuable.

(6) *Axiological problems*: Philosophy is very much concerned with value. Axiology is the science of value. It discusses value from the philosophical point of view. Its main problems are: What is value? What are the fundamental values? What is good? What is beauty? What is art? etc. Without discussing these fundamental problems regarding values, we cannot solve many problems concerning values in our every day life. The philosopher synthesizes the facts with values in his *Weltanschauung*. While the philosophy of science discusses facts, the discussion of values falls within the scope of axiology.

(7) *Problems of aesthetics*: Aesthetics is the philosophical study of beauty. Art creates beauty. Hence, the nature of art is an aesthetic problem. This, in its turn, raises many questions such as: Does art lie in the artist or in his creation of art? Is there beauty in music, drama, picture, statue, dance, woman or is it in our mind? The artist creates beauty, then is it in the content of his mind? What are basic characteristics of art? What are the criteria of judging beauty and art? All these are problems falling within the field of aesthetics.

(8) *Ethical problems*: Ethics is the science of good, the right and wrong. Its main problems are: What is right? What is wrong? What is good? What is conscience? What is responsibility? What are rights and duties and what is their interrelation? What is

justice and how can it be attained? Thus, ethics discusses the ultimate good and explains rights and duties in its light.

(9) *Problems of philosophy of religion*: Philosophy of religion, as is clear by the title, raises philosophical problems in the field of religion. For example, Is there a common element in different religions? What are the fundamental elements of religion? What is the relation of religion with ethics? How far is religion based on Reality? What is God? Is God one or many?

(10) *Problems of social sciences*: While philosophy of science discusses problems of physical sciences, different branches of philosophy have been developed for discussing different problems of social sciences. The important among these social sciences are education, sociology, economics, political science, history, etc. Philosophy discusses the philosophical questions arising in these social sciences. This has given rise to different special branches of philosophy, *e.g.*, philosophy of education, social philosophy, economic philosophy, political philosophy, philosophy of history, etc. These philosophical disciplines based on social sciences raise general and fundamental problems in their field. For example, philosophy of education raises the fundamental question about the aim of education. Political philosophy discusses the nature of state and government, their rights and duties and their limitations. Social philosophy discusses the philosophical questions in the social relationships. Economic philosophy raises questions of fundamental importance in the fields of production, consumption and exchange. Philosophy of history examines the nature of historical and cultural processes and finds out their place in the total cosmic process. Besides problems of these special branches of philosophy, there are some other philosophical problems concerning matters of social importance, for example, the philosophical basis of marriage, family, physical development and even of dress.

Problems of Philosophy as a Comprehensive Science

As has been already pointed out, philosophy also acts as a comprehensive science. In this aspect, its important problems are as follows:

(1) *Criticism of different sciences*: This philosophical problem is two-fold—(*a*) criticism of the basic postulates of different sciences, (*b*) criticism of the conclusions of different sciences.

The critical analysis of the law of causality is an example of a problem of first type. A problem regarding the conclusions of different sciences arises in the form of the question whether man is determined by his circumstances or whether he is free. While psychology, biology and other social sciences conclude that man is determined by his circumstances and is bound to act according to them, jurisprudence, ethics and religion consider him free to act according to his will. Whether man is determined or free, this is an important question because it is closely connected with the concept of responsibility. A man can be held responsible for his acts before law only when he is free to choose among several alternatives. It is only then that his act can be considered to be wrong or unlawful and punishable. If a man is determined by his circumstances, the responsibility for his acts lies not on him but on his circumstances and he cannot be punished for what he has done. As different sciences have presented different conclusions regarding the question of man's freedom in his circumstances, this problem cannot be solved by sciences alone. On the other hand, different sciences present mutually conflicting conclusions on this issue. Such problems arising from the conflict in the conclusions of different sciences are philosophical problems. They are also considered philosophical because they are concerned not with any one particular science but fail within the field of several sciences and because each scientist is confined within his own limited field, no scientist can solve such problems. They are, therefore, left for the philosopher.

(2) *Synthesis of different sciences*: According to A. N. Whitehead, Philosophy is not one among the sciences with its own little scheme of abstractions which it works away at perfecting and improving. It is the survey of sciences, with the special object of their harmony and of their completion"[1] Thus the problem of philosophy, as a comprehensive science, is to weld the conclusions of different sciences into a world-view. Without this the conclusions of different sciences will remain scattered and cannot present a complete picture. Thus man cannot arrive at a total world-view without the help of philosophy. A world-view based on science alone will be one-sided, inadequate and deformed. The synthetic function of philosophy can be understood by the example of an

1. Whitehead, A. N., *Science and the Modern World*, The MacMillan Co., New York (1926), pp. 126-127.

elephant and several blind men. Each blind man touches some part of the elephant's body and takes it to be the whole animal because he does not know other parts of its body. The total picture of the elephant's body can be clear to a person who has eyes to see. The blind men will only form a distorted picture of the elephant Similar is the case with scientists regarding the nature of the world. Each scientist presents a picture of the world according to the conclusions arrived at in his own field. Thus, different scientists interpret the world differently. While for the biologists the world is moved by biological laws, the psychologists lay more emphasis on psychological principles. Only a philosopher can give a total world-view by a synthesis of the conclusions of different sciences. Hence, the importance of the function of philosophy as a synthetic discipline.

(3) *Historical problems of the origin of sciences*: It is a widely known fact that every science originally had its beginning in philosophy. It is hence that philosophy is called the mother of all sciences. One Finds the influence of the thought of ancient philosophers like Socrates, Plato and Aristotle in the fields of several sciences. Basically, both philosophy and science have their origin in man's curiosity and his wonder at the natural phenomena. The philosophers of the Vedas wondered as to how the hard, black cow gives soft white milk. They were amazed to see that though all the rivers flow to the sea yet the sea is never full. While these were philosophical problems, they were equally scientific. In the beginning of human knowledge, philosophy and science were intermixed. It was only after gradual specialization and subtle study that division of labour resulted in the form of different sciences, separated from the main stem of philosophy. These sciences were again divided into separate branches which were gradually considered to be independent sciences. As mother of sciences, philosophy also performs a much more important function. In the process of scientific progress, philosophy is always found at the apex. It always transcends science and goes further. It is hence that the philosophical problems of today become Scientific problems of tomorrow. But does it mean that a time will come when the philosopher will be left with no problem of his own? No. The philosopher will always move further than the scientists, transcend scientific conclusions and discover new problems to think. These problems will be taken over by the

scientists of tomorrow but then the future philosopher will again transcend sciences and discover further new problems for his philosophical reflection. Thus, new branches of philosophy will be born from the womb of philosophy and it will retain its title of the mother of sciences.

The above detailed analysis of the philosophical problems shows that philosophy is concerned with the general problems of physical and social sciences. Philosophy examines the conclusions and postulates of sciences, solves their conflict, synthesises them and presents new problems thus giving rise to new branches of science. It is clear that no description of philosophical problems can be considered to be complete and final because while on the one hand ever new problems arise in the field of new sciences, on the other hand the philosopher himself also raises new problems in new fields. A beginner in philosophy will be amazed to see the wide difference of opinion among the philosophers on the solution of different philosophical problems. On the basis of this difference of opinion, some conclude that the philosophical process is useless. But is the arrival at the destination the only reward of the journey? Those who enjoy journey are satisfied even while they do not reach the goal. In fact, the philosopher is a lover of wisdom, never a sole possessor of it. The culmination of philosophical process lies in an ever burning thirst for new knowledge and not in arriving at final conclusions.

SCOPE OF PHILOSOPHY

The above discussion of philosophical problems also clarifies its scope. Thus, the scope of philosophy can be divided into the following two parts:

(1) *Field of philosophical sciences*: The scope of philosophy includes different philosophical sciences such as metaphysics, epistemology, logic, sementics, philosophy of science, axiology, aesthetics, ethics, philosophy of religion, political philosophy, philosophy of education, philosophy of history, economic philosophy, etc. All these sciences are important parts of the field of philosophy.

(2) *Field of philosophy as a comprehensive science*: Philosophy is the science of sciences, the mother of all sciences. From this point of view, its scope includes the criticism and synthesis of the postulates and conclusions of the physical and social sciences.

(3) *Subject matter of philosophy*: The scope of philosophy clarifies its subject matter. Its subject matter includes the conclusions and postulates of all the physical and social sciences besides their general problems. In the words of C. D. Broad, "The object of philosophy is to take over the results of the various sciences, add to them the result of religious and ethical experiences of mankind and then reflect upon the whole, hoping to be able to reach some general conclusions as to the nature of the universe and as to our position and prospects in it".[1]

The above discussion makes it clear that the philosophical problems, scope and subject matter depend on philosophical sciences and the conclusions and postulates of different sciences.

BRANCHES OF PHILOSOPHY

While studying the philosophical thoughts of a philosopher, we study his thinking in different branches of philosophy. These branches of philosophy are as follows:

1. Epistemology: Philosophy is the search for knowledge. This search is critical. Hence, the first problem which arises before a philosopher is about the nature of knowledge and its limitation. Therefore, epistemology is the most fundamental branch of philosophy. It discusses philosophically truth and falsehood, validity of knowledge, limits of knowledge and nature of knowledge, knower and known, etc.

2. Metaphysics: This is the study of existence, reality or essence. Its main branches are as follows:

(*i*) *Cosmogony*: This is a study of creation. Is the world created, or is it eternal? How was world created? Why was it created? Who created the world? What is the purpose in creation? All these are the problems of cosmogony.

(*ii*) *Cosmology*: The main problems of cosmology are: Is the world one or is it many, or is it both one and many?

(*iii*) *Ontology*: Ontology is the study of ultimate reality. Is the reality one—or is it many or is it both one and many? If reality is many, what is the relation between these many elements? All these are ontological questions.

(*iv*) *Philosophy of self*: This is mainly concerned with the philosophical analysis of self. What is self? What is its relation

1. Broad, C. D., *Scientific Thought*, Harcourt Brace Co.. New York (963), p. 20.

with the body? Is it free or does it depend on the body? Is it one or many? All these are problems of philosophy of self.

(*v*) *Eschatology*: The discussion of the condition of soul after death, the nature of the other world, etc. form the subject matter of this branch of philosophy.

3. Axiology: This branch of philosophy philosophically studies value. It has been divided into the following three branches:

(*i*) *Ethics*: Ethics discusses the criteria of right and good.

(*ii*) *Aesthetics*: Aesthetics discusses the nature and criteria of beauty.

(*iii*) *Logic studies truth*: The subject-matter of logic includes the methods of judgment, types of propositions, hypothesis, definition, comparison, division, classification and fundamental laws of thoughts, etc.

4. Philosophy of science: This branch of philosophy is concerned with the philosophical examination of the postulates and conclusions of different sciences.

5. Philosophies of social sciences: The philosophical problems in different social sciences give birth to different branches of philosophy of which the main are as follows:

(*i*) *Philosophy of education*: This is concerned with the aim of education and the basic philosophical problems arising in the field of education.

(*ii*) *Social philosophy*: This branch of philosophy discusses the philosophical basis of social processes and social institutions.

(*iii*) *Political philosophy*: This branch of philosophy is concerned with the forms of government, forms of state and other basic problems arising in the political field.

(*iv*) *Philosophy of history*: The subject-matter of this branch of philosophy is the nature of historical process, its purpose and its relation with the cosmic process.

(*v*) *Philosophy of economics*: This branch of philosophy studies the aim of man's economic activities and the fundamental problems arising in the economic field.

Besides the above mentioned branches of philosophy based on sciences, there may be certain comparatively lesser branches of philosophy such as philosophy of physics, philosophy of commerce, philosophy of physical education, philosophy of marriage, philosophy of family, etc. These, however, are not sufficient to form independent branches of philosophy.

6. Sementics: The most important branch of philosophy, according to the contemporary school of Logical Positivism, is sementics which is concerned with the determination of the meanings of different words used in different languages.

PHILOSOPHICAL ATTITUDE

It is said that one day Gautama Buddha went out in the city and saw a dead body, a patient and an old man. He was much perturbed to see their miserable condition. His thinking was disturbed and he felt that the world is momentary and full of misery. His faith in the life was disturbed. He began to meditate upon the cause of misery in the world. He deliberated on various alternatives in this connection. For years together he remained wandering in the forests, meditating on the causes of misery and the ways to remove it. Though in the beginning he was much disturbed at the state of misery in the world but while meditating on its causes his attitude was detached and unemotional. His mind was open and his view comprehensive. He meditated on the experiences of his life and tried to find out root cause of misery and the ways to remove it.

The above mentioned situation shows the fundamental characteristics of philosophical attitude. Sometimes one finds a bit different philosophical attitude than that of Buddha. When the ancient sages of the age of Vedas wondered at the phenomena of Nature their philosophical attitude was that of wonder. On the other hand, the philosophy of the French philosopher Descartes began in doubt. He doubted in the efficiency of his sensations and perceptions. How can I know that my senses are not deceiving me? What is the proof that I exist? How can I be sure about the existence of the world around me? Thus, failing to find any solid proof of the existence of things around him and also of his own, Descartes' mind was full of doubt. This doubt was fundamental in his philosophical attitude.

Characteristics of Philosophical Attitude

The above mentioned example of the philosophical attitude of Gautama Buddha, the seers of the Vedas and Descartes, the father of modern Western philosophy, shows the following chief characteristics of philosophical attitude:

(1) *Sense of wonder*: Most of us are so much used to the world around us that we do not wonder even at things which are marvelous otherwise. The philosopher is a man who is given a childlike sense of wonder. He wonders at the system, sequence, variety and mutually contradictory phenomena in the world around him and tries to find out the cause behind all this. This was the beginning of philosophy in India and elsewhere.

(2) *Doubt*: Philosophical attitude is against dogmatism. It examines every belief, it doubts in everything not because doubting is a philosophical habit but because the philosopher is in search of some solid proof for the existence of things around him and also that of himself.

(3) *Criticism*: Thus, the philosophical attitude is critical. The philosopher does not accept a thing as it is but examines it and arrives at rational conclusions.

(4) *Reflection*: Critical thinking involves reflection. Hence the philosophical attitude is reflective.

(5) *Tolerance*: The philosopher is prepared to see every aspect of a problem. His mind is open and his standpoint liberal and tolerant.

(6) *Acceptance of the guidance of experience and reason*: The philosopher thinks in the light of his experience and with the help of his reasoning. He has no prejudice and preconception of his own. He is prepared to go wherever his reason might take him, however, this may hit at his hitherto held beliefs. It is hence that the great social reformer Sankara of India declared the world as Maya.

(7) Absence of hurry in arriving at the conclusions: The philosopher does not arrive at any conclusions unless he has some solid proofs for them. He does not worry about the amount of time involved in the process as he is in no hurry to reach the conclusions.

(8) *Detachment*: The philosopher is neither a sceptic nor a dogmatist. He reflects with a detached and unemotional attitude.

(9) *Persistence*: The philosopher ceaselessly persists in his thinking unless he arrives at some satisfactory conclusion. And because his conclusions are never final his search continues throughout his life.

To conclude, the philosophical attitude involves a sense of wonder, doubt, criticism, reflective thinking, tolerance, acceptance of the guidance of experience and reason, absence of hurry in arriving at the conclusions, detached attitude and a persistent effort for the search of truth.

As a comprehensive science, philosophy has two aspects—critical and synthetic. This synthetic aspect of philosophy is known as speculative aspect because the philosopher has to take recourse to speculation in his philosophical synthesis. The philosophical synthesis is not merely a putting together of bits of knowledge. It involves speculation. It is hence that the philosopher arrives at new truths and sees further than the scientist. The critical philosophy critically examines the postulates and conclusions of different sciences. On the other hand the synthetic philosophy presents a world-view by a synthesis of the conclusions of different sciences. The former type of philosophy is inadequate without the latter. The critical philosophy is discursive. The synthetic philosophy is constructive. The critical philosophy finds out the validity of the postulates of different sciences and examines their conclusions. It solves the problems which fall in the field of more than one sciences. On the other hand, the synthetic philosophy presents a total picture of the world arrived at by a synthesis of the conclusions of science. Thus, it synthesizes various sciences and also points out to those fields of knowledge where no research has been made so far. Thus it leads to the birth of new sciences. It is not that the critical philosophy examines the postulates and conclusions of sciences only, the philosopher also examines postulates and conclusions of other philosophers and presents a more comprehensive world-view by a synthesis of different philosophies.

PHILOSOPHY AND COMMON SENSE

Though the philosophical process is different from the process of common sense, it cannot be said that the two are entirely different. As Aldous Huxley has said, "Men live in accordance with their philosophy of life, their conception of the world." Common sense involves the intelligence required in understanding our day-to-day life. Life is impossible without it. On the other hand, in philosophy one solves the basic and general problems arising in his experience. While common sense is concerned with particular questions it is in adequate without the understanding of basic and general problems. Therefore, philosophy and common sense are mutually complementary. Common sense is certainly not the maximum of philosophy but it is definitely the minimum of it. The systematic form of common sense observations provide the basis for science and the systematization of scientific conclusions leads to philosophy. Thus while common sense is narrow, philosophy is comprehensive. It is hence that some Indian philosophers have equated common sense with ignorance. But ignorance is not the contradictory of knowledge. It points out to knowledge negatively. This shows the intimate relationship of philosophy and common sense. In his everyday life the man finds much conflict and contradiction in the matters of common sense. When this conflict becomes excessive it gives rise to philosophical problems because the man is in need of going to the depth of the common sense problems and find out the harmony lying under the apparent contradictions. This is done by philosophy. Therefore, philosophy is not only required by the philosopher but also by the common man. The philosopher should never leave common sense. By being a philosopher he should be rather more successful in his everyday life though while engaged in the philosophical process he might forget the world around him. However high may be the mind of the philosopher, his feet should always rest on the solid earth because ultimately man is the son of this terrestrial world and he has to grow here. Thus, it is clear that the philosopher cannot do without common sense.

VALUE OF PHILOSOPHY

Philosophy influences both the personal and social aspects of human life. Most of the Western philosophers have considered the goal of philosophy to be the achievement of knowledge, but the aim of philosophy is not merely intellectual. It is true that philosophy gives us knowledge but, as Sri Aurobindo has pointed out, "Still the truth once discovered must be realisable in our inner being and our outer activities; if it is not, it may have an intellectual but not an integral importance; a truth for the intellect, for our life, it would be no more than the solution of a thought puzzle or an abstract reality or a dead letter". The existentialist school of our time has emphasised the life of the individual, his feelings, expectations and frustrations, in philosophical thinking. It is a revolt against logical and naturalistic system building, analytic intellect and dead thought which make philosophy a useless search for the ideas which are entirely unconnected with our practical life. Therefore, the contemporary school of pragmatism emphasizes the pragmatic value of truths. Humanism lays emphasis upon the Protegorian principle of *Homo Mensura.* The instrumentalism of John Dewey explains knowledge and intelligence as instruments for success in life. Hence philosophy and life are closely connected. This can be seen particularly in the following points:

1. *Value of philosophy in personal life*: In our personal life we daily come across the problems when we have to decide between right and wrong. This decision requires criterion of right and wrong or good and ultimate good. To present such a criterion is the job of moral philosophy. Thus, it is clear that we are in need of philosophy at every step of our life. Man cannot live a thoughtless life. He has to always think over many types of problems. Is it not strange that though many people think, few know the laws of thought and the ways of thinking? The laws of thought and the ways of thinking form the subject-matter of an important branch of philosophy known as Logic. A man may sometimes think properly even without any knowledge of logic but a knowledge of logic will definitely make his thinking better and more valid. In the modern times, everywhere in urban areas one hears talk about art. Many want to refine their lives. Many want to live amidst beautiful things and beautify their surroundings. But how many persons think about the basic questions as to what is beauty? What is art? These questions are raised by an important branch of philosophy known as Aesthetics. Many people are prepared to sacrifice their lives for the sake of their values. What is this value? What are the ultimate values? These questions are answered by Axiology. Everyman, sometime or the other, tries to know what will happen to him after death? Is there a world other than our own? What happens to the man when he dies? These questions are raised in Eschatology, an important branch of philosophy. Again, some thoughtful persons, when they reach at some crossing in life, think as to where they have to go? Why have they come to this world? What is the aim of life? Who am I? These questions are raised in philosophy of self. When the man looks at the towering tops of the mountains, murmuring sounds of the forests, pitch-dark nights, roaring oceans and ferocious earthquakes and other peculiar natural phenomena a question

rises in his mind as to what is this world? What is its nature? How has it been made? Who made it? Why did he make it? All these questions are discussed in Cosmology and Cosmogony. Thus, numerous types of questions that are raised in our everyday life fall beyond the scope of common sense or science because they are basically philosophical questions. The value of philosophy in a man's life is, therefore, quite clear.

2. *Value in behaviour towards others*: Whereas philosophy influences personal life, it influences social life as well. Our behaviour towards others is determined by our philosophies. If a man considers others as ends in themselves, his behaviour will be different from that of those persons who consider others as mere instruments to achieve their own selfish ends. Every man has divine element in him, this is a philosophical attitude. Everybody is a thief, this is a different philosophical attitude. It can be easily understood that these different philosophical attitudes will lead to different types of behaviour towards others. In fact, it will not be an exaggeration to say that at the root of the behaviour of different persons, there are some philosophical difficulties. For example, the hatred of a communist towards a capitalist is the result of Marxist philosophy.

3. *Value in political life*. Philosophy also influences political life. Various types of political philosophies such as democratic socialism, communism, totalitarianism, anarchism, etc., lead to different types of government and state and to a lot of difference concerning human rights and the different aspects of political life.

4. *Value in economic life*: Every one has to earn money in order to earn his livelihood. The question is as to what is the aim of life. Is money an end or merely a means to it? This is a philosophical question and on the answer to it, depend not only the economic activities of the individuals but also those of nations. The form of production, consumption and exchange very much depends on the answer to this philosophical question. According to Gandhi, capitalists are the trustees of the capital of society. On the other hand, according to Karl Marx, the capitalists are the exploiters of the proletariat. These two different philosophical attitudes have widely influenced economic life.

5. *Value in social life*: Society is a web of social relationships. These relationships are found in different institutions such as family, marriage, business, etc., and in thousands of associations. All

these are influenced by philosophy. For example, whether the wedlock between male and female is a social contract or whether marriage is a religious sacrament, this is a philosophical question on the answer to which depends the form, stability and result of marriage in a particular society. Similarly, the relationships between parents and their children in a family do not depend on the biological and psychological attachments alone but also on their philosophical attitude towards life. Whether the children should be brought up as ends in themselves or whether they are mere instruments for the progress of the family, this is a philosophical question the answer to which determines many important issues in a joint family. Similarly, what are the rights of society over the individual and do these rights have a limit? How far should the individual accept social control and how far can he evade it? All these are philosophical questions which have important social influence.

6. *Value in cultural life*: The philosophy of a nation is the index of its cultural progress. Thus, philosophy influences each aspect of culture. The forms of dance, music, art, literature, etc., are very much influenced by philosophy. A healthy philosophy will lead to a healthy attitude towards all these. To illustrate, Indian philosophy is mainly spiritual, therefore, one finds the stamp of spirituality on Indian dance, music, art, literature, etc. On the other hand. Western philosophy is materialistic and, therefore, Western culture bears the stamp of materialism. To quote John Dewey, "Thus philosophy makes a change of culture. In forming patterns to be conformed to in future thought and action it is additive and transforming in its role in the history of civilization'.[1] This is expressed in even more clear terms by Archie J. Bahm when he says, "Without philosophy then there would be no civilization, and civilizations differ from one another as romantic, rationalistic, pacific, aggressive, mystical and mundane, partly because of their philosophical differences".[2]

The philosophy of a nation represents the infancy, adolescence and maturity of a nation's culture. Philosophical progress manifests cultural progress. In a nation where there is no philosophical progress, its culture is dead. Cultural revolutions

1. John Dewey, *Philosophy and Civilization*, G. P. Putnam's Sons, New York, 1931, p. 6.
2. Bahm, A. J., *Philosophy—An Introduction*, p. 27.

have also coincided with philosophical crises. In Greece when Socrates was made to drink hemlock it was not because of the enmity of people against him only but also because of his opposition to philosophy of the community of his time. Similarly, many other great men have sacrificed their lives by challenging the philosophies of their contemporary philosophers and thus changing it through their blood.

7. *Value in educational field*: Though now-a-days, the number of students of philosophy and departments of its teaching in Indian universities is gradually becoming less and less, no thoughtful person denies the value of philosophy in educational field. In the words of Blanshard and others, "The function of philosophy in universities is properly the same as its function in the cultural development of a society to be the intellectual conscience of the community".[1]

The most fundamental question in the field of education is concerning its aim? This question raises another question as to what is man, because what he is not, he cannot become. He can become only that which is already implicit in him. Man's nature is, therefore, a philosophical question on the answer to which have developed so many philosophies of education which are the foundations of different modern methods of teaching.

8. *Value in the field of knowledge*: In the modern times, many educated persons who swear by science, consider philosophy to be useless in the age of science because they are ignorant of the function of philosophy in the field of science. It can be said without exaggeration that without a philosophical basis, any knowledge is imperfect, because no total picture can be presented without the synthetic function of philosophy. Without this total picture there will always be tension in the field of knowledge which leads to philosophical activities. As Aristotle has said, "Whether we philosophise or not, we must philosophise". This has been expressed by Perry in somewhat different terms when he says, "Philosophy is neither accidental nor supernatural, but inevitable and normal"[2]. Besides its synthetic function, another important function of philosophy is the criticism of the postulates and conclusions of different sciences. Whenever a scientist delves

1. Blanshard and Others, *Philosophy in American Education*, Harper & Bros., New York (1945), p. 80.
2. Perry, *The Approach to Philosophy*, p. 22.

deeper in his own particular field, he reaches a depth where the process of his thinking is not scientific but philosophical. This can be seen in the thinking of many a great scientists of the world. The importance of philosophy in the field of knowledge is, therefore, quite clear.

From the point of view of different aspects of the individual and social life, and in different fields of knowledge, the discussion of the value of philosophy shows the utility of its study. In the words of J.W. Cunningham, "Philosophy thus grows directly out of life and its needs. Everyone who lives, if he lives at all reflectively, is in some degree a philosopher".[1] In the words of Chestertan,' 'The most practical and important thing about a man is his view of universe—his philosophy. The employee is at the mercy of the philosophy of this employer and the employer stakes his business on the philosophy of his employees".[2]

---

1. Cunningham, J.W., *Problems of Philosophy*, p. 5.
2. Quoted by Hocking, *Types of Philosophy*, p. 4.

2

Philosophy and Education

In order to comprehend the close relationship of philosophy and education the aspirant should first know the various branches of philosophy and then study their relationship with education. The most important branches of philosophy are: Metaphysics, Epistemology and Axiology. Again, the relationship of Philosophy and Education should be sought in different fields of education such as the aims and ideals, the methods of teaching, the curriculum, the school administration, discipline and finally evaluation. All these branches of education are based upon philosophical foundation. Needless to say that as the philosophical foundation differs so differ the aims and ideals, the teaching methods, the school administration and discipline in different educational systems. This will be explained in details in our study of the different systems of philosophy of education. At present, our discussion will be confined to provide a summary picture of the close relationship of philosophy and education.

METAPHYSICS AND EDUCATION

Aristotle developed the study of Metaphysics to be studied after physics. While physics studies the laws of the external form of existence, metaphysics thinks over the real essence of things. Its main problems are: What is the nature of existence? What is reality? What is truth? What are its different forms? Is the world one or many? What is time? What is substance? What is causality? What is fact? What is the purpose or aim? What is change? What is novelty? What is similarity? Who am I? Is there a purpose in creation? Is the world determined or free? Is there a God? Has the world progressed? etc. Thus the subject-matter of metaphysics includes the self, the world, and the God. Its scope includes ontology, philosophy of self, cosmogony, cosmology and theology. Ontology is the science of reality.

The metaphysics, in brief, deals with reality in man, world and hereafter. This has a close bearing upon the aims and ideals of education. The metaphysical attitude provides the educationists the proper perspective for devising aims and ideals of education. What we want to make out of man depends upon his nature and place in the universe. Again, the concept of self is the basis of the development of character, the central aim of education. Know thyself and be thyself is the universally acknowledged aim of education. The concept of world is directly concerned with the individual's relationships with society and nature. While Indian philosophy emphasises harmony between man and the world the Western philosophers have made too much of man's desire to overpower Nature. While the former philosophy has been the foundation of educational institutions like Vishwabharati or Sri Aurobindo's International University, the other approach is the philosophy behind the technological and scientific education of today. In fact the more integral is the world-view the more multi-sided will be the education based upon it. In the end, moral and religious education is based upon the metaphysical concept of God. This does not mean that moral education must necessarily be linked to religious education. It only shows that our explanation of the ultimate reality or the total reality, call it God or anything else, has important bearing upon education particularly its aims and ideals and therefore its means and plans.

The most important metaphysical theories which have influenced education are: Naturalism, Idealism, Pragmatism and Realism. Naturalism has been manifest in different types of theories such as Atomic naturalism, Scientific naturalism, Mechanistic naturalism and Historical naturalism. These will be discussed in detail in our chapter on Naturalism as a philosophy of education. The most important metaphysical theory in the field of education is idealism. Idealism has been subjective, objective, phenomenalistic and absolute. These will be discussed in details in our chapter on Idealism as a philosophy of education. The most influential metaphysical theory in today's field of education, however, is pragmatism. This is closely linked to Instrumentalism and Humanism. These will be discussed in our chapter on Pragmatism as a philosophy of education. In the end the metaphysical theory known as Realism has very much influenced education concerning science and technology. This will be discussed in sequence.

EPISTEMOLOGY AND EDUCATION

Epistemology is the branch of philosophy which is concerned with the discussion of the problems concerning knowledge. Its main problems are: What is the relation between the knower and known? Is the content of knowledge identical with the external object or is it different from it? How can we know that our knowledge is a real knowledge of the object? What are the limits of knowledge? What are the sources of knowledge? etc. Besides, the epistemologist raises certain other questions such as: What is knowledge? Is the knowledge of knower possible, if not, then what is known? If the known is an object then what is this object? Is the knowledge of the existence of an object possible without its being known? How can we distinguish between true and false knowledge? What is ignorance? Is it a form of knowledge or different from it? What is the process of knowledge? Do we know something which was already existent before our knowledge of it? What is the meaning of forgetting of knowledge? What is the basis of validity of knowledge? What are the errors possible in the process of knowledge? Is our knowledge definite or is the definiteness based purely on our feeling and faith? How is it that some beliefs are considered to be more valid than others? What are the distinctions between different types of knowledge? What are the relations of knowledge with science and philosophy?

The above mentioned description of epistemological problems clarifies the scope of epistemology. Its subject matter is the process, methods, object characteristics, conditions, validity and fallacies of knowledge. Epistemology is the philosophical discussion of all these problems. It should be remembered here that epistemology uses the philosophical methods of induction and deduction, synthesis and analysis. In it is adopted the philosophical attitude which is detached, tolerant, persistent and guided by experience and reasoning. One finds different conclusions presented by different epistemologists regarding epistemogical problems. While according to the realist philosophers knowledge is the knowledge of objects, the idealists define it as the knowledge of ideas. While some epistemologists think that the presence of object is necessary for knowledge, and therefore, every knowledge is a knowledge of both knower and known, others think that the knowledge of known is different from the knowledge of knower. Thus, we find realists, idealists and empiricists, rationalists and critical philosophers in the field of epistemological problems. About the possibility of knowledge one finds different approaches such as agnostic, sceptic and mystic. All these approaches have thrown light on different aspects of knowledge. Besides, different epistemologists have criticized the views of other fellow epistemologists and this discussion has given rise to an interesting literature. Kant's famous book *Critique of Pure Reason* is a permanent contribution to epistemological literature.

The explanation given above shows the importance of epistemology for education. Empiricist school of philosophy discussed the methods and value of empirical knowledge. Its opposite Rationalist school pointed out how some of the knowledge is innate. Skepticism shows the limits of knowledge. David Hume rightly pointed out that certainty can be possible only in mathematics and not in the field of sciences. Agnosticism shows the relativity of human knowledge. Criticism shows that our knowledge is neither *a-priori* nor *a-posteriori.* It shows that knowledge is synthetic, requiring sensibility, understanding and reasoning. Intuitionism shows that intellect and intuition are complementary. Mysticism shows the value of spiritual experiences in the field of religion. Pragmatism rightly maintains that the value of knowledge is in its use. Instrumentalism rightly points out that reason is an instrument for the satisfaction of human needs. Humanism rightly shows that the criterion of all knowledge is man himself and there is no ultimate knowledge. Experimentalism and relativism rightly point out that knowledge is experimental and relative. Thus all the schools of epistemology show the methods, limits and value of knowledge. They supply the necessary foundation for all knowledge, scientific and otherwise.

AXIOLOGY AND EDUCATION

Axiology includes three normative sciences: Logic, Ethics and Aesthetics. All these three are intimately related to education.

LOGIC AND EDUCATION

The term logic is derived from the Greek word 'Logos', which means reason or expression of reason in words, that is, discourse. Etymologically, therefore, Logic is the science of reasoning or argument. According to Dewey and Stabbing reasoning is reflective thinking, and reflective thinking is a process of finding way out of some difficulty or problem by weighing the evidence on the basis of a tentative hypothesis and thereby reaching some conclusion. The reasoning can be either deductive or inductive. In the deductive reasoning we argue from a general principle to a particular conclusion. For example, we say that since all men are mortal, an X, who is a man, is mortal. But if we argue that since X, Y, Z, who are men are subject to death, every man must be subject to death, we are arguing inductively. In logic we study the general principles governing both types of reasoning. Accordingly, we may define Logic as the science of laws of thought and reasoning. According to Morris R. Cohen and Ernest Negel, "Logic may be said to be concerned with the question of the adequacy or probative value of different kinds of evidence Thus, according to this definition of logic, logic is concerned with both conclusive as well as partial evidence. Traditionally, logic was concerned only with conclusive evidence. These authors, however, represent the modern approach which includes not only conclusive but also partial evidence as the subject-matter of logic. In the words of Cohen and Negel, "Logic may, therefore, be also defined as the science of implication, or of valid inference (based on such implication)". Thus logic is not concerned with the factual questions such as about the psychological processes of reasoning actually happening in mind, etc. Factual questions are material issues. They crop-up in an enquiry along with the questions concerning the implication. While evidence includes facts it also includes premises and conclusions the relation between which is known as implication. The former is the subject-matter of physical sciences or human sciences, while the latter comes within the field of logic. In the words of Cohen and Negel, "Logic as a distinctive science is concerned only with the second—with the relation of implication between propositions. Thus the specific task of logic is the study of the conditions under which one proposition necessarily follows and may therefore be deduced from one or more others, regardless of whether the latter are in fact true".

The above discussion shows that logic is the basis of all knowledge. It is hence called the science of sciences. It studies various intellectual processes such as thinking, reasoning and judgement. All education is concerned with theory and practice. While the theory is arrival at by induction, the practice depends upon deduction. Both induction and deduction are the two important branches of logic. The knowledge of logic helps us in avoiding error and arriving at correct generalisation in every field of knowledge. It resolves doubts and points out fallacies. It is intellectual exercise necessary for all the serious students. The teacher must know logic in order to have successful communication.

ETHICS AND EDUCATION

According to philology, the word ethics is derived from the word Ethos, which means character. In this way, ethics is the science of character, habits of activity or behaviour of human beings. Ethics is also called Moral Philosophy. The word moral is a derivative from the Latin word 'mores' meaning conventions or practice. In this way ethics literally means the science of convention or practice. Ethics is the science of human conduct. Habits and behaviour are related to the permanent peculiarities of human character. Conduct is the mirror of character. Thus ethics is the science of character or habit. It evaluates human habits, character and voluntary determinations and discusses their propriety or otherwise.

Ethics considers the duties of human beings. It is an ethical science and it pronounces ethical decisions upon conduct. There is a motive in conduct. In it there is voluntary determination. It manifests character. Character is manifested in determinations. Determination is the activated form of character. Therefore, it studies what is right and what is wrong in character. But the propriety of habits and determination can be determined by measuring them with the ideals of life. These goods too have classes. Supreme good determines the propriety of the immediate good. For example, every student must take the examination, it being his immediate good because he has laboured for it throughout the year. But in some conditions it may be improper to do so. To take an example, he may have to desist from taking the examination in order to nurse his mother. Here the propriety of the immediate good of sitting for the examination is determined by the supreme good of postulating the superiority of duty to oneself. Thus ethics is above all the science of the supreme good. It studies the ideals of human life. It shows what ought to be done and what ought not to be done. In the words of James Seth,"As the science of the Good, it is the science *par excellence* of the ideal and the ought".[1]

Ethics is the science of character. But it is different from the natural and factual sciences. It is a normative science. In Muirnead's words, "It is related not merely to temporal behaviour but to behaviour in the form of the basis of legal decision".[2] Its function is to give decisions on behaviour, whether the behaviour is right or wrong.

According to Mackenzie, 'Ethics can be defined as the study of what is right or good in conduct".[3] In this definition ethics has been accepted as the study of both right and good. But there is difference between right and good. 'Rectus' the Latin word from which right has been derived, means straight or according to law. Thus, good behaviour will correspond to law. Good comes from the German 'gut', meaning that which is useful for the supreme good. In this instance, good is that which leads to supreme good. Mostly good is taken to mean an end, not a means to an end.

According to Prof. J.S. Mackenzie, the study of ethics admits classification into at least four divisions: "(1) Psychology of ethical consciousness; (2) Sociology of an ethical life; (3) Theories of ethical criterion; and (4) The application of this criterion in ethical life".[4] These four divisions of ethics are the foundations of all education. The most widely accepted aim of education is man making or character building. As the science of character ethics analyses the psychology of ethical consciousness. It shows how different moral norms evolve in different circumstances but then it examines the validity of these norms and provides solid basis for social ethos of the educand. It examines the theories moral of standard and shows the possibility of arriving at a correct ethical criterion.

1. Seth, J., *A Study of Ethical Principles*, William Blackwood and Sons Ltd., London (1908), p. 37.
2. Muirnead, J.H., *The Elements of Ethics*, John Murray, London (1895), p. 33.
3. Mackenzie, J.S., *A Manual of Ethics*, University Tutorial Press Ltd., London (1929), p. 1.
4. *Ibid*, p. 25.

Ethics is not only theoretical, it also helps in the application of moral principles in actual life. Ethical activities are accompanied by a feeling of vice and virtue. Ethics details the criterion for this vice and virtue. Its scope includes the descriptions of good qualities and bad qualities. Due to the relation of good and bad to every human activity, the field of ethics includes the conclusions of other sciences and arts. Ethics gives moral judgments on these too. In this way, many psychological, political, economic, sociological, religious and philosophical problems come to be included in the field of ethics. Philosophical problems like the real form of human personality, voluntary nature of volition, immortality of the soul, the existence of God, and unity and the moral order in the universe, etc., are included in ethics. The sociological problem relating the relation between the individual and the society is also an ethical problem. In this way, in brief, it may be said that wherever there is human behaviour and human volitions, there is scope for ethics. In John Dewey's words, "The foremost conclusion is that morals have to do with all activity into which alternative possibilities enter. For wherever they enter, a difference between better and worse arises".[1]

AESTHETICS AND EDUCATION

Aesthetics is the science of beauty, as logic is the science of truth and ethics is the science of good. Education seeks to realise the true, the good and the beautiful. Therefore, it requires not only logic and ethics but also aesthetics. The aim of education is to realise all-round development of the educand. In this development moral and aesthetic developments occupy foremost place. While moral development requires knowledge of ethics, aesthetic development requires training in aesthetics. Aesthetics again, is the basis of all literary and artistic criticism. It supplies the philosophical basis to literature and art. As literature and art contribute significantly to education, the value of aesthetics in education is clear.

SOCIAL PHILOSOPHY AND EDUCATION

The term 'Social Philosophy' includes two words, social and philosophy. Literally, it is the philosophy of the society. What is society? Society is the network of social relations. Here society

1. John Dewey, *Human Nature and Conduct* in "The World's Great Thinkers Series", "The Social Philosophers," Edited by Commins and Linscott. p. 449.

means general society, not any particular society, because philosophical view points towards universality even though, in actuality, it may become limited. Hence the subject of social philosophy is the human society as a whole. It does not concern itself with creatures other than the man, for, in the first place, they do not have any society, and in the second place, if at all they have one, their society is fundamentally different from the human society. Social philosophy is not concerned with nature either, because the relations that exist between the objects of nature are different from social relations. The latter have mental or psychic elements and are linked with consciousness. They are also coloured with feelings, emotions, instincts and passions. Bereft of these psychological elements, human relations are nothing more than the relations that exist between objects. Mere co-existence, either among the people of one nation or among the nations themselves, is not enough for social relations. In the field of social relations, social change and regulation cause integrative and disintegrative processes. Both similarity and dissimilarity' are to be found in society though the former is more important. Unity in diversity is the basic trait of social relations. That explains why in the modern world, which is inhabited by various races, nations and states, etc., the consciousness of one world has become so powerful and the notion of world government so popular. Dissimilarity breeds inter-dependence among the social units, causes division of labour, differentiation and specialisation, and then leads to mutual co-operation and organisation. Society is to be measured not by men and their groups but by the interactions and inter-relations that exist among them. Precisely, these are the subjects studied by a social philosophy. It seeks to determine the facts and values involved in the network of social relations. It looks at the human society in all its perspectives, past, present and future; east, west and universal. Its approach is all-pervasive. It evaluates the human achievements in the light of eternal values and pronounces judgements upon them. It analyses various groups, committees, institutions, associations and their inter-relations from the philosophical viewpoint.

The social philosopher examines the basic principles of human behaviour and supreme values of human life, and thus prepares a solid ground for social sciences. Just as the philosophy of science provides philosophical basis for physical sciences, social philosophy provides philosophical basis for social sciences. It studies the philosophical questions involved in social phenomena and processes. It views the problems of the social scientist from the philosophical point of view, and evaluates the social facts in the light of supreme social values. Different social sciences study different aspects of social life. Social philosophy seeks to harmonise the different conclusions of different social sciences and to fulfil the chasm amongst them. Without social philosophy, the knowledge of social sciences would be incomplete and scattered. In regard to the analysis of supreme issues, every social scientist has to consult the social philosopher. For example, the impact of Plato's and Aristotle's social philosophy may be seen on the different social scientists. In modern times, American behaviourist thinker, William James, and the utilitarian philosopher, John Dewey, have exercised considerable influence on different social sciences.

The basic problem of education is now to secure man's development. For this it is necessary to know what is man. Social philosophy analyses human nature and finds out how far man is naturally social and how far not. While prescribing syllabi for educational institutions it is essential to keep in view what type of society we want to create. It is clear that social philosophy constructs the philosophical foundations of the educational system.

3

Philosophy of Education

Our discussion of the concept of education and the concept of philosophy form the basis of arriving at the definition of philosophy of education. Thus philosophy of education is essentially a method of approaching educational experience rather than a body of conclusions. It is the specific method which makes it philosophical. Philosophical method is critical, comprehensive and synthetic. Therefore, philosophy of education is the criticism of the general theory of education. It consists of critical evaluation and systematic reflection upon general theories. It is a synthesis of educational facts with educational values. In brief it is a philosophical process of solving educational problems through philosophical method, from a philosophical attitude to arrive at philosophical conclusions and results. Thus it aims at achieving general and comprehensive results. This clarification of the definition of education will be further clarified by a discussion of the scope and nature of philosophy of education. It should be noted here that philosophy of education is a species of the genus philosophy, with the differentia that its proper scope is confined to the field of education. Thus it is philosophy in the field of education.

SCOPE AND NATURE OF PHILOSOPHY OF EDUCATION

The scope of a subject directly follows from its definition. Therefore, the scope of philosophy of education is concerned with the problems of education. These problems are general in nature, such as the interpretation of Nature, the world and the universe, explanation of aims and ideals, the relationship of the various constituents of the field of education. The main problems of philosophy of education include aims and ideals of education, analysis of human nature, relationship of education and state, educational values, theory of knowledge and its relationship to education, economic system and education, the place of school in educational system, the curriculum and the process of education and finally the relationship of education and social progress.

The above mentioned problems of philosophy of education constitute its scope and clarify its nature. Its scope includes a critical evaluation of the different aims of education held and propagated from time to time such as character building, man making, human development, preparation for adult life, development of citizenship, utilisation of leisure; training for civic life, training for international living, total development of personality, evolution of democratic society, realisation of social change, realisation of cultural man, adjustment of society and individual and finally self-realisation and spiritual emancipation, These and other aims of education presented by educational thinkers in different times and climes are scrutinised and evaluated. It should be remembered here that the chief function of philosophy everywhere is critical evaluation as well as construction. Thus philosophy of education critically evaluates different aims and ideals of education to arrive at the most sound and cogent aim of education. Here again, it is more concerned with the general and universal aim rather than any specific and particular aim of education. It is so since philosophy everywhere deals with most general. Again, philosophical process is comprehensive and total. Therefore, philosophy of education aims at presenting a synthesis of various aims and ideals of education.

The same philosophical attitude pervades the discussion of human nature in philosophy of education. A philosophical picture of human nature is a result of the synthesis of the facts borrowed from all the human sciences with the values discussed in different normative sciences. The philosophical picture, therefore, is more integral as compared to the picture of man drawn by biology, sociology, psychology, economics and anthropology and so many other human sciences.

The most important part of the scope of the philosophy of education is formed by the educational values. Value is typically a philosophical subject since it is more abstract than concrete, mental than physical, integral than one-sided, universal than particular. Philosophical treatment of values not only evaluates them but also systematises them in a hierarchy. Educational values are determined by philosophical values. Educational values held by different philosophers have been derived from their world-view. Therefore, a scrutiny of the world-views, the specific function of philosophy, is necessary for any treatment of philosophical values.

Education deals with knowledge. It is determined by the source, limits, criteria and means of knowledge. The discussion of all these however falls within the jurisdiction of epistemology, an area of philosophy. Therefore, an important area of the functioning of philosophy of education is concerned with theory of knowledge. The most important service of philosophy of education to the cause of education everywhere, is the prescription of criteria for deciding the relationship of state and education, economic system and education, curriculum administration, discipline, progress, etc. These problems have led to the evolution of different philosophies of education. The criteria of judgment everywhere are determined by philosophy. Therefore, philosophy of education prescribes criteria of judgement in these fields.

The above discussion of the scope of philosophy of education also explains its nature. Thus, philosophy of education is an important branch of applied philosophy. Of the three divisions of philosophy, metaphysics, epistemology and axiology, philosophy of education falls in the third. It is, therefore, mainly concerned with educational values. As a branch of philosophy it utilises philosophical methods for the solution of philosophical problems with a philosophical attitude to arrive at philosophical conclusions. In this comprehensive process it includes facts concerning education and synthesises them with values.

PHILOSOPHY OF EDUCATION AND THE TEACHER

According to John Dewey. "Philosophy of Education is not an external application of readymade ideas to a system of practice having a radically different origin and purpose, it is only an explicit formulation of the problems of the formation of right mental and moral attitudes in respect to the difficulties of contemporary social life. The most penetrating definition of philosophy which can be given is, then, that it is the theory of education in its most general phases".[1] Thus the teacher gets his theory of teaching from the philosophy of education. Teaching methods are very much concerned with the philosophy of education the teacher holds. According to Spencer, only a true philosopher may give a practical shape to education. How he behaves with the students and how he communicates depends very much on how he defines the educands. Different philosophical systems of education have explained human nature in widely different ways. This very much governs the teacher's attitude to the method of teaching. Though philosophy is no substitute for the teacher's knowledge of the subject, it is certainly necessary for his enlightenment. In the words of Bertrand Russell, "Philosophy is to be studied not for the sake of any definite answers to the questions—but rather for the sake of questions themselves; because these questions enlarge our conception of what is possible, enrich our intellectual imagination and diminish the dogmatic assurance which closes the mind against speculation, but above all because through the greatness of the universe which philosophy contemplates, the mind also is rendered great and becomes capable of that union with the universe which constitutes its highest good".[2]

The most important contribution of the philosophy of education to the teacher is how ever, concerned with the aims and ideals of education. Without philosophy of education the teacher will not have any sense of purpose in his teaching. This is not possible by science however we may eulogise the role of science in the present-day education. In fact, while science supplies the means, only philosophy supplies the ends. In the words of John Dewey, "Philosophy is concerned with determining ends of education, while the science of education determines the means to be used."[3]

Again, philosophy of education helps the teacher in the determination of the curriculum of education. Defining a philosopher Plato said, "He, who has a taste for every sort of knowledge and who is curious to learn and is never satisfied, may be justly termed a philosopher".[4] Philosophy provides a comprehensive and total view of the educational situation. It

1. Dewey, J., *Democracy and Education*, p. 386.
2. Bertrand Russell, *The Problems of Philosophy*, pp. 249-50.
3. John Dewey in *Sources of Science of Education*.
4. Plato, *Republic*, Book V.

leads to integral approach. It is a total view-point. Therefore, it is a good prophylactic against all one-sidedness. Criticising the anomaly of one-sidedness in our present educational system, A. M. Schlezinger has rightly pointed out, "We desperately need a rich emotional life, reflecting actual relations between the individual and the community".[1]

The world is faced today with two prominent approaches to life, the Eastern and the Western. These present two different cultural attitudes, two different philosophies of life. Mankind has made experiments for a proper human life in different climes and times. The modern man may do well by synthesising the wisdom of different cultures. An ideal teacher imbibes combination of East and West, philosophy and science. Explaining this viewpoint, Kewal Motwani has said, "Now two types of cultures, with vastly different ideologies and values have come face to face in India and are engaged in a deadly combat. India, with her rural, agricultural, handicraft culture, with an integrated view of life, with its emphasis on indefinable, qualitative values, on individual uniqueness, on dharma, on self-imposed poverty, on social synthesis, on a subjective, broad-based nationalism, on man and machinery of the government, on a life of religious experience and unfoldment, on power through repose is confronted by a culture that stands for machine and science, for an urbanised, industrialized order, for analytical view of life, with its emphasis on neuroses and complexes, for mass production, for quantitative values, for struggle for existence and survival of the fittest, for accumulation of wealth and economic imperialism, for assertive, arrogant nationalism, for democracy and dictatorship, for religion of scientific humanism and rationalism. India has sought the vision of the whole not of the parts, she has been interested in living not merely in the means of livelihood. She has combined philosophic contemplation with action; she has stood for beauty and dignity, not mere utility. But today the culture of machine and science has taken a firm grip of India and is slowly seeping into her soul".[2]

The complex modern civilization, overburdened with technology, is threatening a relapse into babarism or an extinction

---

1. Schlezinger, A.M., *The Politics of Freedom*, 1950, p. 237.
2. Kewal Motwani, "*Sociology*" University of Madras Journal, July 1939, pp. 189-190.

of *Homo Sapiens.* Man is facing today the problems which are characteristic of the atomic age and bred by industrialism. Everywhere, we find chaos and frustration. Solutions have been offered from all sides. Science and international law have proved helpless. Thoughtful men are looking towards religion, morality and spirituality. As an author puts it, "The alternative with which we are faced is: either atrophy of our brain power; degeneration of man, decline of his intellectual and spiritual activities which become more and more mechanical and in the end slavery in new totalitarian regimes with over-centralised control; or a spiritual revolution; an awakening of man to the fact that he, after all, is a spiritual being, with inexhaustible spiritual powers; and a stern determination to defend his liberty and to subordinate the so-called progress of science and technology to the moral and spiritual end of humanity within a democratic order".[1] Therefore, the most essential thing for a teacher is his philosophy of education. The only remedy to cultural or any other type of one sidedness is the philosophical approach. This philosophical approach is expressed in integral viewpoint admirably summed up by Sri Aurobindo in these words, "The heart and the mind are universal Deity and neither a mind without heart nor a heart without mind is the human ideal".[2]

Warning against the neglect of philosophy of education on the part of the teacher Rusk maintained, "Teachers who assume that they can afford to ignore philosophy pay the penalty of their neglect, for their efforts, lacking a co-ordinating principle, are thereby rendered ineffective".[3] Philosophy is needed not only in the determination of aims and ideals and the curriculum but also in the actual day-to-day programme of educational practice. In the words of Adler, "Thus we begin to see, not only the distinct sphere of the philosophy of education, as answering questions, unanswerable by science, but also the need for a philosophy of education for without it there could be no certain determination of the basic practical principles, underlying the policies which direct actual day-to-day educational practices".[4]

1. F.H. Heinemann, *Hibbert Journal*, October 1957, p. 46.
2. Sri Aurobindo, *Views and Reviews*, p. 3.
3. Rusk, R.R., *Philosophical Bases of Education*, p. 9.
4. Adler, *In Defence of The Philosophy of Education*, 41st Year Book of the National Society for the Study of Education, p. 206.

In the end the teacher is not only supposed to have a sound philosophy of education but he is required to develop a philosophical viewpoint among his students as well. In the words of K.L. Shrimali, "Thus, not merely must the teacher have a philosophy of education, he must come prepared to develop among his students a philosophy of life"[1] The teacher provides information and knowledge to the educands but his personal stamp is always in the form of a philosophy of life. What the great teachers have given to the world is philosophy and not information.

METHODOLOGY OF PHILOSOPHY OF EDUCATION

The nature of a subject determines its methods. In the words of Sri Aurobindo, "The description of the status of knowledge to which we aspire determines the means of knowledge which we shall use".[2] Philosophy of education is concerned both with facts and values about all the aspects of human being, the world around him and his status in the cosmos. Such a comprehensive field cannot be dealt with mind alone. In the words of Sri Aurobindo, "What the mind conceives must be need not be the measure of will be".[3] This, however, does not mean the neglect of the importance of language and logic in philosophy of education. To quote Sri Aurobindo again, "A language has to be created which is at once intuitively metaphysical and revealingly poetical, admitting significant and living images as the vehicle of a close, suggestive and vivid indication".[4] While a rational method alone is not sufficient to realise the purpose of philosophy of education, the same is true about an empirical method as well. In the words of Sri Aurobindo, "So long as we confine ourselves to sense evidence and physical consciousness, we can conceive nothing and know nothing except the material world and its phenomena" Only a synthesis of reason and experience may give us an insight into the problems of philosophy of education. As Sri Aurobindo has rightly pointed out, "Every concept is incomplete for us and to a part of our nature almost unreal unless it becomes an experience".[5] Philosophy of education is both a criticism as well

1. Shrimali, K.L., *Better Teacher Education*, Ministry of Education, Government of India, 1954, p. 2.
2. Sri Aurobindo, *Synthesis of Yoga*, p. 351.
3. Sri Aurobindo, *Letters on The Mother*, p. 87.
4. Sri Aurobindo, *The Life Divine*, Vol. II, p. 43.
5. *Ibid.*, p. 74.

as realisation. Therefore, "In each case", as Aurobindo points out, "Understanding, discrimination, verification are necessary, but the subjective and the supraphysical must have another method of verification, than that which we apply successfully to the physical and external objective".[1]

Pointing out the function of philosophy Sri Aurobindo said, "It is an attempt to fix the fundamental realities and principles of being as distinct from its processes and the phenomena which result from those processes".[2] Therefore, neither synthesis nor analysis alone can be ideal methods of philosophy of education. Rational analysis is insufficient to solve the problems concerning educational values. To quote Sri Aurobindo, "All this labour of speculation has its utility in training the human mind and helping to keep before it the idea of something beyond and ultimate towards which it must turn. But the intellectual reason can only point vaguely or feel gropingly towards it or try to indicate partial and even conflicting aspects of its manifestation here, it cannot enter it and know it".[3] This, however, does not mean a total rejection of intellectual processes in the field of philosophy of education. Even in the field of psychical and spiritual development reason and logic may play some role. To quote Sri Aurobindo again, "Reason is not the supreme light and yet it is always a necessary light bringer and unless it has been given its rights and allowed to judge and purify our first infrarational instincts, impulses, rash favours, crude beliefs and blind prejudgments, we are not altogether ready for the full unveiling of a greater inner illumination".[4]

Therefore, philosophy of education cannot do without utilising intuitive method. The intuitive method is a knowledge by identity, a knowledge by intimate direct contact. In the words of Sri Aurobindo, it is inclusion, indwelling and identity. He has rightly said, "Intuition, therefore, is present at the beginning of things and in their middle as well as at their consummation."[5] This intuition is not only mental but psychical and spiritual. Explaining

1. *Ibid*, Vol. II, p. 434.
2. *Ibid*, p. 456.
3. *The Riddle of This World*, p. 24.
4. Sri Aurobindo, *Evolution*, p. 29.
5. Sri Aurobindo, *Letters*, 1st Scries, p. 5.

spiritual intuition, the sure foundation of any philosophy of education, Sri Aurobindo has said, "The spiritual intuition lays hold always upon the reality, it is the luminous harbinger of the spiritual realisation or else its illuminative light, it sees that which the other powers of our being are labouring to explore, it gets at the firm truth of the abstract representations of the heart and life, a truth which is itself neither remotely abstract nor outwardly concrete, but something else for which these are only two aides of its psychological manifestation to us".[1] Spiritual intuition does not negate the experiences gained through physical, vital or mental instruments. Whereas the latter seek to abstract one particular type of experience from the whole, it is a knowledge through whole being. "It is a direct vision, an authentic seeing, a comprehensive intuitive apprehension".[2]

Thus, educational philosophy utilises deductive and inductive reasoning, experiences of different types and the intuitions to arrive at inner as well as total truths. The utilisation of these methods however requires a constant development of the philosopher and the educator, his constant grappling with the actual problems arising in the everyday process of education.

NEED OF PHILOSOPHY OF EDUCATION IN MODERN TIMES

All modern educationists hold the view that not only should the educator be equipped with knowledge of a variety of subjects, but also that he should have his own philosophy of education, without which he cannot efficiently solve the problems that face in teaching from day-to-day. Fichte correctly pointed out that the art of education will never attain complete clearness in itself without philosophy. Hence, there is an interaction between the two, and either without the other is incomplete and unserviceable. Some people are so impressed by the achievements of science that they give a higher place to science than to philosophy in education. Psychologists are of the opinion that education should be based on psychological principles, while sociologists, impressed by the significance of social phenomena, suggest that education should be more influenced by their findings. But all these people forget that even sociologists and psychologists have failed to solve

1. Sri Aurobindo, *The Synthesis of Yoga*, p. 663.
2. Sharma, R. N., *The Philosophy of Sri Aurobindo*, IIIrd Ed. 1977, Kedar Nath Ram Nath, Meerut, pp. 57-58.

many difficulties that have arisen in connection with the aims of education, curriculum, teaching methods, discipline, etc. They have failed to provide a satisfactory criterion for determining techniques of assessment, standards of evaluation, selection of text-books or of teaching methods. In actual fact, there is no rivalry between educational philosophy and educational practice because philosophy gives adequate importance to the principles enunciated by psychology and sociology. The only real difference is that philosophy of education is concerned with more fundamental problems, that it delves far more deeply than any one science, that its attitude is far more comprehensive and liberal and that it is an attempt at synthesizing most of the viewpoints from which any phenomenon is examined. Hence, the educator can do nothing without philosophy.

The educator is often faced with problems in the sphere of education which can be solved only on the basis of his conception of the universe. Every behaviour or action has its own principles. Hence educational behaviour, too, must have its own principles. The principles underlying all educational behaviour are derived from philosophy of education. It is only through a philosophy of education that one determines the curriculum, the text-books, the methods of teaching, methods and standards of evaluation, the methods of maintaining discipline, etc. Hence the educator should study educational philosophy.

"The educational system which we attempt to set up," says G.D.H. Cole, "must depend on the kind of society we mean to live in, on the qualities in men and women on which we set the highest value, and on the estimates which we make of the educability of both of those who are endowed with the higher intellectual or aesthetic capacities and of ordinary people".[1] Philosophy of education is theoretical, the theory, however, aims at the guidance to practice. In the words of John Dewey, "Whenever philosophy has been taken seriously, it has always been assumed that it signified achieving a wisdom that would influence the conduct of life".[2] Idealism has been the most ancient and the most prominent school in philosophy. In the words of Adams, "Idealism in one form or other permeates the whole of the history of philosophy",[3]

1. Cole, G.D.H., *Essays in Social Theory*, p. 47.
2. John Dewey, *Democracy and Education*, p. 378.
3. Adams, *The Educational Theory*, Macmillan & Co.

This idealism has been the most fundamental theory underlying educational principles. In the words of Robert R. Rusk, "It bestows dignity and grandeur upon human life by emphasising the distinctiveness of man's nature, attributing to him powers, not possessed by animals, which issue in ideals—logical and aesthetic, it admits the existence of a Supreme Being, by its respect for human personality it provides the basis for democracy".[1]

The most fundamental question in the field of education is concerning its aim. This question raises queries about the nature of man and the possibility of its modification and transformation. Man's nature is very much concerned with his place in the cosmos. Therefore, the question of the aim of education is very much concerned with the question of the nature of the universe. Again, it is intimately concerned with the concept of culture prevalent in a society. This makes for the close relation between philosophy and education. In the words of Blanshard and others, "The function of philosophy in universities is properly the same as its function in the cultural development of a society, to be the intellectual conscience of the community".[2] Education is based upon the distinctions between animal and human nature. It has generally aimed to develop the characteristics peculiar to man. In the words of Robert R. Rusk, "Those powers and their products are peculiar to man, and differentiate him from other animals. They lie beyond the range of the positive sciences—biological and even psychological, they raise problems which only philosophy can hope to solve and make the only satisfactory basis of education a philosophical one".[3]

Education aims at imparting knowledge. Knowledge, however, requires a global outlook and a synthesis of various types of informations and experiences. This is a philosophical activity without which no education is possible. Therefore, the need of philosophical basis of education is rooted in the branch of philosophy known as epistemology. This has been expressed by Perry in somewhat different terms when he says, "Philosophy is neither accidental nor supernatural, but inevitable and normal".[4]

---

1. Robert R. Rusk, *The Philosophical Bases of Education*, University of London Press, p. 154.
2. Blanshard and Others. *Philosophy in American Education*, Harper & Bros., New York (1945). p. 80.
3. Rusk, R.R., *The Philosophical Basis of Education*, p. 154.
4. Perry, *The Approach to Philosophy*, p. 22.

Besides its synthetic function, another important function of philosophy is the criticism of the postulates and conclusions of different sciences. Whenever a scientist delves deeper in his own particular field, he reaches a depth where the process of his thinking is not scientific but philosophical. This can be seen in the thinking of many a great scientist of the world. The importance of philosophy in the field of knowledge is, therefore, quite clear. From the point of view of different aspects of the individual and social life, and in different fields of knowledge, the discussion of the value of philosophy shows the utility of philosophy of education. In the words of J.W. Cunningham, "Philosophy thus grows directly out of life and its needs. Everyone who lives, if he lives at all reflectively, is in some degree a philosopher".[1] In the words of Chesterton, "The most practical and important thing about a man is his view of universe—his philosophy".[2]

1. Cunningham, J. K., *Problems of Philosophy*, p. 5.
2. Quoted by Hocking. *Types of Philosophy*, p. 4.

4

Idealism

Idealism is one of the oldest schools of thought in the world of philosophy, originating in human nature itself, continuing from the primitive man to his present counterpart in some modified form or the other, the metaphysical standpoint has overtones of spirituality since it believes that the ultimate existing element is spiritual in nature. The entire universe is an extension of the mind or soul. From the epistemological standpoint it is better called idealism, implying thereby that thought or ideal has greater validity than the physical object. From the normative standpoint it is accurately represented by the term idealism which means that it attaches greater importance to ideal than to facts in this world. Obviously, the term idealism connotes different concepts when placed in various contexts. Whatever the context, the word definitely represents a particular theory in philosophy.

Summing up the importance of idealism in the history of philosophy, Adams has remarked, "Idealism in one form or other permeates the whole of the history of philosophy".[1] The essence of idealism has been admirably explained in brief in the words of G.T.W. Patrick as follows: "Idealists refuse to believe that the world is a great machine. They deny the supreme importance of matter, mechanism and the conservation of energy, as explaining our world. They feel that somehow certain sciences, such as psychology, logic, ethics, aesthetics, have to do with things basal and intrinsic, that they are quite as much a key to nature's secrets as are physics and chemistry. They believe that the world has a meaning, a purpose, perhaps a goal, and that there is a kind of inner harmony between the heart of the universe and the soul of

1. Adams, *The Evolution of Educational Theory*, MacMillan & Co. (1912) p. 28.

man, such that human intelligence can pierce through the outer crust of nature and penetrate to its inner being, at least in some measure". This explanation of idealism highlights its distinction from materialism.

Idealism has been also compared to realism. In the words of Brubachar, "Some realists take the view that mental functions can be reduced to bodily ones, while certain idealists make matter a function of the mind. The idealists arrive at their monism by pointing out that it is mind that is central in understanding the world".

CHIEF CHARACTERISTICS OF IDEALISM

The following are the chief characteristics of idealism:

1. The universe exists in spirit: According to idealism, the spirit is the fundamental constituent of the universe. It points out that only mental life can be known, because the mind is capable of knowing only its own states and its adjuncts. Every individual human mind is a part of the universal mind, outside which nothing exists. For this reason, rational or spiritual knowledge is the only true knowledge. By virtue of this distinction, philosophy and the other social sciences are far more important than the physical or natural sciences.

2. Mechanical explanation of the universe is inadequate: Idealists believe that the mechanical explanation of the universe is inadequate because it does not succeed in explaining human values. Idealists also refute the concept of mechanical determinism.

3. Teleological explanation of the universe: In the words of Stella V. Henderson, "Idealism emphasizes the spiritual side of man. Because, to the idealist, spiritual values are the most important growing out of metaphysical, idealism would emphasize spiritual growth". Idealism propounds that human life and natural phenomena have a common goal, and that both man and nature try to achieve this goal. This concept finds its best explanation in the contemporary Indian philosopher Sri Aurobindo's thought. Idealists do not challenge or deny the importance of science, but they do not completely accept its explanation of the universe since it finds no place for spiritual values.

4. Man is central in creation: Idealists point out that man is at the centre of the universe. In the words of Rude, "It bestows dignity and grandeur upon human life by emphasising the distinctiveness of man's nature, attributing to him powers not possessed by animals, which issues in ideals—logical, ethical and aesthetic: it admits the existence of a Supreme Being: by its respect for human personality it provides the basis for democracy".[1]

5. Emphasis upon normative and social sciences: In the field of education, idealists place greater stress upon normative and social sciences than upon the natural and physical. The normative sciences are—ethics, logic and aesthetics. Of the social sciences the main ones are sociology and psychology. Idealists explain the universe on the basis of these sciences.

6. Normative description of the universe: Idealists have offered a normative and value-oriented explanation of the universe. For the idealist, facts alone are not sufficient explanation. The universe as a whole is explicable in terms of the ideals of truth, good and beauty.

7. Conceptualism: In its epistemology, idealism is conceptualism, for it believes that objects have no existence apart from the concepts related to them. An object and its qualities are not independent of the knowledge of the object. Knowledge influences the object, and this knowledge is obtained, not through perception but indirectly, through the medium of concepts or ideas. Objects have no public reality, for they appear different to different individuals. All existence is related to consciousness.

8. Universe is knowable: Idealists believe that the universe can be comprehended through the mind, because both the mind and the universe are constituted of the same elements, intellect and spiritual essence. Hegel has gone so far as to identify nature and mind by saying that the various categories of knowledge or mind are the different stages of the universe's development.

9. Greater emphasis upon the mental or spiritual aspect of the universe: The idealist conception of the universe does not either deny or neglect the physical aspect of it but it is based on the mental or spiritual aspect. It is this higher aspect of reality which grants a measure of meaning to the lower reality.

---

1. Rusk, R.R., *The Philosophical Bases of Education*, University of London Press, p. 154.

IDEALISM IN EDUCATION

Ever since knowledge dawned in human mind man has been thinking about problems ontological, epistemological, eschatological and axiological. The questions of philosophy in the beginning of human knowledge were everywhere mixed with psychological problems. Thus, psychology in the beginning was concerned with the nature of the mind and the processes of consciousness. As men lived in small groups and the society was generally confined to a particular village, city or group of villages, the solutions offered were simple. There was hardly any distinction between social and political problems as the political institutions were developed as a means to social welfare. Therefore, most of the ancient thinkers did not distinguish between social philosophy and political philosophy. As the life was simple and social stratification and differentiation was not complex the thinkers offered solutions working in more than one field of knowledge. Most of the thinkers were teachers and men of education who used to pass their life completely free from worldly affairs. The state and the society generally extended support to these scholars and they were generally respected and followed. The job of instruction and education of the younger generation was generally entrusted to these men of letters. The state supported finance but not interfered in the process of education. These great teachers formed their own personal institutions where their disciples collected to hear their learned discourses and learn through their lives. In this way, society was generally governed by the teachings of these great scholars though the administrative machinery was almost everywhere in the hands of the state.

The most important contributions of the idealistic philosophers in the field of education have been made by Plato, John Amos Comenius, Jean Jacques Rousseau, John Henrick Pestalozzi, Johann Friedrich, Friedrich August Froebel and R.R. Rusk.

CONTRIBUTION OF PLATO

According to Plato, man's mind is always active. Man is attracted towards all things that he sees in his surroundings, and he runs after them. Educator should take advantage of this propensity in the child and educate him. He should pay attention to the objects which surround the child. Such objects should be beautiful so that the child is naturally attracted to them and his curiosity is aroused. The process of education advances through this constant interaction between these objects and the mind. A beautiful environment provides the right stimulus by which the mind develops. For this reason the child should be kept in a beautiful environment. In fact, the human individual requires such an environment not only in infancy but throughout his entire life, because, according to Plato, the process of education is never complete. It continues throughout one's life. Plato has laid the greatest stress on mental development in education. He conceives of the state as an advanced mind. Education aims not merely at providing information but at training the individual in his duties and rights as a citizen. Just as the state evolves from the mind, the mind itself passes through all those stages of development through which the state passes. In Plato's opinion, the aim of education is human perfection, and with this end in view, he suggests a curriculum which comprehends all subjects.

Curriculum

Plato has divided curriculum into three parts:

1. *Bodily development*: Plato's philosophy believes bodily development to be of utmost importance in education, but this bodily development is achieved not merely through exercise and gymnastic activity but also through a regulated and controlled diet. The educator must guide and train the educand to attend to his food. He must be a kind of doctor who advises a particular kind of diet after acquainting himself with the weaknesses of the educand's body. This must be done in order to get rid of these debilities and finally to lead to complete development of the body.

2. *Educational impressions*: But it must be remembered that bodily development is only a means to mental development, because a healthy mind resides only in a healthy body. Although much importance is attached to bodily development, even greater importance is attached to mental development. Being under the influence of Pythagoras, Plato recommended the teaching of mathematics as of supreme importance. The first step in the teaching of mathematics is the teaching of arithmetic. Geometry and algebra should then be taught. Plato believed that the teaching of mathematics can remove many mental defects. In addition to mathematics, Plato considered the teaching of astronomy as of great significance, as part of higher education.

3. *Training in music*: In order to achieve balance in education, Plato stressed the value of musical training as a supplement to training in gymnastics. Exercise is the source of bodily development while music helps in the development of the soul. But music and literature taught to the student must be capable of building character. Plato suggested that the child's curriculum should be purged of all literature and musical epics which tended to generate such qualities as cowardice, weakness, selfishness, egoism, etc. He was critical of the epics of Homer and other contemporary poets on this ground. Plato considered balance in human life to be of the greatest importance, because in the absence of such a balance, man should neither fulfil his social obligations nor enjoy his own private life to the full.

Hence it can be concluded that Plato suggested a balanced curriculum for education.

Role of Educator

In Plato's plan of education, the educator is considered to have the greatest importance. He is like the torch-bearer who leads a man, lying in a dark cave, out of the darkness into the bright light of the outside world. His task is to bring the educand out of the darkness of the cave into the light of the day. He is, thus, the guide.

In his methods of teaching Plato believes imitation to be of the greatest importance, for he realizes that the child learns a great deal through imitation. He will acquire the behaviour of the people among whom he is made to live. Hence, keeping in mind the status of the child, he should be made to live among people from whom he can learn good habits and avoid bad ones.

Education According to Classes

Plato's plan of education does not envisage uniform education for one and all. He accepted the concept of social stratification, and suggested that since different individuals had to perform different tasks in society, they should also be educated differently, in order to train each one in his own respective sphere. He believed that different individuals are made of different metals. Those made of gold should take up administration and government, while those made of silver were best suited for trade and defence. Others made of iron and the baser metals should become labourers and agriculturists. The state must make different arrangements for the education of these different kinds of people, although Plato implicitly agrees that education of governing classes is of the greatest importance. The education of the other classes in society does not concern him very much.

Faced with the problem of determining the classes of each individual, Plato suggested various kinds of tests to be conducted at different age levels. In the first place, primary education will be given to all between the ages of seven and twenty, following which a test shall be administered to everyone. Those who fail the test are to be sent to labour in the various occupations and productive trades. The successful candidates will be sent to the armed forces where training will be imparted to them for the next few years. This will again be followed by a test, the failures will be compelled to remain in the armed forces while the successful ones will be sent to join the government. Then this governing class will be subjected to further education in science. Later on, one from among the governing class will be elected as the philosopher administrator whose task it will be to look after government and education of the state. This individual will occupy the highest position in the land, his word will be the law of the land. Apart from this supreme individual, all other members of the governing class will continue to receive education throughout their lives, most of this education consisting of teachings in philosophy. It is thus evident that Plato granted the highest place to philosophy in his educational scheme.

Evaluation

As has been pointed out earlier, Rousseau was correct when he commented that Plato's *Republic* is the finest text-book on education. But it must be admitted that Plato's scheme of education suffers from certain defects and shortcomings, which have been enumerated below:

1. Little education of the productive class: In any society the labouring or productive class is invariably the largest in size. In Plato's scheme of education, this class is granted only primary education, which implies that higher education of all kinds is intended only for the soldiers and the governing classes, assuming that the labouring class has no need for such an education. Plato's dictum was that the productive class actually required no more than primary education.

2. Absence of variety: Plato's educational plan pays no attention to the individual differences between one individual and another. He suggested the same kind of education to be given to an entire class of people, according to a uniform curriculum. This will inevitably lead to deadening monotony and lack of variety, which kills all future progress.

3. Stress on philosophy: Some people get the impression that Plato's insistence on philosophy is exaggerated, and that it could only lead to an increase in the number of contemplative individuals at the expense of more practical members. But it must be remembered that Plato has stressed the importance of both bodily and mental development and in this respect, he has achieved a remarkable harmony of both.

4. Neglect of literary education: Plato's curriculum also neglects training in literature by stressing the importance of training in mathematics.

In spite of the above defects, Plato's concept of education has influenced educational philosophy in almost all ages. In particular his influence can be seen in the idealist philosophy of education. And, many of the finest teachers still consider Plato as their only true guide.

CONTRIBUTION OF RUSK

Rusk's idealism establishes a synthesis between man and nature, and also stresses the superiority of man over animal beings. In fact, the chief difference in human and animal education is due to the special qualities of man. In Rusk's words, "Those powers and their products are peculiar to man, and differentiate him from other animals, they lie beyond the range of the positive sciences—biological and even psychological; they raise problems which only philosophy can hope to solve, and make the only satisfactory basis of education a philosophical one". Education is not an end in itself, but only a means to an end, for through the medium of education, parents acquaint their own ideals. It is through education that the state creates ideal citizens. Morality is spread by religious institutions through education. Where the idealists are concerned, they want to use education to spread democratic conceptions in society. They also want to attach more purpose to education and make it more utilitarian. On the one hand they believe in knowledge for its own sake, but on the other they also want to use such knowledge for progress in life. They believe in the importance of ideals. Man's life changes due to his ideals. Literary men, artists, scientists and philosophers develop according to their own ideals. Accordingly, then, the idealist aims at creating an ideal social organisation in the society and the race, a social organisation essentially democratic in nature, which attaches the greatest importance to the human personality.

JOHN AMOS COMENIUS (1592-1670)

According to Comenius, God is the ideal of education. Education includes knowledge concerning the world and its relationship with man. Thus, Comenius was influenced by the religious aims of education. However, he also opened the gates of secular ideals of education. Education, according to him, starts in the lap of the mother. The mother makes a significant contribution to the first six years of the child development. The development of his tendencies in the next six years very much depends upon the school. In the next six years more intelligent students may be allowed to study in the Latin schools. Those who successfully pass through it may study at the university for another six years. The method of education, according to Comenius, should adhere to the rules of child's nature. His interests should be developed and intellectual development should be realised through the use of his senses. Perception should be given emphasis in learning.

According to Comenius there are three sources of knowledge—inner knowledge, observation and idea. The means of attainment of knowledge are: senses, intelligence and talent. The three aims of education are:

1. To give knowledge to man for success in life.
2. To give wisdom for moral and character-development.
3. To create devotion to God in man.

From the point of view of teaching methods, Comenius has laid down the following nine principles meant for the reform of the educational system of his time:

1. Whatever is to be taught to the child should be told in direct and clear words.
2. The thing to be taught should have practical utility.
3. Education should not be complex.
4. The purpose of whatever is to be taught should be clearly stated.

5. General rules should be explained before-hand.
6. It is necessary to teach everything or all aspects of a subject in a proper order, proper place and proper relationship.
7. All subjects should be taught in a proper order.
8. The subject should not be left unless the child understands it properly.

The above principles were summarised in the following rules for the development of the child:

1. Proceed from concrete to abstract.
2. If possible, present mutual co-relation.
3. Adopt result method.
4. Prompt the interest of the child.
5. It is necessary to proceed towards 'to prove' instead of 'to assure', 'to see' instead of 'to discuss' and 'to know' instead of 'to believe'.

School Management

Comenius has classified schools according to different stages of the development of the child. Thus school may be organised for infants, children, adolescents and the adults. Infancy schools may admit infants from birth to six years of age. Childhood schools may admit children from six years to twelve years to be taught through mother tongue. Adolescence schools provide education to adolescents from 12 to 18 years of age through Latin. These are also called Latin schools. Beyond 18 years of age the educand may be admitted to schools for adulthood. The functions of all these categories of schools are:

1. Teaching of language.
2. To develop faculties through the study of science and art.
3. To develop morality.
4. To create true devotion in God.

Establishment of New System of Education

The following characteristics show that Comenius established a new system of education in 17th century:

1. Practical: Children should be taught practical things having utility in their life and at the same time they should understand them as well.

2. Self-experience: The child should understand the reality by his self-experience, should explore things himself and should not depend on others.

3. Mother-tongue: The medium of education should be mother-tongue. Only then education will be enjoyable, easy and useful.

4. No pressure: No pressure should be exerted on child. If the child does not take interest in studies, it means there is some defect in the teaching method of the teacher.

5. No punishment: The child should not be given corporal punishment if he is unable to read.

6. Equal opportunities: Boys and girls should be given equal opportunities for education.

7. Physical development: It is necessary to make proper arrangement for the physical development of children. Provision of games only is not sufficient.

8. Greek and Latin: It is necessary to teach Greek and Latin through the mother-tongue. But these languages should be taught only to those who have interest in them.

9. Scientific methods: Education is a science. All subjects should be taught by scientific methods. By finding natural law and order it is necessary to base education on them. Object-knowledge should be given first and then word-knowledge. In order to develop the mind of children properly, it is better to discuss about the things before telling them the rule.

10. Psychological education: First easy and then difficult things should be taught. Proceed from concrete to abstract with objects so that they can understand them well. The children should take interest in analysis and should not study books only.

Evaluation

Though it is undeniable that reforms suggested by Comenius made all-round improvement in the existing system of education, criticisms have been advanced by educationists upon the philosophy of education given by Comenius. The most important evaluation has been advanced as follows:

1. He considered the child as inheritor of human-race but could not present an educational system accordingly. He forgot ancient culture in his zeal for scientific study. He thought it necessary to teach the works of contemporary authors only.

2. Comparison is useful only when it is explained. In his principles he takes inspiration from nature and compares man to trees and birds. But he forgets human nature. He begins to give importance to nature, without man. Reality lies in proof.

3. On the basis of Divine-voice, he imagined that man should learn everything, but did not estimate 'knowledge' and 'human-power' properly. This made his educational system defective. Later on, in his old age Comenius admitted that his books did not fulfil the need of the time.

4. It is not proper to give the essence of 'worldly knowledge' to the children.

5. It is not proper to explain general rules first.

6. Comenius was of the view that the essence of language should be taught to the child, but this is not suitable because there are many words in the language which we do not know nor is there any need of knowing.

In spite of the above mentioned criticism, it should be remembered that Comenius has been compared to Copernicus and Newton in science so far as his contribution to education is concerned.

JOHN HENRICK PESTALOZZI (1746-1827)

According to Pestalozzi education depends on the inner development of the child. Therefore it should not be imposed from outside. The principles of education should be discovered through observation and experiment in the field of education. The success of the teacher depends upon teaching according to the interests of the child. Childhood is the most important period in a person's education. Education is the birth right of every individual. It aims at the all-round development of his capacities and abilities. The teacher should not only know various subjects but should also be conversant with best teaching methods.

JOHANN FRIEDRICH HERBART (1776-1841)

The ideal of education, according to Herbart, is the development of moral character in the educand. Moral education is helped by the education in history, literature, science and mathematics. The child's interest is the most important basis of his education. As long as he does not take interest, education cannot realise any significant aim in him. Various subjects of teaching are correlated. Preparation is the first step in teaching. After it teaching proceeds by presentation, comparison, generalisation and application. Thus in aims and ideals, methods of teaching, curriculum and school organisation Herbart presented an idealistic system of education.

FRIEDRICH AUGUST FROEBEL

Froebel has been considered to be the most idealistic philosopher of education. He believed that right since birth man possesses dormant capacities and abilities. The sole function of education is to arouse these dormant capacities and abilities and leave them to complete development. Therefore, education should be based upon the natural principles of inner development. As God is the source of creation, therefore there may be one common element among all living beings. Hence, the child should realise integrated development of his powers. According to Froebel self-activity is the chief method of child's education. Therefore, his creativity must be encouraged. The school is a mini-society and social environment is very much important for the development of the child. These ideas of Froebel have been found to be particularly important in the field of primary education.

SIR T. PERCY NUNN (1870-1944)

Among contemporary idealistic philosophers of education the most important name is T. P. Nunn. He believed that out of society the man's personality was flawless. The society contributed both positively and negatively to the development of man's personality. Social environment has a far reaching effect upon the individual's development. This development must be natural and individualistic. It requires self-realisation. Therefore, the chief aim of education is self-realisation or development of personality. It is the duty of the society and the state to provide proper environment for the development of the child.

According to T. P. Nunn, man's mind may be classified into horme and mneme. While horme is a drive or urge, mneme is the power of conservation. While the former keeps us active, moving, organising and planning, the latter conserves our experiences. Thus mneme is closely relative to memory and includes it. It conserves all the experiences including those memorised. Heredity is the unchangeable impact of past generations as engrains. There should be harmony between heredity and environment since both determine the development of the individuals. Thus both horme and mneme are important for the child's education.

The first eight years of the child should be educated by kindergarten and montessory methods. Primary education continues from the eight years of age to 13 years. After it five years are to be devoted to secondary education which is the pivot of educational system. In the adolescence stage boys and girls are developed as men and women respectively. Therefore, one's future depends upon his adolescent education.

As has been already pointed out, the aim of education according to Nunn, is self-realisation. This self-realisation, however, is both individual and social since man's personality is equally determined by heredity and environment. It is in the environment that the individual traits develop. On the other hand, it is the individual who is the vanguard of all progress and advancement in the society. These views of T. P. Nunn have been echoed among almost all contemporary idealist philosophers of education in West and East. One may find parallel statements in the philosophy of education of contemporary Indian thinkers including Vivekanand, Sri Aurobindo, M. K. Gandhi, Radhakrishnan and R. N. Tagore.

According to T. P. Nunn the curriculum should be balanced and integrated. The school should impart knowledge of culture and civilisation, both national and human. The aim and function of education is to develop inner traits of the educand. This requires study of humanities, social sciences, art and literature as much as that of science. Besides, music, science and mathematics are equally relevant. Knowledge and practice of all these subjects is required for an all-round development of the educand.

As has been already pointed out, with Rousseau, T. P. Nunn believes that man is free at birth. He requires freedom for natural growth. However, freedom should not hamper man's development. Real freedom is realised in the harmony of heredity and environment. It is not unrestrained behaviour but included self-control. Therefore, along with freedom, discipline is equally important in the educational system. Discipline includes prevention of unrestrained expression of inner tendencies. Discipline, however, cannot be imposed from outside since this hampers natural development of the child. Like all other contemporary thinkers T. P. Nunn declares that real freedom is discipline and real discipline is self-discipline. Very young children, however, may be given instruction about behaviour. The most important element in the growth of discipline, however, is the example set by the teacher.

AIMS AND IDEALS OF EDUCATION

Idealism has influenced every sphere of education. In the first place we will glance at the impact of idealism on the aims of education. Since idealism believes human personality to be the most important, it wants education to aim at the development of human personality culminating in self-realization. In the words of Home, "The end of ends, the goal of goals, according to Idealism, is the increasing realization of the Absolute Idea for the individual, society and the race". Further explaining this aim of education, Rusk has commented, "We may accept that the aim of education is the enhancement or enrichment of personality, the differentiating feature of which is the embodiment of universal values".[1] These universal values are expressed as the beauty, goodness and truth, and the aim of education is to concretise these values in the child's life. Thus the idealists cherish the following aims and ideals of education:

1. Development of personality: As has been already pointed out, the most important aim of education, according to the idealist thinkers, both ancient and modern, Eastern and Western, is the development of personality. This has been called man-making by Vivekanand. Explaining this ideal of education, Heraman Harell Horne says, "The forces that make men and women I find to be heredity, environment and will. Education is not a fourth elemental force, but it does its work in co-operation with these three. Education, through public-opinion influences and may come to control, the force of heredity, it is itself a part of the physical and social environment, it assists in the formation of will. By consciously directing, through education and otherwise, these forces shall in time have the true superman of our modern dreams, as well as the ideal people of Plato's Republic. But unlike Plato and Shaw, we shall have to work through, not without, the family as an institution"[2]

1. Rusk Robert R., *The Philosophical Bases of Education*, p. 194.
2. Herman Harrell Home, *Idealism in Education, Preface*, p. 10, MacMillan.

The idealists believe that man is God's finest and ultimate creation. That is why development of the human personality has been accepted as the aim of education, and stress has been laid on the teaching of humanitarian subjects such a literature, art, religion, ethics, etc. Through education the cultural and social heritage of the community must be maintained and transmitted to the following generations. Some other idealists believe that the aim of education is to guide the individual to self-realization, for this also includes the development of the personality. Such development, in fact, is the development of those divine qualities which are inherent in human beings but which are dormant at his birth. The educator's task is to manifest these qualities. And for this reason every human being has an equal right to education.

2. Self-realisation: As has been already pointed out, according to idealists the aim of education is self-realisation. This is the individualist aim of education emphasised by the idealist.

3. Development of will power: Self-realisation requires development of will power. H.H. Horne has given eight points for the realisation of this ideal:

(*i*) The training of the will should be indirect, by activity rather than idea.

(*ii*) The object lesson method according to time and context should be used.

(*iii*) The power of will should be increased by self-suggestion, knowledge and practice.

(*iv*) Practice is the only way to acquire will power.

(*v*) Proper discipline leads to will power.

(*vi*) The educands should be acquainted of facts concerning nature and society.

(*vii*) Development of moral character by ethical instruction.

(*viii*) Freedom to make choice in most of the matters concerning the individual.

4. Synthesis of man and nature: Another aspect of the idealistic conception of education is the synthesis between nature and human beings. Adams has suggested that education must aim at achieving an understanding of nature in human beings and educating them to achieve harmony with it. This can be done by acquainting the educand with the permanent laws which guide and control natural phenomena. These laws of nature are the causes of all natural activity. Only through such knowledge can the educand arrive at a harmony with all that lies around him.

5. Cultural development: Greatest significance is attached to the cultural environment created by religion, morality, art, literature, mathematics, science, etc. That is why the idealist tendency is to stress the teaching of humanities so that the cultural and social heritage is maintained intact and allowed to grow. Education is also concerned with enabling the individual to make his own contribution to the cultural development of the community. The ideals of beauty, goodness and truth are the spiritual ideals of the human race, and the child has to be trained to achieve them in reality. Education must transform the child into a true human being by educating him to manifest the divine qualities which are invested in him. The idealists argue that there is system in every part of the universe, and hence the individual must also be taught to create some system in his life through intellectual and spiritual guidance. For this it is essential to develop every aspect of his life—the physical, moral, ethical, intellectual, spiritual and the aesthetic. Failure to develop anyone of these would create an imbalance in the individual's personality. In the words of Froebel, "The object of education is the realisation of a faithful, pure, inviolable and hence holy life. Education should lead and guide man to clearness concerning himself, and in himself, to face with nature, and to unity with God".

6. Exploration of universal values. Idealism places more emphasis upon more universal objects of education. Ross puts it thus, "The function of education is to help us in our exploration of the ultimate universal values so that the truth of the universe may become our truth and give power to our life. Education must aim at adapting not only to the physical environment but to every kind of environment".[1] Rusk points out, "The purpose of education is to enable the child to reconcile himself to reality in all its manifestations, not merely to adapt himself to a natural environment". From among all these various kinds of environment, the cultural environment is considered to be the most important because man's cultural characteristics are his most distinctive qualities.

1. Ross, *The Philosophical Bases of Education*, p. 196.

IDEALISM AND CURRICULUM

Explaining the idealist bases of curriculum as the imparting of spiritual and cultural heritage to the child along with his self and personality development, Herman H. Home writes, "It is better to centre education in ideals for children and the race rather than in children themselves. After all children are immature, dependent and plastic members of the race. They are often irrational in their individuality". As Socrates said in effect to the sophists, "Not man but reason is the measure of all things, not individuality but universality; not percepts, but concepts. Ideals are the norms for all human experience, including that of children. After all, it is still true that obedience to just law is a virtue, that following physical laws leads to health, that truth is something to be discovered, rather than made, that conformity is a large element even in creativity, that repression is a necessary phase of expression. Under the influence of paidocentrism (what a hybrid), self-expression may easily become self-explosion".

Idealists insist on emphasis being placed on the study of humanities such as literature, art, religion, morality, etc., along with the teaching of science. All the elements necessary for attaining God are included in the curriculum suggested by idealistic followers of Plato, who laid down that education must aim to realize the ideals of truth, beauty and goodness. Hence, he has suggested the inclusion of all those subjects or disciplines which help in the realization of these ideals. Most significant among man's activities are the intellectual, the aesthetic and the moral. The teaching of language, literature, history, geography, mathematics and science will encourage intellectual activity while the aesthetic impulse can be reinforced through art and poetry. Moral activities can be taught and instilled in the educand through the teaching of religion, ethics, etc. This curriculum is determined on the basis of the goals to be realized through education and by the criterion that it must reflect the experience, culture and glory of the human race. Man's experiences relate not only to his physical or natural environment but also to his social experiences, knowledge of which can be obtained through a study of the natural and the social sciences.

James Ross, the educationist, has classified human activity in two groups—physical actions and spiritual activity. Physical activity includes the entire range of actions relating to bodily welfare and to motor skills. The teaching of these must also be a part of education and they can be taught through physiology, exercise, medicine, hygiene, etc. Spiritual activity comprehends all intellectual, ethical, aesthetic and religious activity, all of which can be taught through history, geography, science, mathematics, language, ethics, art and religion. Herbart, the idealist philosopher of education, grants these subjects the main place in the curriculum because these subjects can contribute more than any other to the spiritual progress of man. But this is the shortcoming of the idealistic philosophy because it does not attach any significance to the teaching of science. Herbart points out that the part that literature and history can play in the spiritual development of man, cannot be played by science. For that reason, scientific subjects such as the natural sciences, mathematics and even history and geography are granted a secondary role.

T. P. Nunn, another educationist, has glanced at the idealistic conception of the educational curriculum, and has remarked, "The school is to consolidate the nation's spiritual strength, to maintain its historic continuity, to secure its achievements, and to guarantee its future".[1] In order to achieve all these goals, education in the school should consider two kinds of activities. In the first group fall such activities which create conditions by which the individual and social life is ensured and maintained, and this can be done through physical health, customs, social organisations, ethical conduct, etiquette, religion, etc. Education must provide opportunities, therefore, for physical training, ethics, religion, etc. The second group of activities is the one which is more important outside the sphere of the school. In this group lie those activities which maintain the cultural life of the community because they are creative. In order to evolve skills for such activities, educationists advocate teaching of literature, art, music, various kinds of handicrafts and manual skills, sciences, mathematics, history, etc. Hence the curriculum must be so designed that it can help to acquaint the individual with his social and cultural heritage and also to enable him to make some positive contribution to this heritage. Nunn writes, "In the school curriculum all these activities should be represented. For these are the grand expression of the human spirit, and theirs are the forms in which the creative energies of every generation must

1. Nunn ,T. P., *Education: Its Data and First Principles*, London (1923), p. 221.

be disciplined if the movement of civilization is to be worthily maintained".[1]

IDEALISM AND THE EDUCATOR

Idealistic pattern of education grants the highest place to the educator, and conceives of the educator and educand as two parts of an organic plan. The educator creates a specific environment for the educand's development and provides guidance so that the latter may progress towards perfection and a rounded personality. The most precise explanation of the educator's role is manifested in Froebel's kindergarten pattern of education, in which the school is treated as a garden, the educand as a delicate plant which requires nurturing and the educator as the cautious gardener. Although even in the absence of the gardener the plant will continue to grow and will inevitably follow the laws governing its nature, the gardener has a certain significance in that he has the skill to develop plants. He may be unable to change a rose into a cabbage, but he certainly can contribute his mite to the plant's development. His efforts help in achieving perfection in this development, a level of perfection which would otherwise have been impossible. The educator plays a parallel role in the school. He can guide the educand appropriately because he knows the rules which govern the latter's development. Through his guidance he can make this natural development into a process leading to perfection and beauty. Ross explains, "The naturalist may be content with briars, but the idealist wants fine developing according to the laws of nature, to attain levels that would otherwise be denied to him".[2] Clearly, the idealists attach much more value to the educator than do the naturalists. Adams opined that both the educator and the educand are two parts of the intellectual universe both of which should be considered equally important. The educator inspires the educand to realize the ideals of truth, goodness and beauty, and guides him along the path to its realization.

IDEALISM AND EDUCATIONAL METHODS

Turning to methodology in education, idealists suggest that the method must be oriented to achieving the complete development

---

1. *Ibid.*
2. Ross, James, S., *Groundwork of Educational Theory*, p. 121.

of all the innate abilities of the child and to train him for self-realization. In Rivers' words, "The process of education in childhood consists, or should consist, in the direction of innate or instinctive tendencies towards an end in harmony with the highest good of society of which the child is an active member. Idealists believe in a harmony between individual and social objectives. The child must be provided with a liberal environment for his development and his education should be related to present experience. One finds, therefore, that many elements of the idealist methodology are common with those of the naturalist, realist and pragmatist methodology."

The idealist methodology in education lays special stress on the three following processes:

1. *Instruction*: The term instruction as used here implies educational instruction which is believed by Herbart to be essential to education. But instruction does not mean that the child's mind should be stuffed with various scraps of information. It implies a modification and a refinement of the child's mind. For this it is essential that the educator must provide sympathetic guidance. The idealists believe that training of all kinds must be provided in the school.

2. *Activity*: Like the naturalist methodology, the educational methods recommended by the idealists also are based on activity. The child must learn through doing. Although the child can learn much by asking questions after lectures in the school, creative activity is much more important. This creative activity should be natural, continuous and progressive. This helps in moving towards self-realization, because it encourages the child to manifest his innate tendencies. Through mental activity the child learns cheerfully and happily and this also helps in the development of his personality. Besides, by these means the child learns rapidly. Hence, idealists also stress that instruction should be active.

3. *Experience*: Idealist methodology also places considerable stress on experience. Every educand must base all his education on his own experience. The educator's task is not to stuff his own experience in the educand's mind but to provide the latter some insight into his own experience. The guidance given by the educator helps to manifest many frustrated and repressed tendencies and drives of the educand. Independence is an

essential pre-requisite for experience. For this reason idealists believe freedom to be an essential part of education but it must be remembered that this freedom is not absolute, but controlled and guided.

It is evident from the foregoing account that idealists believe the experiences of both the educator and the educand to be of great importance. Both of them should be active and they should indulge in the mutual exchange of experience so that they can progress. The teaching method should be such that the child should recognise it as a mode of self-instruction.

IDEALISM AND DISCIPLINE

Discipline is a part of the question concerning educational methods and some people feel that idealists are in complete opposition to the naturalists for the latter believe in complete freedom while the former insist on discipline. The only grain of truth in this assumption is that idealists stress the value of discipline as part of the educative process, without, in any way, detracting from the importance of freedom and liberty. In fact, idealists interpret discipline as being based on independence, and they try to harmonize the two. Rigorous discipline is never accepted by the idealists. Discipline must always take the shape of self-discipline, because only then can it guide the educand along the path of self-realization. Education basically aims at training the child in true independence. It is argued that the child is not independent at birth. This independence is granted to him or acquired by him in the process of education because, in the absence of education, there is no self-realisation, and without self-realization there is no independence. Rousseau believed that the individual was born free but that later on he is bound in chains. On the contrary, Froebel expressed the conviction that man is born in chains, and that he has to steadily win this freedom for himself, for, no one can grant it to him. Independence is not a divine gift, because even God cannot give independence. True independence can be won only by oneself, by one's own acts. Through the medium of education the individual can break the chains which bind him at birth. The educator must develop in his educands the capability of reasoning and arriving at a decision by the use of which the educand can achieve his own development, naturally and by his own inspiration. Independence lies not in a revolt against the environment but in achieving harmony with it. Hence, the child must be trained for independence in the school. He should be taught to discipline himself and to contribute to the disciplined behaviour of others, besides himself. Through a steady development of this kind, the individual becomes the member of a group of self-disciplined individuals. It can thus be concluded that the idealists do not favour the notion of allowing the child to roam free of any restraint but prefer to guide his freedom. For this reason, the child's activities are controlled in the school. Physical punishment and external restraints are not the methods of achieving this. It is better realized through developing such qualities as self-resignation, obedience, humanity, politeness, etc. Once these qualities are evolved in the individual, he achieves a stage of self-discipline. Froebel denies any importance to any system of punishment. Instead, he believes that it is better to encourage self-control and self-guidance in the child through sympathy. He believes that the child should not be submitted to any external pressure. It is only through discipline that the child can realize the ideals of education, and once it has understood this, it can discipline itself. Idealists, therefore, believe in the efficacy of discipline through influence and impression, not through fear and coercion.

But, discipline can be created among the educands only when the educators themselves create and present good models of discipline. Their own conduct and behaviour should be conditioned by a knowledge of the child's interests and inclinations. In their own behaviour, they must present the highest ideal of self-discipline, for only then can any discipline be expected from the educand. Idealists have criticised the establishment of discipline through threats, repression and punishment. They believe that the entire natural, social and spiritual environment in which the child lives should be fashioned in such a way that it should encourage the desire for self-discipline in the child. Plato believed that the child in the school is restrained with the intention that he may be granted greater liberty gradually as he develops higher. As the individual develops to a level of higher responsibility, he should be granted successively more liberty.

CRITICAL EVALUATION

Though idealism may have been very much left aside in the contemporary field of education, it is undoubtedly the most ancient school which has influenced education throughout its history. Even now the following points may be noted concerning the influence of idealism in the contemporary field of education:

1. *Wider and higher aims*: As the nationalist aims of education are giving place to humanist aim, idealism has become more relevant to the modern educationist. The idealists present the highest and the widest aims and ideals of education summed up in such terms as self-realisation, man-making, development of personality, harmony of man and nature, realisation of truth, goodness and beauty and realisation of heaven upon earth. All these aims have been emphasised by contemporary philosophers of education in East and West.

2. *The ideal teacher*: In this age of science the model of ideal teacher is still presented by idealism. Whatever may be said about the need of practical education and the utilisation of scientific means, no teacher can influence the educands without some sort of idealism. Teaching involves communication which very much depends upon rapport between the teacher and the taught. This is possible only when the teacher considers the taught as a part of his self and thus becomes selfless in his profession. The ideal of character building cannot be achieved unless the teacher himself presents the model of ideal character.

3. *Integrated and multisided curriculum*: While other systems of philosophy of education lay emphasis upon science and technology, the idealists point out the eternal value of humanities, social sciences, art and literature. In fact, they lay emphasis upon an integrated curriculum which may include every branch of knowledge. Thus the idealist curriculum is the most liberal, the most dynamic, the most multisided and therefore, most conducive to the cultural development of the individual and society.

4. *Moral education*: Thinkers everywhere today lament at the general loss of moral character. Everywhere development of moral character is being considered as an urgent need, to save the world from future catastrophe. The idealists explain the aims and means of moral education.

5. *Self-discipline*: The idealist concept of freedom as self-discipline has come to stay. It prescribes central place to the child in the system of education and lays emphasis upon natural development. Natural development requires freedom but freedom cannot be enjoyed without self-discipline. Contemporary educationists

unanimously accept the need of freedom and discipline and agree that self-discipline is the only way for proper development.

6. *Psychological methods*: Even the pragmatists agree that some sort of idealism is necessary for teaching, particularly that of humanities, art and literature. The idealists include instruction, activity and experience in their methods of teaching. The idealist method of teaching is most effective in religious and moral teaching. It is a solid ground for character building and realisation of intimate relations between the teacher and the taught.

In spite of the above mentioned contribution of idealism to education, today it is more and more being left in the background while pragmatism and realism are coming to the front. This is due to the following disadvantages of the idealist philosophy of education:

1. *Utopian aims*: Plato, the first idealist philosopher of education, presented a scheme which was through and through utopian in spite of its deep insight into human life here and there. In fact, in his idealistic flight the thinker often leaves the solid ground and presents aims and ideals which can be neither realised nor cherished.

2. *Theoretical methods*: The idealist method of teaching makes too much of memory, personal contact and brain faculties. They lay less emphasis upon the development of various types of interests and abilities which help the educand in playing important role in society.

3. *Lack of specialization*: The idealist curriculum is too wide and lacks specialisation which is a growing demand of modern education.

4. *Neglect of science and technology*: The idealist thinkers have laid emphasis upon culture in education and neglected science and technology. Therefore, today most of the educational institutions have rejected idealistic curriculum.

5. *Teacher centered*: While modern education is child-centred or educand-centred, the idealist system is teacher-centred. By expecting too much from the teacher it does not allow him to live as a human being with a multisided personality. Too much expectation from the teacher ultimately results in his criticism by the students and society. The role of teacher today is very much different from his role in ancient times. Education today is a

life-long but limited part of life. It goes on even without the teacher. Various audio-visual means are replacing the all important role of the teacher. Therefore, neither the modern teacher nor the taught accept the ancient idealist concept and status of the teacher.

From the perusal of the above mentioned advantages and disadvantages of the idealist philosophy of education it is clear that though some sort of idealism must stay in every field of education, the aims and ideals, the methods, the curriculum and the school management, etc., the ideal of education cannot be realised without the help of naturalism, pragmatism and realism.

5

Realism

Realism is the theory which holds that the existence of objects is real. For this reason it is also sometimes called objectivism. Both realism and objectivism are metaphysical theories concerned with the existence of things. In epistemology realism holds that in the process of knowledge things are independent of the existence and influence of the knower. Hence the main tenet of this theory in the epistemological field is that object audits qualities are independent of and uninfluenced by the knower and the process of knowledge.

Chief Tenets of Realism

As a general rule the chief tenets of realism are the following:

(1) Existence of objects is independent of knowledge: According to the naive realists objects exist irrespective of our knowledge of them. Scientific realism accepts this notion but according to it thoughts concerning the objects are based on the mind.

(2) Qualities are inherent in known objects: According to the naive realists the qualities that are experienced in the objects are part and parcel of the object while the scientific realist distinguishes between primary and secondary qualities, maintaining that primary qualities belong to the object while the secondary are attributed to the object by the mind in the process of knowledge.

(3) Knowledge does not affect the object or its qualities: According to the naive realists the objects or its qualities do not suffer by becoming the subjects of knowledge but according to the scientific realists this theory does not hold true for secondary qualities.

(4) Knowledge of objects is direct: According to the naive realists, knowledge of the object is direct and perceptual. According to representationism, this is true of simple thoughts, for in complex thought knowledge is indirect since complex thoughts are compounded of simple ones.

(5) Objects are common: According to the analytical realists objects are common while according to the representationists objects are commonly available only for the purposes of primary or elementary thought. Scientific realists hold that the same object may be experienced differently by different individuals.

(6) Relation between object and thought: Naive realism holds that there is relation between object and its thought, but the scientific realist rejects this theory.

MAIN TYPES OF REALISM

The main types of realism are the following:

(1) Naive realism: This is a theory propounded by common-sense according to which objects are independent of mind whether they are known or not. Object possesses its own qualities. Knowledge does not affect the object. The object is precisely what it is seen to be. Objects are known directly and objects are common for all.

(2) Representationism: This theory is the product of Locke's mind. It states that the object's existence is independent of knowledge but metaphysical thought depends upon the mind. Primary, objective, individual and secondary qualities are inherent in the object. Knowledge does not impress upon the object but it can influence metaphysical thought. Thoughts are the representations of objects. Knowledge of objects is direct in the case of simple thoughts but indirect in the case of complex ones. In simple thoughts objects are common or universal but not so in complex thinking.

(3) Neo realism: This is a novel approach to the Platonic theory of reality. In this theory it is believed that the total object is not the subject of knowledge but its aspects are, and they are independent of knowledge. The qualities of the object are its own and knowledge does not affect them. An object is what it is manifestly seen to be. Knowledge of the aspects of an object is direct while logical entities are universal.

(4) Critical realism: The theory was first propounded in America at the turn of the century and is critical in nature. It also believes that the existence of objects does not depend upon knowledge in any way. The object is possessed of qualities and is directly known. Objects may or may not be universal. Critical realism does not hold that the object is precisely what it is seen to be or that it is seen to be exactly what it is. When the object becomes object of knowledge it is influenced by knowledge. Knowledge can be direct as well as indirect. The relation between the knower and known is not direct but takes place through the medium of thought, which is the subject matter of knowledge. Different people can have different knowledge of an identical object.

These different theories of realism have been arranged in order of their historical appearance and none of them has been found to satisfy completely. Each and everyone has been objected to and found wanting in some respect.

IDEALISM AND REALISM

In the varied fields of epistemology, metaphysics and evolution, idealism and realism present two almost completely differing theories. They differ in the following respects:

(1) Difference in epistemology: Idealism and realism differ in the following respects on the various questions of epistemology:

(*i*) According to idealism objects have no existence apart from their ideas, while according to realism, objects have an existence independent of any knowledge of them.

(*ii*) Idealism maintains that qualities are imposed on the object by the mind while realism holds that qualities are a part of the object.

(*iii*) The idealistic tenet is that knowledge influences the object and its qualities while the realist theory is that objects cannot be affected in this way.

(*iv*) According to idealism objects are known indirectly through the medium of their ideas but realism holds that objects are known directly.

(*v*) In idealism it is believed that different objects appear differently to different people but in realism it is believed that objects are universal.

(*vi*) According to idealism objects are not what they appear to be since their knowledge is indirect but realism maintains that objects are precisely what they appear to be.

(2) Metaphysical differences: From the metaphysical standpoint realism and idealism differ in the following respects:

(*i*) According to the idealists the universe exists within the mind while the realists are of the opinion that the natural world is independent of the mind.

(*ii*) The idealists believe in some kind of synthesis between man and nature while the realists deny the existence of any such synthesis.

(*iii*) Idealism states that man is the centre of the universe while realism does not attach the same importance to man with reference to universe.

(*iv*) Idealists are idealistic while the realists are realistic.

(3) Difference in cosmology: Realism and idealism differ in the following respects on questions regarding cosmology:

(*i*) According to idealism the mechanistic explanation of the universe is not adequate while realists propound this mechanistic explanation.

(*ii*) Idealism holds that creation of the universe is teleological while the realists do not believe in there being any purpose in creation.

(*iii*) In explaining creation the idealists lay the stress on normative and social sciences while the realists rely more heavily on the natural sciences in their explanation of creation.

(*iv*) Idealism puts forth a value judgement of the creation while realism is more factual in this analysis.

(*v*) According to the idealists the world is known through the mind while realists do not attach so much importance to the mind in understanding the universe.

(*vi*) Idealism stresses the mental and spiritual in its explanation of the world and realism the material and physical.

From the above analysis of idealism and realism it should be fairly obvious that the two theories are almost contradictory and mutually exclusive. In evaluating the two it must be said that idealism seems more appropriate for understanding the values of human life, which is, in fact, the aim of all our knowledge and science. A more comprehensive standpoint, on the other hand, will make it clear that both idealism and realism view the universe from different standpoints, and hence the difference in their respective metaphysics, epistemology and cosmology. To a liberal, dynamic philosopher with broad vision the two will appear to be complementary. In their respective ways both show glimpses of truth and according to one's standpoint one may be as satisfied with one as one may be with the other. It depends on one's mental make up as to which will appeal to one. Nevertheless, it must be said that idealism, on the whole, is a philosophy that is more mature, refined, optimistic, comprehensive and it elevates the lot of mankind. Nothing can be gained by denigrating realism but there can be no denying superiority of idealism.

HISTORICAL BACKGROUND

The following may be considered landmarks in the field of realistic thinking in education:

1. Erasmus (1446-1537): According to Erasmus knowledge is of two kinds: Object knowledge and world knowledge. Of these the world knowledge comes first and then comes object knowledge. However, object knowledge is more important than world knowledge. In the curriculum Greek, Latin and Grammar should be taught first of all. This helps in gaining proper object knowledge after which teaching in other subjects may be started.

2. Rabelais (1483-1533): Rabelais supported social, moral, religious and physical education in place of classical, linguistic and literary education. He pleaded for free thinking. According to him books should be not only mastered but also practised. The teaching should be made interesting. This is also true in physical education. The aim of education is to make practical life better.

3. John Milton (1608-1674): Milton's philosophy of education is available in his book entitled, *Tractate on Education*. According to Milton the aim of education is to know God, to love Him and to be one with Him. Milton presented a plan of education for the child from 12 to 21 years of age. First of all, Latin, Grammar, Arithmetic, Geometry and morality should be taught. After it education may be imparted in agriculture, physiology, handicraft, natural philosophy, geography, etc. Poetry, literature, languages, economics, politics, history, etc., may be taught as supplementary studies. Milton gives more importance to ideas than words, to practical efficiency than ostentatious achievements. He defined education in these words, "I call, therefore, a complete and generous education that which fits a man to perform justly, skillfully and magnanimously all the offices, both private and public of peace and war".

4. Michael de Montaigne (1533-1592): Montaigne represented socialistic realism which aimed at making child a worldly man. Socialistic realism supported utilitarian viewpoint in education. It criticised bookish knowledge and supported the idea to make knowledge practical. Montaigne was a humanist and a naturalist. He was a realist and a socialist. In fact, he was a socialistic realist. The aim of knowledge, according to him, is to enhance knowledge and reasoning power. Nothing should be admitted without understanding. It is improper to take abnormal interest in goods. Knowledge must be practical. The child should be trained for worldly activities. Virtues should be created since these are the bases of enjoyment of the world. The function of philosophy is not only to tell about thinking but about the livelihood. It gives us a knowledge of virtues. Moral knowledge should be gathered from the biographies of great persons.

5. Richard Mulcaster (1531-1621): Mulcaster represented sensuous or empirical realism. According to empirical realism real education emphasises training of senses and not the memory. Education is a natural process and should be based in nature. Philosophy of education should be scientific and not imaginary. Word knowledge should follow the perception of the object. New practical ways should be adopted. According to Mulcaster the aim of education is to develop physical and mental power. Child is the centre of education. Mother tongue should be the medium of education. The teachers should have a sound knowledge of the method of teaching.

6. Francis Bacon (1561-1626): Bacon was also a supporter of empirical realism. He condemned bookish education and tried to make it practical. According to him practical knowledge may be gained through the study of Nature. Subjects such as philosophy, literature and language should be considered secondary. Knowledge can be gained by inductive method. This is particularly true in the field of science. Bacon is known as a great supporter of the inductive method in science.

7. Ratke (1571-1635): Ratke was also a supporter of empirical realism. He favoured education through mother tongue. He maintained that one thing should be taught at one time.

Teaching should be done in free environment. Learning should be discouraged. Object knowledge should be acquired by direct experience and experiment.

8. Comenius (1592-1670): Comenius presented far more clear ideas than other realist philosophers. He laid emphasis upon mother tongue, graded curriculum, suitable text-books, practical application of teaching and four stages of educational structure.

9. Johann Friedrich Herbart (1776-1841): The aim of education according to Herbart, is the multisided development of interests. The child should be made interested in his social environment. The aim of education is character development. This, however, cannot be achieved by preaching but by presenting moral example before the children.

10. Herbert Spencer (1820-1903): Herbert Spencer was a naturalist as well as a realist. Complete living is the aim of education and also the aim of life. This may be realised by doing the following activities:

1. Self-preservation, *i.e.*, care of health.
2. Earning a living (Preparation for vocation).
3. Fulfilling duties regarding race-preservation.
4. Fulfilling duties of a citizen.
5. Utilization of leisure.

All these activities should be done scientifically.

AIMS OF EDUCATION

The realistic aim of education is a happy and integrated life. According to the American educationist Franklin Bobit, happiness in life may be achieved by fulfilment of human responsibilities and obligations such as:

1. Activities concerned with language,
2 Activities concerned with hygiene,
3. Citizenship activities,
4. Ordinary social activities,
5. Leisure activities,
6. Activities of mental health,
7. Religious activities,
8. Activities concerning race-preservation,

9. Vocational behaviour activities,
10. Vocational activities.

The child should be provided complete knowledge of society. He should know the social circumstances, social organisation and natural environment. Learning is the art of leading practical life. This requires scientific attitude. Scientific attitude is a rational attitude. It is objective and sensuous. The aim of education is to enable the child to acquire knowledge of definite and real objects and to analyse it through reason.

In the sphere of education, realism made its appearance as the revolt against theoretical and verbal education. From the earliest ages educationists have been trying to relate education to the social and natural environment, but very often this truth was forgotten and the process of education was allowed to become very theoretical and merely verbal. At all such times, realism has appeared as the reaction to this tendency. At the root of realism were two factors—the disutility of ancient and medieval ideals, and the development of the scientific tendency. By the sixteenth century an awareness had broken upon men that ancient ideals could not satisfy their needs because they were impractical. In Europe, during the Renaissance, there was a reaction to old Monasticism and Scholasticism. It came to be believed that men must aim at evolving humane qualities, and for this it was felt that a study of the literature in Greek and Latin was essential. After the Renaissance, the next tendency which became prominent was Humanism in which the Greek and Latin literatures came to be called humanistic because of their unique contribution to the progress of mankind. Individuals in favour of these literatures came to be called Humanists and their ideas on education gave rise to the concept of Humanitarian education.

But very soon it was realised that the only thing which could be derived from Greek and Roman literature was a definite style and grammar. When Cicero's style became the object and aim of education, humanitarian education was converted to Ciceroism. An unnecessary emphasis upon the study of dead languages and bookish language within (he school drew education far away from real life, and bore little relation to the life outside it.

After the period of humanism came the period of Reformation. This, too, did not go beyond obeying a set of rules and concepts, but it gave a tremendous fillip to research by showing a deep inclination towards reason and intelligence which encouraged free thinking. It was the unprecedented growth of science. A revolution in the sphere of knowledge was created by the researches of Copernicus, Galileo, Newton, Kepler, Harvey, Bacon and others. In this manner, realism came into existence as the result of the growth of science and an inclination to search for the truth. According to the realists, education should be made to conform to the social and individual needs of the child so that he may lead a happy and contented life in the future. Whatever the other ideals of education, its primary purpose was to prepare the child for real life, and the criterion of successful education lay in its ability to prepare the child for adult life. One of the major problems which the individual has to face in adult life is the problem of earning one's livelihood. Hence, education must take care that it enables a man to earn his livelihood. And when the emphasis came to be laid on livelihood, it was only natural that the realist pattern of education should stress the need for teaching scientific subjects rather than artistic or literary subjects. In this, efforts are made to harmonise the child's education with real life. The environment of the school should be such that it creates qualities which are required in the life outside the school. Ancient and medieval education was both bookish and exclusively mental. According to the realists, the first function of education was to develop the qualities of determination, reason and intelligence so that he should facilely solve the problems of life. For this reason realists favour the empirical methods of teaching in which all education is done through actual experience. The realist thinkers also favour education through the medium of the mother-tongue through the medium of demonstrations, tours and actual experiments. This brings education nearer to life, and also stimulates the use of one's own intelligence instead of making demands only upon the educand's memory. In this manner, it can be concluded that the realists want education to keep in mind the social and individual needs of the educands.

CURRICULUM

According to the realists the child should be allowed to choose subjects according to his ability from detailed curriculum. He should be taught what is useful in his life. Learning according to one's abilities results in success in practical life. Subjects should be related to one another. They should be planned according to the needs of the society. Education should enable the student to adjust to changing social circumstances. Phrases such as, 'knowledge for the sake of knowledge', 'art for the sake of art', etc., are meaningless. The curriculum should have utility. Subjects such as literature, art, music, dance, etc., are unnecessary. The curriculum should lay emphasis upon science subjects—physics, chemistry, biology, astrology, etc.

METHODS OF TEACHING

Realist thinkers emphasise objectivity, knowledge of scientific facts and the knowledge of the real. Students should be helped to know objectively. This requires knowledge through sense organs. Words are symbols to convey experience. They help in communication of knowledge. Practical verification is the test of all knowledge. Propositions which cannot be verified are non-sense. Facts are related to the present. The teacher should enable the student to know the world. He should not give personal opinions but clarify the facts. In fact, the facts should themselves be revealed without any distortion. Thus, the realists support fact-centred method of teaching.

According to the realist the knowledge of the real involves two laws: Law of aggregation and the law of conversion of simplicity. There is continuity in nature. In concept formation the feelings should not be allowed to interfere. In the law of conversions of simplicity, it has been pointed out that space and time are divided for the sake of convenience. The whole is the aggregate of parts. The parts do not loose their existence in the whole. Therefore, the proper method of teaching is to begin with the part and reach the whole. Knowledge should be analysed, into principles, and principles into hypothesis. Facts should be analysed into propositions. Thus, the method of teaching should involve analysis and rational classification.

Realist approach to education is child-centred. The method of teaching should change according to the requirement of the child. The intellect of the child should be developed to enable him to know the facts. Experimentation should be the basis of facts. Knowledge is uniform in nature. The teacher should have firm faith in science. He should have a scientific attitude and develop the same in the educand. He should himself investigate and encourage the educands to do so. He should know the experimental method and train the educands in it. He Should understand the needs of the student and fulfil them. He should render a clear, lucid and systematic understanding of scientific facts to the student. He should keep his personal opinion apart from objective teaching. He should keep an eye upon child psychology and adolescence psychology and mould his methods of teaching accordingly. He should make a selection of subject matter according to the interests of the student.

SCHOOL ORGANISATION

According to the realist the school should be organised on the basis of needs of society. Educational institutions should be opened according to local needs and not by political pressure. Science teaching must be done in every school as academic and literary subjects alone do not fulfil the needs of society. Science gives us an understanding of the real world.

Educational institutions may have co-education since the two sexes have to adjust in society. Living together is the best way to learn this adjustment. Sex education may also be imparted to boys and girls in order to check population growth in future. Population education may also form a part of curriculum. The school should minor the society and encourage all types of activities required in society. It is a miniature society and it should present a realistic picture of the world outside it.

DISCIPLINE

The school should be organised in such a way that the child should learn self-discipline. He should learn to control his feelings and desires and to perform his duties. Discipline is adjustment to objectivity. It is required to enable the child to adjust to his environment. It helps the child in concentrating on his studies. Every student is a part of the world and he should learn to adjust in his circumstances. Discipline, however, is not withdrawal. The students should remain in close touch with the harsh realities of life.

CRITICAL EVALUATION

Like other systems of philosophy of education realism has its advantages and disadvantages. Its impact can be seen everywhere. The realist philosophers influence practical education. In seventeenth century academies for the teaching of natural sciences developed everywhere in Europe and later on in America in 18th century. Technical and vocational education has become a common feature of education everywhere. Thus, the following may be considered to be the contribution of realism to education:

1. Education in technical and vocational subject: Every society needs technocrats and people trained in different vocations. Therefore, in every country of the world today the plan of education is based upon the needs of such persons in the development of the nation.

2. Practical bias: The realist insisted upon the practical nature of education. Modern education is empirical, experimental and practical.

3. Practical aims: Even in the field of ideals of education practical aims such as national development, earning a livelihood, personality development or realisation of happiness are being emphasised. These aims conform to real social aspirations.

4. Widening of scope: Realists have widened the scope of education to include scientific and technical subjects as well as social sciences and humanities.

5. Scientific teaching methods: Modern teaching methods are more scientific. Help is taken from audio-visual means of education particularly in the teaching of science subjects. Laboratory training is a must for science teaching. More stress is laid on inductive method. The universities are encouraging research in sciences and humanities.

6. Objective attitude: Today's education is objective. Personal opinions and feelings are ignored while objective facts are emphasised.

7. Sense training: Modern education is empirical, particularly in primary and nursery stages. Stress is laid on sense training so that the child may use his different senses with maximum efficiency in order to directly gain knowledge of the world around him.

8. Realistic school organisation: Modern school is organised to be a mini-society. Discipline means self-control and adjustment to facts. The students are required to develop all the traits of personality required in social life. The programmes in the school are geared to make him a responsible member of society.

In spite of the above mentioned advantages and favourable influences of realism on education, there have been certain disadvantages and limitations in realistic philosophy of education. Of these the most important are as follows:

1. Too much emphasis on objectivity: The terms objective and subjective are relative. Absolute objectivity is impossible. No scientist claims absolute objectivity. Knowledge as well as ignorance, both are subjective as well as objective. Realist's exclusive emphasis on objectivity ignores so much content of knowledge. It neglects imagination, feeling, emotion and sentiments which are also important facts of individual and social life. This leads to negligence of values which, of course, are not facts.

2. Too much emphasis on facts: Facts and values are interwoven in the fabric of individual and social life. By their exclusive emphasis upon facts the realists tend to ignore values. The theory that values are social facts has led to immoral and corrupt implications. In a sense, values are *sui-generis.* They are self-evident. No real human life is possible without values. The realistic attitude often becomes factual but not value-oriented. Practice, of course, is useful but theory has also its value. Facts and ideas, both are part of knowledge.

3. Positivism and meliorism: Positivism pleads that science alone is the real knowledge. According to meliorism we can make this world better only through science. Both these have some grain of truth but they have their limitations as well. Science cannot substitute philosophy, art and literature. Liberal education should find a place for all these. Some persons have better talents in philosophy, art and literature. Therefore, it is wrong to make science compulsory at all stages of education. Not only academic subjects but even some sort of training in ethics and religion are necessary for a happy life. Exclusive emphasis upon science makes education one-sided.

The above criticism is no condemnation. The contribution of realism is undeniable. The above discussion only shows its limitations. As has been already pointed out earlier, every type of philosophy has its positive and negative contribution to education. This is as much true of realism as of idealism, naturalism and other types of philosophies of education.

6

Naturalism: Jean Jacques Rousseau

In the history of philosophy of education naturalism is also as old as idealism. The term naturalism, by its ordinary meaning, means the ism laying emphasis upon nature in every field of education. Thus, the naturalist philosopher derives the aims and ideals, the means, the methods of teaching and the principles of curriculum and school management from the Nature. The most ancient form of naturalism was presented by Democritus (460-360 BC) in the form of atomistic naturalism. In Greece, Democritus explained the composition of universe in terms of innumerable, individual and indestructible atoms. This materialistic explanation of the world was the ground of naturalism in education. This theory was partly amended by Epicurus (341-270 BC). This atomistic naturalism was the beginning of naturalism in the West. This, however, is not the basis of modern naturalism as a philosophy of education.

PHILOSOPHICAL PRESUPPOSITIONS

In metaphysics, the ultimate reality, according to naturalism, is the Nature and Nature is material. In epistemology, the naturalists are empiricists. They believe that knowledge is acquired through sense organs and with the help of the brain. They do not accept the rationalist's position that all knowledge is innate. In modern western philosophy John Locke, Bishop Berkeley and David Hume, the British philosophers were empiricists. They believed in the possibility of direct knowledge. In axiology, the naturalists believe in living according to Nature as the best type of life. 'Follow Nature' is their slogan. Be natural is their motto. They are pluralists since Nature has made all persons different.

THREE PHILOSOPHICAL FORMS OF NATURALISM

From the standpoint of philosophical principles, the following three forms of naturalism are distinguished:

1. Naturalism of physical world: This principle seeks to explain human actions, individual experiences, emotions and feelings on the basis of physical sciences. It seeks to explain the entire universe in the light of the principles of physical sciences. It has little or no influence in the sphere of education, because all that it has done is to place knowledge of science above every kind of knowledge. It points out that not only is science one form of knowledge, but that it is the only form of valid knowledge. It is a concept of positivism, and it holds that even philosophical knowledge is worthless.

2. Mechanical positivism: According to this principle, the entire universe is a machine made of matter and is possessed of a self driving energy that ensures its functioning. This is materialism, for it suggests that matter is the only reality, and anything that exists is a form of matter. The human being is conceived of as nothing more than an active machine which is activated by certain environmental influences. The impact of this kind of positivism led to the emergence of the behavioural school in psychology which explained all human behaviour in terms of stimulus and response Behaviourists do not believe in the existence of any consciousness distinguished from the material element. All processes of the mental faculty such as imagination, memory, thinking, etc., are explained in physiological terms. This school also makes no distinction between human and animal, because both can be explained in terms of stimulus and response. Behaviourism thus seeks to explain the entire range of human activity as a mechanical process. As naturalism it has had a tremendous impact on education.

3. Biological naturalism: It is naturalism in this form, as biological naturalism, which has had the greatest impact upon education. It has elaborated the theory of the natural man, and has explained that the evolution of man and animal is a single process. It refuses to admit the spiritual nature of man and expounds that his nature is the heritage he has received from his ancestors. That is why it traces many similarities between human and animal behaviour. Biological naturalism contends that all the processes of Nature and the entire existence of the universe cannot be explained in terms of mechanical and physical processes, because in the biological world, evolution is a more important phenomenon. All living beings have an instinct to live and for this reason life evolves from lower forms to higher and more complex ones. One can find all the characteristics of evolution in man's life. The principles underlying evolution can explain the form that a human being will ultimately assume and the manner in which he will progress. At the animal level, the process of evolution stops at the material or physical level, but in the case of human beings it is also manifested in the mental, moral and spiritual levels. This instinctive evolution is found not only in individual human beings but also in groups of human beings, because these groups also evolve to a stage of greater complexity. But this evolution is also governed by the same principles which govern the individual's evolution. In this process of evolution, the principles of struggle for existence and survival of the fittest have been considered the most important by Charles Darwin, because in his opinion the principle of self-preservation is the strongest law of nature.

HISTORICAL BACKGROUND

As has been pointed out earlier, naturalism, like other isms, started in ancient Greece and ancient India. Democritus (460 BC), Leucippus (793-57 BC), Thales (640-546 BC), Epicurus (341-270 BC) and Lucretius (96-55 BC) were prominent naturalists in ancient Greece. In ancient India the philosophers known as *Charvakas* were naturalists. In medieval period no significant naturalists prospered since religion had a wide influence upon thinkers. From the sixteenth to eighteenth century, the most important naturalist thinkers were Rousseau (1712-1788), Bacon (1561-1626) and Hobbes (1588-1679). Herbert Spencer (1820-1903 AD) presented a naturalist philosophy of education in contemporary times. Before an exposition of the views of modern naturalists, a review of its influence in education will be useful.

As a philosophy, naturalism has influenced education by determining the aims and objectives of education, apart from explaining the methods of education and means or agencies of education, through an explanation of human nature. In the sphere of education, naturalism is neither the positivism of the physical world nor mechanical positivism or even biological naturalism. It is an entirely different concept which seeks to base education on the experience of the child, and thus is a repudiation of all text-book teaching. In the eighteenth century Rousseau launched a bitter offensive against all traditional forms of formal education, and instead advocated the basing of all education on education according to nature. Ever since then, so much stress has been placed on studying the nature of the child, that it has led to a veritable revolution in the field of education because it has motivated considerable research in this sphere and applied the principles discovered through this research. Nineteenth century saw comprehensive educational reforms all over Europe, and the appearance of a tendency to make all education scientific. Naturalism adopts a scientific posture in as much that it wants the educational process to follow the natural inclination of the child, and it is thus opposed to all traditional and static methods of education. It stresses the value of dynamic methods. It seeks to base all education on psychology. Adam has pointed out that naturalism is a word obscurely applied to those principles of training which do not depend upon books but instead upon the laws of the natural life of the educand. Hence all those systems which oppose the use of text-books and prefer to centre education on the child can be called naturalistic. This principle is opposed to making education complex, for its motto is "Follow Nature". It is against artificiality of any kind. Naturalism is the inevitable reaction in education when education had been practically killed by the oppressive weight of tradition, stern discipline, rules of the school, dry curriculum, the formal behaviour of the teacher, etc.

JEAN JACQUES ROUSSEAU (1712-1778)

As has been already pointed out, in modern times Rousseau was undoubtedly, the most important naturalist philosopher of education. His writings were published since 1750 AD onwards. Some of his famous works are: (1) *The Progress of Arts and Sciences;* (2) *Social Contract,* (3) *New Heloise:* and (4) *Emile.* Of these the most important are *Emile* and *Social Contract. Emile* is a novel in which the author has described the education of Emile, an imaginary child. The author described the methods of bringing the child in contact with Nature and removing social evils. The child is left under the guidance of an ideal teacher away from school and society. The teacher teaches the child in a natural environment. The book *Emile* consists of five parts respectively devoted to infancy, childhood, adolescence, youth and the imaginary wife of Emile named Sofia.

Rousseau was particularly impressed by the poverty and suffering of the people. He hated society for the evils and wanted to reform it. He realised, "Everything is good as it comes from the hands of the author of the nature but everything degenerates in the hands of man". Thus Rousseau, on the one hand, opposed society and praised Nature on the other hand. His book *Social Contract* portrays his ideas concerning society and politics. He gave the slogan 'Return to Nature.' His work *Emile* aroused reactions everywhere, favourable as well as unfavourable. France and Switzerland banned this book. It was burnt at so many places. Rousseau had to leave France for England in 1766. Alter 11 years he returned to France and wrote his last book entitled *Confessions*. He died in 1778. His thoughts influenced French revolution. He was acclaimed as a great revolutionary and reformer.

Rousseau's naturalist philosophy shows three forms: Social naturalism, Psychological naturalism and Physical naturalism. In his social naturalism he devices education as a method to develop society. According to him one cannot become a man and citizen at the same time. Every new culture is born out of the old. The past mistakes or evils must be removed though old ideals may be honoured. As a bitter critic of society Rousseau condemned old traditions opposing new reforms. He said, "Whatever is generally banned today you should do just the opposite, then you will find the right path". Rousseau's social naturalism may be found in his book *Social Contract.* His aim is man making and not the making of social man and citizen. In man making the man should follow his own inner feelings and natural tendencies. The child should be left to behave naturally. He learns in the contact of plants, animals, birds and natural objects. Society and man spoil the child. From moral and physical point of view the city is opposed to human good. The people should organise government to fulfil their needs. Wealth should not be concentrated in few hands. Thus, Rousseau pleaded for liberty and equality. According to him education means, "natural development of organs and powers of the child".

Negative Education

According to Rousseau, the first education ought to be purely negative. It consists not at all in teaching virtue or truth but in shielding the heart from vices and mind from errors. Thus

Rousseau was against imparting any education to the child. According to him, "In childhood the aim of education is not to utilise time but to loose it". Elsewhere he said, "A twelve-year old child should know nothing. The teacher should pay attention to the child only and not to knowledge".

In Rousseau's time the children were given moral and religious education through various types of books in order to prepare them for adult life. Explaining his new system of education Rousseau said, "Give me a twelve-year old child who does not know anything. By 15 years of age, I will teach him so much as other children read in 15 years of early life. The only difference will be that your student remembers only knowledge and my student will be able to use it in practical life". Thus, Rousseau precisely reversed the old order. As he said, "Take the reverse of the accepted practice and you will almost always do right". This was what he called, negative education.

Criticising the educational system of his time Rousseau said, "What must we think then, of that barbarous education which sacrifices the present to an uncertain future, which loads a child with chains of every sort and begins by making him miserable in order to prepare for him long in advance, some pretended happiness, which it is probable, he will never enjoy". This was positive education emphasising the mind and trying to make the child an adult. Negative education, on the other hand, strengthens the sense organs and the power of reasoning. As Rousseau said, "Nature wants that the child should remain a child before he becomes an adult. By changing this sequence we shall get raw fruits which shall soon perish. The child has his own ways of seeing, thinking and experiencing. We should not impose our own methods on him. It will be a folly".[1] We do not understand the child and assume our ideas as his ideas.[2] Elsewhere he said, "I want that some wise man should tell us the art of counselling the child. This art will be valuable for us. The teachers have not learnt even its elementary rule".[3]

Thus, negative education is self-education. It is the education of sense organs and body. This may be more possible in the playground rather than in the classroom. As Rousseau said, "We

1. Emile, p. 75.
2. *Ibid.*, p. 185.
3. *Ibid.*, p. 114.

give too much importance to words. We produce by chattering education chatterers only. If you are all the time teaching morals to the child, you will make him a fool. If your mind is always giving instructions to the child, then his mind will become useless. Whatever the child learns in playground is four times more useful than what he learns in the classroom". According to Rousseau man's development may be classified into the following four stages:

1. *Infancy,* from birth to 5 years of age.
2. *Childhood,* from 5 years to 12 years of age.
8. *Adolescence,* from 12 years to 15 years of age.
4. *Youth,* from 15 years to 20 years of age.

Rousseau has suggested suitable education in all these stages in his book *Emile.*

Aims of Education

In the opinion of Rousseau, education aimed at the natural development of the child's inner faculties and powers. Education should help the child to remain alive. Life implies not merely the taking of breath but working. To live is to work, to develop and to properly utilise the various parts of the body, the sense organs and the various other powers of the body. In his book *Emile,* Rousseau seeks to train Emile in the profession of living so that he may become a human being before becoming a soldier, a churchman or a magistrate. Education, thus, in Rousseau's opinion, must aim at making the child a real human being.

But the aims of education change at different stages of the child's development, because at each stage something different needs stress. The following are the various aims of education according to each level of the child's development:

1. Infancy: This stage begins at birth and continues up to five years of age. The chief objective during these five years is bodily development, the development and strengthening of every part of the body. This is essential if the child is to grow up healthy and strong. It forms the basis of subsequent healthy development of the mind. Rousseau expressed the opinion, "All wickedness comes from weakness. The child should be made strong so that he will do nothing which is bad". When the child is allowed to freely engage in playing and exercising his body, he remains active and has no time to indulge in undesirable activities. Nothing need be done to develop his instincts other than to give him complete liberty. If such freedom is given, he naturally develops his own instincts.

2. Childhood: This stage lasts from the fifth year to the twelfth, and it is the period of developing the child's sense organs. This development is achieved through experience and observation. Hence the child should be made to observe and experience those things in his environment which will assist the development of his sense organs.

3. Adolescence: For Emile, adolescence was believed to last from the twelfth to the fifteenth year. The child has, by this time, achieved the development of his body and his sense organs, and is, therefore, prepared, for systematic education. At this stage, education aims at developing the adolescent personality through hard work, guidance and study. During adolescence the individual should be given knowledge of various kinds so that he is enabled to fulfil his needs.

4. Youth: The individual passes through his youth between his fifteenth and twentieth year and undergoes development of emotions and sentiments. Rousseau pointed out, "We have formed his body, his senses and intelligence, it remains to give him a heart". Development of the sentiments will lead to development of moral and social qualities, but it is essential to pay attention to the development of religious emotions also. Summing up, the aim of education is to achieve the bodily, sensory, mental, social and moral development of the individual.

Curriculum of Education

It is possible to arrive at Rousseau's concept of a curriculum from an analysis of the various stages of development described in his *Emile.* Even in framing the curriculum, Rousseau paid attention to these four stages in development, and it will be better to consider the curriculum in the same fashion.

1. Infancy: Rousseau was very critical of the contemporary curriculum laid down for the education of infants, because he stressed the fact that infants should be treated as infants and not as adults in the miniature. The child is not a young adult, because his instincts and tendencies are dissimilar to those of the adult. For this reason, it is imperative to first understand child psychology and then to frame a curriculum. Instead of giving him controlled information of various subjects at this stage, it is far more important to pay attention to the development of his body and his senses. Before thinking of making the child a successful engineer or doctor, it is desirable to make him a healthy and self-sufficient young animal. In this age, the child can be taught a great deal through normal conversation carried on in the child's mother tongue. This will develop his linguistic ability. It is better not to try and instill any kind of habits in the child at this stage. Rousseau stated, "The only habit the child should be allowed to contract is that of having no habits".

2. Childhood: Even in childhood, Rousseau objected to the use of any textbooks for education, because he wanted to keep Emile away from books of any kind up to the twelfth year. He thought it necessary to give the child a chance to learn everything through direct experience and observation. Education of this kind is based on the concept of negative education which suggests that the child's mind should not be stuffed with information of different kinds. Instead he should be given liberty to learn through experience, because experience develops the sense organs which in turn lead to mental development, reason and development of the power of argument and reasoning. When the child is free to play, move, act at his own will during his childhood, he goes through a variety of experiences and learns all kinds of activities. During childhood, the child should not be given any verbal lessons on history, geography or even language. It is not desirable even to do any moral preaching. Rousseau opined that the child will learn his morality by the natural consequences of his own actions. Hence, up to the childhood stage no curriculum of any kind is required.

3. Adolescence: Having arrived at the appropriate level of bodily and sensory development, the child can now be exposed to teaching according to a formal curriculum consisting of education in natural science, language, mathematics, woodwork, music, painting, social life and some kind of professional training. Even here, Rousseau opined, more stress should be laid on the use of the sense organs than books. The very object of training in all these various subjects is the training and development of the sense organs. The study of science will enhance the child's curiosity and his inclination towards research, invention and self-education. Painting helps to train the muscles and eyes. Handicrafts help in developing the ability to work, apart from the mental development which is part of the process. Passing through various phases of social life, the individual learns that men depend upon each other, and thereby the child learns to assume and fulfil social responsibility. Rousseau gave it as his opinion that books do not give knowledge, but only train one to talk. Hence it is better if the curriculum for adolescence is based on active work than on books. During this period the adolescent must get adequate opportunity and time for hard work, education and study.

4. Youth: In the curriculum for youth, special stress has been laid on moral and religious education. But even moral education is to be derived through actual experience rather than through formal lectures. The youth learns a moral lesson when the sight of a physically handicapped person arouses in him the emotions of pity, sympathy and love. Religious education also follows the same pattern, but it can be assisted by the teaching of history, mythological stories and religious stories. The youth derives many lessons from these stories. Apart from moral and religious education, Rousseau gave appropriate importance to education in bodily health, music and sex.

Educational Method

Pointing out the importance of experience in education Rousseau said, "To be alive does not mean to breathe, but it means to work and to develop our organs, senses and other powers. That man is not happy who has a long life but happy is one who has gained experiences of life". As the method generally pursued in education in his time was mainly oral and theoretical, Rousseau criticised the prevalent teaching methods. He said, "I want that some wise man should tell us the art of counselling the child. This art will be valuable for us. The teachers have not learn even its elementary rule". Rousseau wanted to adopt play way method in education in place of verbal teaching. He maintained, "Education should be practical rather than oral. The child will not have to read through books, he will have to stop reading words". Then, what should be the proper method of teaching the child? For Rousseau education to the child should be provided by play. "Thus, real education is self-education. The infant himself learns to develop by utilisation of his sense organs and reacting to the environment".

Principles of Education

Rousseau is a naturalist in his methodology of education just as much as he is a naturalist in the curriculum of education. He has stressed the importance of the two following principles governing the process of education:

1. Learning through self-experience: Rousseau wanted to educate Emile through experience and not through books. He was opposed to bookish education, because he contended that books try to teach one to talk about those things which one does not, in fact, know. That is why he wanted to keep Emile away from books for twelve years, so much so that he did not want Emile even to know what a book is. Rousseau has praised only one book, *Robinson Crusoe,* because it presents the natural needs of human beings in such a simple manner that the child can easily comprehend them. From this book the child can also learn the manner in which these needs are to be satisfied.

2. Learning through doing: Rousseau opposed the rote method of learning on the ground that knowledge acquired through actual doing or actual experience is far more permanent than knowledge acquired through words He wanted the child's power of reasoning and not his power of memorising things to be developed. That is why Rousseau was so severely critical of the existing methods of education. He wanted the child to become educated through his own observation, experience and analysis. Instead of stuffing the child's mind with his own knowledge, the educator's task is to arouse the child's curiosity so that the child is inspired to find out things for himself, thus developing his own mind. Science is best taught through curiosity and the desire to experiment and research. Rousseau's insistence on these elements was later manifested in the evolution of the Heuristic method. If the child is to give moral education to himself he must be active. Long lectures bore the child, and instead of contributing to his education, only hinder it because they blunt the child's appetite for new things. Hence, instead of delivering long lectures to the child, it is better to give him the opportunity to act for himself. In education, the object is more important than the word. It is undesirable to fashion a method of education and to mould the child accordingly.

Discipline

Rousseau, being a naturalist, wanted complete freedom as the first step towards inducing discipline in the child. He wanted a total absence of any restraints on the child, because he felt that they hindered the development of discipline. It is better to leave the child free in free environment so that he can develop his natural powers. Rousseau's plan also did not include any arrangement for punishment, because he felt that punishment should be the natural outcome of their own mistakes. This is the naturalist conception of punishment. In this theory it is assumed that the child has no know ledge of good and bad, but he suffers pain when he makes a mistake and pleasure when he does something right. Hence, he gets the reward of his actions. This is the natural pattern of punishment and it is this which will instill discipline in the child. This is natural discipline, which implied obedience of natural laws, because neglect or violation of these laws invariably leads to pain and suffering. Hence, it is not necessary to lecture to the child. He is naturally possessed of a fine character, and this character is defiled by long lectures. He will learn better discipline, if he is left to himself.

School Organisation

The title given above may be a little misleading because Rousseau objected to the system of school education. He contended that the child is born innocent and pure, that he is only defiled and distorted by the defective environment of the school. In fact, the only suitable environment of every kind is defective and impure. It is better to separate the child from his parents, to take him away from school, and leave him by himself in a natural environment. The educator's only task is to look after the child, because in natural surroundings the child will himself look after the development of his natural abilities. Even if schools are created, they can be utilised by stressing the natural surroundings instead of insisting on creating a social atmosphere. In the predominantly natural surroundings the child will be able to develop naturally.

HERBERT SPENCER (1820-1903)

Herbert Spencer published his book *Education* in 1861. This book shows his naturalist philosophy of education. Like Rousseau he criticised the curriculums and methods of teaching of the schools of his times. He pointed out that they were too much theoretical.

Aims and Ideals

The aim of education, according to Herbert Spencer, is to prepare the child for complete living. The aim of life is complete living and is a means to know the techniques of this art. Complete living is a happy life. It requires development of body and mind. This development is acquired by full utilisation of natural resources and the use of organised powers.

Responsibilities of Man

The aims and ideals of education follow from the five responsibilities of man:

1. Self-preservation: The first and foremost responsibility of man is self-preservation. This is not individual but social. The individuals should help each other in realising this ideal. Self-preservation means the preservation of both the body and the mind. To realise this ideal the child should be given practical knowledge of physiology and hygiene. The knowledge itself, however, is not sufficient. It requires practice of its implications. This practice is the function of education. Thus, self-preservation is the most primary aim of education. It goes without saying that this aim is naturalist.

2. Earning a living: In youth self-preservation requires earning a living. This is realised by means of education. Education develops one's capacity for earning a living. Its utility lies in vocation. Science particularly helps in this process. Not only in work and vocation but also in our daily life the knowledge of science is required in construction of houses, agriculture, etc. Different sciences such as geology, chemistry, astrology, physics, etc., prepare us for various vocations in life. Therefore, Spencer prescribes education in all the sciences. Different science subjects should be taught according to the talents of different children. Science experts should be consulted for this purpose Spencer prescribes teaching of all science subjects to the children. This, however, is far from possible. Therefore, educationists have not accepted such a wide prescription of science in the curriculum. However, earning a living remains the aim of education in the present time.

3. Up-bringing of children: After getting employment one marries and begets children. These children should be brought up for complete living. In order to realise this aim the boys and girls should be taught subjects which make them successful parents in future. This aim of education has also been generally accepted by educationists now-a-days.

4. Citizenship: An important area of man's responsibility is citizenship. As a citizen the individual has to perform duties prescribed by the state. Therefore, in almost all the states since ancient times the children were taught things concerning citizenship. In order to develop citizenship, Spencer prescribes scientific study of history. He criticises non-scientific approach in history. According to him history should be taught with reference to the principles of political science. Its importance consists in the growth of liberalism and international understanding.

5. Use of leisure time: As mechanisation and scientific progress was realised, man found more leisure to utilise. One of the important responsibilities of man is worthy use of leisure time. Education helps in this process. For example, leisure time may be devoted to painting, music, sculpture, poetry and also recreation by natural scenes. These arts are developed through education. However, Spencer insists that even leisure time utilisation depends on scientific approach. Even success in music and other arts is not possible without the knowledge of physiology and mechanics. Therefore, Spencer prescribes the combination of innate powers and science. However, this too much insistence on science has not been accepted by modern educationists. It is not accepted that excellence in literature and arts requires a foundation in science, nor is science accepted to be more valuable than arts. In fact, by his too much emphasis on science Herbert Spencer leaves the ideal of complete living. In order to realise the aim of complete living literature, fine arts and science, all should be given proper place in the curriculum. It is wrong to say, as Spencer did, that science is more useful than language. It is again wrong to say that science develops memory and thinking. The value of science is unquestionable but to say that it develops moral values like truth, self-reliance and perseverance is to confuse science with ethics. What we lack today is not science but ethics. In fact, too much subordination of culture to science has led to the present crisis in human culture.

Principles of Teaching

Though not original but Herbert Spencer's principles of teaching admirably sum up the fundamental maxims to be followed by the teacher. These principles are as follows:

1. From easy to difficult: Both curriculum construction and teaching method should proceed from easy to difficult as this is the law of the mind.

2. From known to unknown: For association and integration of the newly achieved information both the curriculum and teaching method should proceed from known to unknown. While this will help in the assimilation of new knowledge, it will also facilitate interest and memory.

3. From indefinite to definite: In the development of man he proceeds from indefinite to definite. This maxim is the foundation of the educational process. The teacher teaches only because his knowledge is definite while the knowledge of the child is indefinite. The child develops from vague to clear knowledge. Therefore, the teacher should all the time proceed from indefinite to definite knowledge. As the knowledge grows, the area of definiteness increases. In the field of indefinite the scientists are always struggling to achieve definite knowledge.

4. Concrete to abstract: In the process of mental development the child first perceives and then ideates. Concept formation depends upon knowledge through sense organs. We first know concrete things and then arrive at abstract concepts. Therefore, it is a set principle of curriculum formation and teaching methods that one should start with concrete experiences and gradually reach abstract equations, concepts and formula, etc.

5. Principle of stages of human development: Since ancient times to present day it has been an accepted principle of curriculum formation and teaching methods that these should vary according to the different stages of human development. The man passes through the stages of infancy, childhood, adolescence, adult and old age in his development. In all these stages his physical and mental powers constantly change. Therefore, the curriculum and the teaching method should be according to the stage of human development. While this will sustain interest, it will make education a success. In the construction of curriculum and teaching methods the environment should also be given new consideration along with stages of human development.

6. From experimental to rational knowledge: Like Rousseau Herbert Spencer was also against bookish education. According to him, the child should be allowed to experiment with things around him. This experimentation will develop his talent and give him experience. This will prepare him to imbibe and retain rational knowledge given in books.

7. Principle of interesting teaching method: Interest is intimately related to attention and memory. Therefore, the teacher should always make his method interesting according to the individuality and development of the educands. Audiovisual aids may be utilised to create interest, particularly in science subjects.

Moral Teaching

Herbert Spencer followed Rousseau in the case of moral teaching. Like Rousseau he prescribed the formula of return to nature as the basis of moral teaching. He criticised the cruel and immoral practices concerning punishment to the child in the family. He pointed out that the child's conduct can develop only when the parents and family provide proper atmosphere. According to Spencer natural consequence is the best punishment. Therefore, the child should be allowed to learn by natural consequences. This point, however, cannot be stressed too far. It may be remembered that the child cannot be left free to make all sorts of experiments, such as playing with knife and fire. In such cases he should be forewarned as he does not know the consequences of so many actions.

Physical Education

In order to realise the aim of complete living, Herbert Spencer prescribed physical education. His physical education is based on science. He points out four different defects in the prevailing physical education system. Firstly, the children are not given full food, secondly, they do not get sufficient clothes. Thirdly, they do not get enough physical exercises. Fourthly, they are asked to do too much mental work. Spencer insists upon provision of balanced food and sufficient clothes according to laws of physiology. The physical and mental work should be balanced with the viewpoint of efficiency and good health. Good health alone leads to joy of life and success. Therefore, it is the duty of the parents and teachers to provide physical education for good health.

Critical Evaluation

The above mentioned philosophy of Herbert Spencer made the following changes in the field of education:

1. Aim: Herbert Spencer, like Rousseau, made the aim of education more practical.

2. Curriculum: Due to the influence of Spencer science was given an important place in the curriculum of schools. Science was included in secondary school in different countries. Similarly, it was included in the curriculum of primary school. It was included in the curriculum in Protestant universities. Science academies were opened at several places. Gradually, all the universities in different European countries started science departments and awarded bachelor and doctorate degree in science.

In spite of the above useful impact of Spencer on education the following drawbacks in his philosophy of education have been pointed out by the critics:

1. As Spencer did not study education, one hardly finds any originality in his views.

2. Spencer preached reform but without any scientific basis.

3. Spencer exclusively stressed the teaching of science from primary to university stage. He even proposed for a scientific form to be given to every subject of study. He neglected the value of literature, art and history.

4. Spencer was against traditional methods of study. He made education more practical. However, he neglected the importance of language in education.

5. According to Dewey educational aim as preparation for future is too limited. It is vitiated by utilitarian bias.

AIMS OF EDUCATION

Concerning the aims of education, naturalists adopt a biological and evolutionist attitude. Even among the different forms of naturalism one finds a variation in the objectives assigned to education. Mechanical naturalism suggests that education should aim at the efficiency and perfection of the human machine. But this concept does not represent completely the naturalist school. Biological evolution uses education to ensure the proper adjustment or adaptation of the child to his environment.

McDougall points out that education aims at the transformation, synthesis and sublimation of instincts. Darwinists argue that education must train the individual to struggle successfully for his own survival. Lamarck and his followers agree with the concept of biological evolution, because for them also the aim of education is to adapt to the environment. On the other hand, Herbert Spencer believed education to be a preparation and a training for the complete life. Bernard Shaw believed that education must aim not only at the individual's development but also at making the individual capable of stimulating and sustaining social development, for this will add to the social heritage of the succeeding generations. T. P. Nunn prefers to use education as a means of making the individual capable of developing his own individuality and of contributing to society. Naturalists of the nineteenth and twentieth centuries believe that education should achieve a synthesis and adjustment between individual and society and also between man and nature. Rousseau believed that education should develop the child according to his natural ability. And it is accepted today that education should conform to the childs abilities. To quote Rousseau's words, "Now of the three factors in education, nature is wholly beyond our control; things are only partly in our power; the education of men is the only one controlled by us; and even here our power is largely illusory, for who can hope to direct every word and deed of all with whom the child has to do .

What is the goal? As we have just shown it is the goal of nature since all three modes of education must work together, the two that we can control must follow the lead of that which is beyond our control".[1] The naturalist approach to the aims of education is rather narrow in that it fails to include the spiritual aspect of man's nature. Its inclusion would almost naturally remove the distance between idealism and naturalism and this is what is being attempted now.

NATURALISM AND CURRICULA

As a system of philosophy, naturalism has been exceptionally susceptible to the development of science, and by virtue of this influence it has attached much importance to evolutionary

1. Jean Jacques Rousseau, *Emile*, Barbara Foxley, Translator. New York E. P. Dutton & Co, Inc. Every man's Library, 1911.

theory, empirical teaching and scientific analysis, etc. As a result of the significance ascribed to scientific study naturalists want to introduce physical and social sciences at every level of education because they believe these to be more important than the humanities. Language and mathematics for the naturalists, are tools for the learning of science and both should be taught only so long as they assist the learning of science. Literature, in any case should not completely absorb the students' interest and attention. Curricula should be so constructed as to encourage the educand to take an interest in science and to gain knowledge which is factual and objective.

Granting that the present is more important than the future, the naturalists have not fallen into the mistake of neglecting the past, because the past contains many valuable suggestions for the educand. For this reason, naturalists believe in the value of historical study. Such a study will enable them to construct a new social structure and thus plan for the future.

Since evolutionists believe man to have developed or evolved, from the animal stage, and since they also believe that there is no gap or discontinuity in the transition from the animal to the human, they want education to develop the instincts and emotions.

On the subject of curriculum, naturalists have expressed theories which differ from each other to some extent. Comenius wanted the educand to study every subject, without making any selection. Locke refuted this notion by demonstrating that every individual cannot be made to study the same subject, because of certain natural handicaps. Hence, much emphasis was laid upon modifying the curriculum to suit the needs of the individual. Herbert Spencer arranged the curriculum with science as its nucleus and tried to synthesise the other subjects to science. The arts were given a secondary place in his programme because he believed that one must first create the basic elements before refining or making them sophisticated. In fact, he wanted to synthesise all subjects to the study of science, arriving at a conception of liberal education arranged around science. T. H. Huxley, another naturalist, attached greater importance to the cultural aspects of life than to the study of science. Thus, his conception of a liberal education differed materially from that of Spencer. In contrast, modern naturalists do not stress the importance of anyone subject against that of any other, although more importance is attached to the sciences. Yet, the arts are not neglected, but given an important place in the curriculum so that it may acquire a definitely wide base.

EDUCATIONAL METHODS

Naturalist education is paidocentric. The child occupies the central place in it. The child, in order to develop, should be left on its own. The society or the state should not interfere in his contact with nature. This will allow the growth of the child in natural circumstances. Therefore, the most important method of teaching, according to the naturalist, is to leave the child free to learn from nature. Naturalism was responsible for a violent denunciation of the traditional methods of education. It opposed all kinds of negative techniques and the stress on rote learning. Instead, it favoured teaching by more positive methods. Being empirical, it preferred to educate the child by giving him actual experience of all that he is to learn. Locke believed that training of the sense organs or sensory training, should be the first stage in the child's education. Naturalists considered experience to be more important than books, for they propounded the principle of do and learn. They felt that the child learns much from natural consequences, and therefore it is best that the child be left to do as he is inclined, so that he may follow the dictates of his own nature.

Much emphasis is laid upon direct experience. It is argued that the child learns more by direct experience of nature, men and objects than through books. By the same reasoning, teaching of science can be more effective if it is done through practical work in the laboratory, just as geometry is better learnt by calculating the configuration of actual objects and spaces than through hypothetical problems posed in the text-books. Geography can be taught better through tours of places of geographical interest than through maps and charts. The same holds true of the teaching of history. Hence, the naturalistic educational methods depend more upon direct experience and personal observation than upon text-books.

Naturalist thinkers suggest the following two methods of education:

1. Positive method: In this the educator tries to inform the child about various subjects. This is the traditional method which the naturalist rejects as old fashioned and ineffective.

2. Negative method: Concerning the negative methods of education, Rousseau has commented, "I call a negative education one that tends to perfect the organs that are the instruments of knowledge before giving them this knowledge directly and that endeavours to prepare the way for reason by the proper exercise of the senses". Hence negative education consists in training the child to use his sense organs and motor organs instead of filling his mind with bits and pieces of information. By using the various bodily powers at his disposal, the child will generate much knowledge for himself

The playway method of education is very popular with naturalists because, during play, the child gets the opportunity to manifest his dormant powers. He is often faced with situations which compel him to use these powers. Irrespective of the definition of play—as recapitulation of man's ancient activities, as a rehearsal for the rough and tumble of future life, as safety valve for letting off excess energy it is undoubtedly the most natural and facile way of developing the child's natural inclinations. That games provide an outlet for man's creative power is true not only of the child's games but also of games played in adult life.

Artificiality of any kind is another thing which the naturalists find objectionable. The atmosphere in the class and the school should be informal, and the time-table should not be rigorously adhered to. Apart from the subjects taught as part of the prescribed syllabus, the child must be encouraged to take active part in various extra curricular programmes. And, in fact, the child should not be burdened by or compelled to submit to any definite teaching method at all. Left to himself the child is perfectly capable of evolving an educational technique which suits him best. If the educator wants to know what this method is, he should observe the child, since through such observation he can learn what the child wants, in which direction he is inclined, in what things he evinces interest. Consequently, the teacher will be enabled to mould his own technique to suit the child.

THE TEACHER

Naturalism opposes the traditional concepts of education in which the educator inflicted any and all kinds of punishment on the child in order to make it progress in the desired direction. Naturalists believe that the period of infancy is important in itself, not merely as a stepping stone to adult life. That explains their extreme emphasis upon the playway technique of education. They opine that the child should be encouraged to enjoy his infancy and childhood as much as he can, with the least possible interference from the teacher. Consequently, the teacher does not occupy as high and respected a position as he does under the idealistic tradition. One example of this is Neil's Summerhill School in which the educator mixed with the educands, played and practically lived with them. Even the matter of discipline was in the hands of the educands who selected a cabinet of five educands for this purpose. This cabinet was even empowered to expel an educand from the school, if it felt the necessity for such an extreme step. Neil's only function was to remove the various difficulties of the educands, after discussing everything with them. Hence, in this school, the educator was no more than just one of the members of the school.

Naturalists suggest that the educator should be a guide and a friend, and that in his behaviour with the child, the educator should try to recollect his own childhood and infancy. The child is naturally inclined to laughter and happiness. Hence the educator should be jolly and not grave, for undue seriousness of manner and behaviour depresses the child. The educator's role is primarily negative inasmuch as he is required to protect the child's inherent goodness from bad influences originating in the environment. He is responsible for creating an environment in which the child can experience the greatest amount of freedom. He must study the child's psychology and intervene in his activity only when some obstacle bars the way to the child's progress.

Hence, the aim of education is, thus, to provide the child with opportunities for completely unrestricted self-expression. The role of educator, therefore, is only to protect the child from repressions, mental conflicts and mental disorders of all kind. Naturalism warns the educator against unnecessary seriousness, the desire to assert his authority, physical punishment, etc., since all these measures have a detrimental influence upon the child's development. The educator must think in terms of what he must avoid doing rather than think of things he must do. He can do even better and become literally a child in dealing with children. But his guidance is apparent when he can give a positive and confident opinion on controversial matters, and for this he must be possessed of unbounded self-confidence. He can also guide the children in their search for new things, and can train them in new techniques of doing things so that in later life they should become capable of doing things on their own. The role of the teacher is most clearly defined by Ross in the following words, "His (educator's) place, if any, is behind the scenes; he is an observer of the child's development rather than a giver of information, ideas, ideals and will power, or a moulder of character. These the child will forge for himself, he knows better than any educator what he should learn, when and how he should learn it. His education is the free development of his interests and motives rather than an artificial effort made on him by an educator. "It is evident, therefore, that the educator should never have recourse to any kind of pressure or force, even to the use of his own authority. His task is simply to provide the theatre for the child's acting, to collect the materials required, to provide the child with an opportunity to do as he likes, to create an ideal environment. As a result of the impact of naturalism, many of the latest techniques of education, such as the Montessori system, Dalton plan, Project method, etc., all grant to the teacher a similar status.

Compared to naturalistic philosophy, the idealistic school grants a more responsible position to the teacher. Adams expressed the opinion that the educator himself has been through the same situations as the educand is experiencing at present. He is no less a part of the intellectual world than anyone else. Both the educator and the educand are two elements of the organic structure of the universe, and both have their own status and role in God's plan. The educator teaches and guides him along the path of perfection.

The educator's role in the naturalist organisation of education is clarified by the example of Froebel's kindergarten system. In this system, the school is conceived to be a garden, the educand to be a delicate plant and the educator the careful, responsible and cautious gardener. The plant grows by itself, it seeks its own nourishment, and its development is governed by natural laws. It is impossible to turn one plant into a plant of another kind. This is beyond the abilities of even the greatest gardener.

His only function is to make sure that the plant and the weed grows-according to its own nature, and that this development is not hindered.

Up to this point, the idealistic conception does not differ very much from the naturalistic conception. But, as Ross has commented, the naturalist may be satisfied with wild flowers, but the idealist can be satisfied only by the finest of roses. The idealist places greater stress on the aims of education, and believes this aim to be self-realisation or perfection. Hence, under the idealistic pattern of education, the educator allows the educand to follow the natural pattern of growth, but he reserves the right to guide the educand towards perfection. It is implied that such perfection cannot be achieved without the educator's guidance, and hence the educator does not remain merely a friend, but becomes a guide and a sage.

DISCIPLINE

As in the case of curriculum and educational methods, the naturalist philosophers oppose the traditional concepts of discipline. And more than anything else, they oppose the method of physical punishment for they believe that this gives rise to undesirable conflict in the child. Rousseau has written, "Children should never receive punishment. Freedom and not power is the greatest good". If the child makes a mistake he will get his reward from nature itself, and thus he will learn to distinguish between the right and the wrong through the consequences of his own actions. For this reason the child should be given every liberty. To the naturalist, liberty does not imply freedom to interfere with the activity of others. The child can never be independent in this sense because he is controlled by many rules and laws which unconsciously or consciously operate in his mind. Only external and obvious discipline should be done away with. All the work of school administration and organisation should be left to the educand, for then he will learn to make the rules and to obey them.

Respect of discipline is sought to be instilled in the child's mind through natural consequences. Spencer writes, "When a child falls, or runs its head against the table, it suffers a pain, the remembrance of which tends to make it more careful; and by repetition of such experiences, it is eventually disciplined into proper guidance of its movement". But, there is a limit to learning through this method. In fact, very often the child is not able to reason out the relation between his various actions and the total consequences. As a result, he repeats even the harmful activity many times. And, hence, in such a situation, as Dewey has hinted, it becomes necessary to scold the child, to caution it, or even to punish it. As T.H. Huxley observes, "Nature's discipline is not even a word and a blow, and the blow first, but the blow without a word. It is left to you to find out why your ears are boxed".[1] Hence, it is not enough to abandon the child to learn for itself through these natural consequences of his actions. They do play a significant role in his training, but it is necessary to caution him at times. He should be warned against certain kinds of activities. The system of reward and punishment has been found effective everywhere. But it must be remembered that the value of the naturalist concept lies in that it hints at the shortcomings of excessive external discipline, although there is no doubt that the theory is definitely one-sided.

SCHOOL ORGANISATION

Naturalism distinguishes between formal and informal agencies. While the formal agency of education is the school and other educational institutions, the informal agencies include family, society, community and state, etc. Of these the informal agency, family starts the education of the child. The state influences the formal agencies of education. The school management, according to naturalists, should be liberal, free and based upon natural laws. According to the naturalist philosophers nature itself is a school where the child is taught according to natural principles. The school should be organised in such a way so that the child may get natural atmosphere for his growth. The naturalists cherish democratic values. The social environment of the school should be based upon the principles of liberty, equality and fraternity. The teacher's role should be reduced to minimum. The students should themselves govern the school. They should receive training in leadership. The time-table of the school should be flexible because a rigid time-table hampers freedom. The naturalist school organisation may be found in Dalton plan where classes

---

1. Quoted by Ross. J.S.: *Ground Work of Educational Theory,* George G. Harrap & Co., London, (1949), pp. 94-95.

are changed into laboratories and there is no definite time-table in the school. The school buildings should have proper arrangement of light and air. Rousseau recommended organisation of schools according to the nature of children and the stages of development of the educands.

CONTRIBUTION OF NATURALISM TO EDUCATION

Like other systems of philosophy of education, naturalism has also made important contribution to education. It made education paidocentric, psychological, free, self-dependent, related to nature and society, based upon developmental psychology, democratic, multisided and natural to the stages of development. These points may now be discussed in detail.

1. Paidocentric education: In the naturalistic conception of education, the child is in the forefront while all other things such as the educator, the books, the curriculum, the school, etc., are all in the background. Sir John Adams called this the conception of paidocentric education. Naturalism stresses the fact that education should be guided by the nature of the child, that the natural inclination of the child is always good. Rousseau said, "Everything is good as it comes from the hands of the Author of Nature but everything degenerates in the hands of man". It is, therefore, argued that the child is naturally invested with all goodness, and all that is necessary is to protect him from a defective environment. He must be provided with the kind of environment which will encourage him to develop his innate goodness, his natural sense of the beautiful. He must be enabled to avoid the ugly, to manifest the natural truth inside him so that he can combat the falsity which is thrust upon him by the defective environment. In this process, the educator can perform only the function of the guide. Naturalists are not inclined to transform the child's nature through education or to apply to him the standards of the adult. Education according to them, is not the preparation for life but life itself. Children should live like children, because infancy has its own significance, and it is not merely a stepping stone to adulthood. The child is not to be prepared and made ready for his fixture, but instead to be allowed to enjoy the present. Munro opines that Rousseau was the first to state the principle, that, "Education finds its purpose, its process and its means wholly within the child life and the child experience". In this manner, it can be summarised that education is the process of living a natural life and moving towards evolution, because the child has within himself the germs of evolution.

2. Emphasis upon psychology: The influence of naturalism was the cause of the psychological tendency gaining so much prominence in the field of education. By stressing the fact of the child's nature, it emphasised the importance of natural development. And, in order to determine what is natural and what is abnormal in child development, the naturalists turned to the psychologists. Thus it came to be understood that education must study the child and observe him. Many psychological researches have established that the child is not a young adult, that he has a distinct psychology which differs from adult psychology. It has been established that the child's mental activities of thinking, memory, imagination, recall, learning, etc., all differ from similar activities in the adult. Hence, naturalism stressed the value of psychology for education. Rousseau is often credited with introducing the psychological tendency in education for he was the first to point out that education should follow the child's nature, which must first be understood. Although Thomas Fuller had stressed even before Rousseau the importance of studying the educand more than books, it was the latter whose theorising in this sphere took practical shape. Rousseau's ideas were put into practice by Pestalozzi, Herbert, Froebel and other educationists. The introduction of psychology into the sphere of education led to considerable research in child psychology, and the entire process finally culminated in the Emergence of a distinct branch of psychology called educational psychology.

William McDougall has made valuable contribution to the literature on and knowledge of child psychology by his analysis of the child's instincts and his definition of the process of character formation, determination and sentiment formation in the child. Thorndike and other psychologists contributed great wealth of knowledge in the sphere of manual skill and other aspects of child learning. By comparing and examining the various stages in the evolution of the child, it was found that child psychology differed considerably in infancy, childhood and adolescence. As a consequence, great stress was placed on adopting different techniques of teaching at each one of these stages. Apart from this, education was further influenced by the discovery that children differed from each other to a very great extent in respect of their physical and mental capabilities, their nature and emotions, etc. It was considered desirable to make education flexible so that it could accommodate all such variations and still contribute to the healthy development of the child.

But probably the greatest impact on education was that of the psychoanalysts. Freud put forward many novel theses about child psychology. Other psychoanalysts were responsible for many interesting and illuminating books on child psychology, and these were avidly read by educators the world over. In the main, the influence of psychoanalysis can be seen in the knowledge it provides of the harmful effects of repression and the fresh attitudes to sex, authority, the child's attitude to authority. Besides, this branch of psychology also warned educators against the harmful effects of threats, physical punishment and asserting oneself, Ross is of the opinion that the greatest benefit derived from psychoanalysis is that it has helped to explain the causes of juvenile delinquency and also suggested ways and means of curing it.

3. Emphasis upon free choice: Naturalists contend that a pre-determined pattern of education must never be foisted upon the child even when the pattern is entirely scientific. Education must give the child an opportunity of making a free choice in everything that he wants to study or play or even the manner in which he wants to behave. No external restraints should be placed on this free choice. Some naturalists even object to the very institution of school education, because they fear that the school is an obstacle in their normal and independent development. They also believe that the atmosphere in the home is freer than the school environment but they are contradicted by others more conscious of the constant interruptions made by parents in the child's activities. Apart from this naturalists, in general, are opposed to all educands in one class being taught in the same manner, or by the same method of education. They even object to the introduction of any kind of time-table. One example of a completely unrestrained environment is to be found in Summerhill School established by A. S. Neil. It was taken for granted at this institution that the child was not expected to be fit for school, but that the school had to prepare itself for the child. Liberty was the first principle in the child's education, so much so that the children could play through the entire day if they were so inclined. They were given no religious education because a child is not naturally religiously inclined. No adult values were forced upon the children who were also taught none of the principles of culture. Naturalists also believe that the child should not be made cultured unless he realises the need for culture. It was, therefore, thought better to leave the child in his more primitive condition. The liberty granted to the children even extended to their being allowed to roam naked if they so wished. It was found that no moral difficulty was raised due to the sex instinct, and it was decided that a healthy attitude to sex could only be generated through co-education. Neil was of the opinion that undesirable behaviour is due to moral and unnatural repression, and that no undesirable incidents take place due to co-education if the environment is completely free and liberal.

4. Place of the teacher: Naturalism grants to the teacher the place of the friend and the guide, not of the administrator, for he is not to interfere in the child's activities, nor to make any attempt at influencing him. He is there merely to observe them, not to give them any information or to fill their minds with facts or to form their characters. It is for the child to decide what he wants to learn. He will learn from experience what he should learn and when, what he should do and what he should avoid. His interests and instincts should be given an opportunity to manifest themselves freely. All this does not imply that the teacher has no role at all in education, for he has a definite role inasmuch as he is the one who will provide the educative material, create the opportunities for learning, create the ideal environment and thus contribute to the child's development. For example, in the Montessori method of education, the child is given many kinds of equipment to play with, while the teacher looks on and observes. Naturalism, thus, favours the concept of self-education. Norman Mancken has gone one step further and suggested that children can even educate each other. Nothing should be done with a view to turning the child's mind in any particular direction. He is not to be taught to read or write, to make use of the various parts of his body, or be taught moral lessons, but merely to be left to himself so that he can develop independently. This is what Rousseau implied by his concept of the educator's negative effort in the process of education. Negative effort did not imply that the teacher was merely to pass his time, but to observe the child, avoid any interference in his activities, to prevent or protect him from defects, to protect him from a defective environment. The educator must be perfectly aware of all that he has not to do, but at the same time this negative attitude is to be supplemented by the positive one of love and sympathy. He can love the child only when he himself has been a child, that is, he has not completely forgotten his childhood. He should have the inclination to laugh and play like the child, to forget that he is an adult, to mix with the children and become one of them himself. Only then can he give anything to them.

At times, one finds children developing some bad tendencies and it becomes necessary to guide them. But even this should be done in the form of an informal conversation with the child. In such a dialogue the educator understands the difficulties of the educand, shows his love and sympathy and encourages the educand to solve them himself. He makes the educand aware of the difficulties he is likely to face. Neil called this re-education. He saw in his own school that many of the children often sought opportunities for such informal dialogues. Whenever the children showed any disinclination for such dialogues, they were immediately abandoned.

5. Direct experience of things: Naturalists believe Rousseau's dictum, "Give your scholar no verbal lesson; he should be taught by experience alone". Hence, the naturalist lays stress on teaching through direct experience. The child will learn more by coming into contact through the objects surrounding him than through books. He should be allowed to examine these objects. Similarly the teaching of science should not take the form of verbal lectures, but actual performance of experiments in the laboratory. Geometry should be taught not by the problems written in books but by the actual measurement of the areas of the school and the height and other dimensions of the school buildings and other objects. If geography is to be taught, the educand should be taken to the various parts of the country, and not taught only through maps and charts produced on the blackboard. Thus naturalists insist that the educand must learn from the things that exist in the school, not through the lectures of the educator.

6. Direct experience of social life: What is true of the natural environment of the child, is also equally true of the social environment in which he lives. He should learn the various duties, obligations and responsibilities of social life not through lectures of the educator but through the natural society of the school, of which the educand is a member. Here, left to himself, he will learn to do those things which should be done and leave alone those which should be avoided. In Neil's Summerhill School the children themselves decided upon the form of behaviour which others found objectionable or which hindered their adjustment, and thus learnt to avoid it. This formed the basis of the child's social education. The concept of co-education is also favoured by the naturalists because then the society within the school resembles more closely the society outside school. Besides, it has been contended that unnatural attitudes to sex are the inevitable result of segregated education of boys and girls. This is a very controversial subject and many educationists fail to agree with the naturalists, although in many cases the results of experiments in co-education favoured the naturalists' thesis. It can undoubtedly be said, however, that the child's experience of the social life within the school, forms the basis of his later social and moral life.

7. Self-government: Another characteristic feature of the naturalist conception of education is the insistence on self-government. Neil's Summerhill School experimented in this direction also by allowing the educands to form their own government. They created a cabinet of five educands whose function it was to reflect on various difficulties, to give decisions in cases of indiscipline and even to inflict punishment for such acts. These five cabinet members met every Saturday night, and one of them was elected to the chair. All problems were then discussed. The cabinet even had the authority to expel an educand from the school, if it so decided, although in fact this right was never exercised. Neil states that this arrangement led to the development of highly democratic qualities in his educands, and it was felt that this weekly meeting had a much greater influence and impact than an entire week of traditional teaching. And, in fact, no one can doubt that such an arrangement of self-government is very beneficial for training educands in democratic living. The condition of self-government does impose certain restrictions on the educand's activities, but because it is imposed through his own rules and regulations, it takes the form of self-government and self-discipline. All kinds of self-control can be learnt through self-government, and it has none of the drawbacks of the method of external control. There is undoubtedly no better way of teaching public morality. And it is only self-government which teaches cultured behaviour and co-operation.

8. Play way of education: Of the many methods of education, naturalists prefer the play way. In this technique, all that the child learns is through a sense of playing or indulging in sport. Psychologists contend that the child best manifests his instincts and tendencies in an independent game, and his development can also be achieved through sport. Whatever the objectives of play—the recapitulation of man's primitive activities, the preparation for future life, or a kind of safety valve for an individual's excessive energy—it is undoubtedly the most natural method of teaching. Playing affords education not only during childhood, for people learn many things through playing even in adult life. It also provides an opportunity for constructive activity. Games are an important medium of constructive or creative education. Naturalists have, therefore, placed adequate stress on the value of games a fact which even modern educationists accept without reservation. Now-a-days the play-way of education is adopted for the education of infants and children, and thus they acquire all the advantages of a naturalist education. Montessori education, for example, is a good instance of this because in this method of teaching the child learns even reading and writing through play. Scouting is another activity in which the child is taught many things through the medium of play. In Neil's Summerhill School, more stress was placed on character than on learning. Children were free to play from morning till evening. There was no system of examination, and books had less importance in the school than most other kinds of activities. Some lessons were taught, but attendance was never compulsory because most of the work, in any case, was done outside the classroom. On the other hand, educands favoured the craftsrooms much more, where they were taught to make things out of wood, plastecine and metal. Educands and educators sat together to write plays. It was found that drama writing is an important means of developing the creative imagination.

9. Development of the child according to its nature: Naturalists stressed the fact that the child must develop according to his own nature, and educational pattern must be modified to suit the various needs of children, because children differ from each other on account of their innate individual differences.

10. Importance of developmental psychology: By stressing the value of studying child development, naturalists made contributions to the progress of developmental psychology which scientifically studies the various stages of man's development.

11. Comprehensive curriculum: Naturalists have favoured the adoption of a multi-faceted and comprehensive curriculum, which reflects, apart from the scientific, sociological and psychological tendencies, the holistic tendency in education. The holistic approach is, in fact, a synthesis of the scientific, sociological and psychological tendencies. Schools make use of all kinds of modern audio-visual aids, and arrange for teaching of sciences and the various arts. Extra curricular programmes and activities are also believed to be of considerable importance.

12. Development of democratic qualities: Naturalism is opposed to repression and vigorous discipline of any kind. It seeks to replace the traditional by the modern, the dogmatic by the liberal and the progressive. It consequently helps in the development of such democratic qualities as liberty, equality and fraternity. It favours a complete rejection of the traditional modes of teaching and instead advocates greater dependence upon self-government.

13. Development of child psychology: Naturalists played a significant role in the development of child psychology as a result of their insistence on education being oriented to the child's nature. As a result of this development in child psychology, it was discovered that the child is not a young adult, but a distinct kind of human being possessed of a different psychology. Naturalists insist that the child is born good, and that education must seek only to protect him from evil.

14. Support of residential schools: Under the naturalist mode of teaching, the educator has the negative role of protecting the educand from evil. For this reason naturalists favour residential schools because the educand's environment can be controlled much better if the educand lives in hostels attached to the school. They also favour the pattern of co-education because this develops more natural attitudes in boys and girls.

15. Revolution in all fields of education: Finally, it can be said that naturalists were responsible for some of the most revolutionary ideas in all spheres of education. As has already been pointed out, naturalists vigorously opposed all traditional thinking on child psychology, educational techniques, curriculum, administration, co-education, etc. Although all their ideas are not found acceptable today, many of the principles propounded by the naturalists are still being applied. For example, such educational principles as learning through activity, going from the simple to the complex, from the concrete to the abstract, from the definite to the indefinite, from the easy to the difficult, and from the known to the unknown, are all principles which were originally propounded by the naturalists. And all these have been established as correct. Modern educationists now agree that the aim of education is not to provide education but to encourage spontaneous development. The significance and efficacy of broad based and comprehensive curricula have been almost universally accepted. Frustration and repression are held to be harmful everywhere. And the role of the teacher is now universally seen as the guide and not the administrator.

CRITICISM OF NATURALISM

The contribution that naturalism made to education is evident from the foregoing account but there are certain elements in it which other educationists find difficult to accept. As a consequence, all such difficulties were used to criticise naturalism on the following grounds:

1. Confused conception of the aims of education: Most educationists find it difficult to accept the aims of education propounded by naturalism. Evolutionists believe that the aim of education is biological development, while Spencer specifies it as self-preservation. Some evolutionists have ascribed more comprehensive aims to education but even these aims do not include everything.

2. Too much emphasis upon the present: Infact, the evolutionist places more emphasis upon the present than upon the future. It can be accepted that infancy is a significant period in life and that the child should be given every opportunity to enjoy it to the full. But if it is agreed that in later life this same individual will have to face the responsibility of earning his livelihood, creating a family and supporting it, it is only desirable that he should be educated and prepared for it. If he is to be a useful citizen of society, he has to be taught his responsibilities and how to fulfil them. The present has its importance, but up to a certain extent it is definitely a preparation for the future.

3. Many explanations of nature: The concept of nature differs from one realist to another. Some evolutionists interpret it in the sense of physical nature while others take it to mean human nature. And even among the latter there is often disagreement about what constitutes normality and abnormality in human nature. Very few, if any, evolutionists have placed any emphasis upon spiritual nature, and for that reason realism separates itself so much from idealism, although both want education to conform to human nature.

4. Defects in the theory of instincts: Evolutionists believe that the child is possessed of some instincts, and they want education to aim at the development of these. But it is difficult to get the evolutionists to agree about the number and nature of these instincts. McDougall counted 14 instincts while L.L. Bernard made a list of 300 so-called instincts. Most of the instincts are common between man and animal, but the latter does not possess the instinct for religion. Besides, in the light of modern anthropological and sociological research, it is difficult to believe that anything is innate in human nature, after one has discounted the influence of the cultural environment. Dewey has gone so far as to say, "All that is human is learned". Modern psychology does not accept the theory of instinct and specifies that it is well nigh impossible to understand human nature after abstracting it from the cultural environment. Consequently, it is not easy to interpret what is meant by an education according to instinct.

5. Isolation of man from environment: Whenever the evolutionist or naturalist talks of adjustment or maturity, his argument often implies a total isolation from the physical or natural environment, as if this has no influence upon man. Such an attitude is not acceptable to other philosophers. It is generally believed that the human personality is the outcome of an interaction between heredity and environment. Without such an interaction with the environment no development is possible. Besides, as soon as the human being reacts with the environment, the latter itself undergoes immediate change.

6. Adaptation requires man's subordination to environment: It is accepted that man can change his environment to a very great extent, but he cannot be believed to be independent of it while interacting with it. Such an interaction demands some subordination from the individual. On the other hand, when adaptation is accepted as the aim of education by the evolutionists, it is often forgotten that struggle has its own significance and value in the process of growth.

7. Defects in the conception of evolution: The naturalist is an evolutionist but he often forgets that it is difficult to accept man's evolution from the animal stage because of man's language, intelligence and certain other characteristics which distinguish him from the animal. Besides, complete evidence has yet to be discovered to completely substantiate Darwin's theories. Evolutionists have also failed to explain the fact of mutation. Weisman's experiment indicated that although some change occurred in the living being of a particular species over a period of several generations, this change was not transferred to the chromosomes of that species. Besides, the biological explanation of evolution cannot be applied to social and spiritual development. This is what the evolutionists have frequently attempted. Social evolution differs from biological evolution in that it combines conflict with co-operation.

8. Limits of free development of the individual: Naturalist believes in the free development of the individual but the question is, is man really independent and can he exist when completely independent of nature and society? If nothing else, so much stress on the freedom of the individual can at least lead to uncontrolled egoism, which in itself is likely to bring many difficulties. And, in fact, in certain situations, much can be gained by becoming one's own individuality. In order to rise above the conflict between the individual and society, it is necessary to believe that man is not only individual, but also universal to a very great extent.

9. Defects of Hedonism: The application of naturalistic principles to ethics leads to the creation of Hedonism. Spencer established the school of evolutionary Hedonism, according to which the aim of life is not the maximum good of the maximum number, but the preservation of life and of social health, implying social balance. Right and wrong are measured by the extent of happiness. In Spencer's own words, "The business of moral science is to deduce from the laws of life what kinds of action necessarily tend to produce happiness, and what kinds tend to produce unhappiness. Its deductions are to be recognised as laws of conduct, and are to be conformed to, irrespective of a direct estimation of happiness or misery". Many arguments have been given to refute this hedonistic principle. Since the biological and the moral worlds differ from each other, the rules of conduct cannot be derived from the history of social conduct. Happiness does not always promote health, neither does misery invariably destroy it. Happiness is not the sole motive of action, just as the longevity of life is not the moral aim of life. In ethics a concept is defined not by its origin but by its objective. Synthesis is not based on ideals. Morality, too, is not an adventitious element of moral consciousness. The concept of a perfect society denies the fundamental tenets of evolutionary theory. The objective of a secular policy is not moral. Many evolutionists have themselves refuted Hedonism as an ethical philosophy. As Rusk puts it, "According to this doctrine there is no moral law, no place for duty for duty's sake: self-sacrifice would be utter foolishness; one's own selfish satisfaction is the greatest good."

10. Defects in education through natural consequences: Naturalism wants to leave the child to the natural consequences of education, on the presumption that he will naturally learn the consequences of his own actions. For example, if he does not wear adequate clothes, he will learn to do so when he feels cold. This is accepted on the presumption that every violation of natural law will bring him pain and thus compel him to change his pattern of behaviour. It is neither proper nor very humane to accept this principle of natural consequences. As T. H. Huxley has commented, "Nature's discipline is not even a word and a blow, and the blow first; but the blow without the word. It is left to you to find out why your ears are boxed". Hence, it cannot be presumed that the child will realise the source of his discomfort when one of his actions leads to some painful consequence. And, besides, in human society such rigid conditions do not prevail. Many people commit mistakes without ever being punished for them. Hence, the child cannot be educated merely by natural results. He also cannot be allowed to completely take the initiative. In many cases it is necessary to warn him, in many cases to prevent him. It is desirable to explain certain casual relationships in order to prevent mistakes.

11. Negative principle: In fact, the evolutionist or naturalist theory is negative because it admits the propriety of an action as long as one can evade the consequences of that action. Can such a principle be applied to social activity? If it is, then it will negative the possibility of achieving any ideal.

12. Negation of all human characteristics: Influenced by the concept of evolution, naturalists believe that man is nothing better than the next step after the animals, but man actually possesses many qualities which animals do not possess even in the rudimentary form. For example, man is not merely conscious but also self-conscious. Spearman put this truth in this way, "Psychology is no mere flower of biology but one of its greatest roots". Recall is a quality found in human beings. Many characteristics of the human mind differ from the nervous system of animals. Man is a rational animal, the only living being capable of thinking.

13. Many interpretations of naturalism: To begin with, the very term naturalism has been-open to several interpretations. It is often accepted to be a reaction against dogmatism and artificiality, but it is also transformed into positivism, which has faith in science, and later on into Hedonism. Naturalists like Herbert Spencer, T. H. Huxley, T. P. Nunn, Glen Johnson, etc., differ from each other in their ideas to a very great extent. Many of Rousseau's concepts are also not palatable to the naturalists.

One cannot justifiably deny the contribution of naturalism to education, for it has influenced all spheres of it, the aims of education, methods, curricula, school administration, discipline, its significance, etc. It achieved the complete refutation of traditional and dogmatic concepts of education by basing child education on the principles of child psychology and developmental psychology. Although the emphasis laid on experimental teaching was justified, it soon gave way to evolutionary influences. Naturalism limited its interpretations of nature to a very narrow field by considering human nature to be nothing more than biological. Had it chosen to integrate with this the spiritual nature of man, the idealistic school would have had no quarrel with the naturalists. In more recent years, one finds that the gap between naturalism and idealism is rapidly filling up. Modern naturalism is more comprehensive, in that it has abandoned the purely biological explanation and has come nearer the idealistic conception.

7

Pragmatism: John Dewey and Bertrand Russell

One of the most important schools of philosophy of education is pragmatism. It is also as old as idealism, naturalism and realism since it is more an attitude, than a philosophy. In the fifth century B. C. Heraclitus said, "One cannot step twice into the same river". Thus Reality is a flux, things are ever changing. Modern pragmatists agree with the Greek sophists. According to Protagores, "Man is the measure of all things". This maxim is the basis of modern humanism. Another famous sophist Gorgias used to say, "Nothing exists and if any thing exists we can never know it". This agnosticism has led to relativism in pragmatic epistemology. In modern times Francis Bacon and Auguste Comte were pragmatists. John Dewey regards Bacon, as the prophet of a pragmatic conception of knowledge.[1] Auguste Comte created positive philosophy which formed the basis of pragmatic social philosophy. Pragmatists agree with Comte that the universe is composed of laws and relations and not substance. John Locke said, "Our business s not to know all things but those which concern our conduct".[2] Immanual Kant used the word pragmatic in a different sense.

MEANING OF PRAGMATISM

According to Robert R. Rusk, the Oxford Dictionary first referred to the term 'pragmatic' in 1643 and the term 'pragmatism' in 1663.[3]

1. John Dewey: *Reconstruction in Philosophy*, p. 38. London, University of London Press Ltd., 1921.
2. John Locke: *An Essay Concerning Human Understanding*, 1960, Introduction.
3. Robert R. Rusk: *Philosophical Bases of Education*, p. 68, footnote. London, University of London Press, 1956.

According to *The Concise Oxford Dictionary* the term 'pragmatic' means dealing with matters according to their practical significance or immediate importance. The term, 'pragmatism', according to the same source, means, "Doctrine that evaluates any assertion solely by its practical consequences and its bearing on human interests"[1]. The term pragmatism has been derived from the Greek term *pragma* which means use. Thus pragmatism is an ism according to which use is the criteria of reality.

In 1870 in Boston and Cambridge a study circle informally but frequently met for discussion. It was called The Metaphysical Club. As Charles Pierce points out, "It was there that the name and doctrine of pragmatism saw the light".[2] Thus historically speaking the doctrine of pragmatism in contemporary time was first referred by Charles Sanders Pierce in his famous essay of 1878 in the *Popular Science* monthly on "How to Make Our Ideas Clear". Pierce gave it its first clear-cut formulation and later decided to use the label "Pragmaticism as one ugly enough to protect his views from unwanted associations going with pragmatism". In point of fact pragmatism is a name which has referred to many varieties of doctrines since Pierce took over from Kant the adjective 'pragmatic' to stress the relation of thought and knowledge to definite human purpose.

PRAGMATISM AND NATURALISM

1. Universality of scientific theories: According to naturalism the scientific conclusions are universal and objective. Pragmatism, however, does not admit any scientific principle to be universal and objective. According to William James, all the laws are determined by space and time, no law is independent of circumstances.

2. Explanation of the world: Pragmatists do not accept the mechanical and impersonal picture of the world drawn by the naturalist which has no place for human values. On the other hand, the pragmatists admit with the idealists that there is a spiritual order behind this mechanical physical world. In the pragmatic world-view, human efforts have been given a respectable place.

3. Opposed to monism: Both the idealists and naturalists are monists, while the pragmatists are pluralists. In the words

1. *The Concise Oxford Dictionary*: Sixth Edition, IIIrd Impression, 1976, p. 868.
2. Pierce: *Chance, Love and Logic* (M.R Cohen, Editor), Harcourt, Brace and Co., 1923, p. 19.

of Robert R. Rusk, "Pragmatism joins issue with Naturalism and Idealism insofar as both the latter are monistic, seeking to explain nature, man and God by reduction to a single principle—Naturalism to life, Idealism to mind or spirit. Pragmatism regards this way of conceiving the universe as singularly unimaginative and lacking in verity". Thus, in the explanation of the world the pragmatists do not mention one but many elements. In comparison to the naturalists the pragmatists find idealistic standpoint more satisfactory in human life, but while idealists place the source of this satisfaction within man, the pragmatists attribute it to external success.

4. Opposed to abstraction: The naturalists establish a single element in the world through abstraction. The pragmatists, on the other hand, are against all abstractions. They give more importance to concrete things and facts. As William James has explained the pragmatist viewpoint, "He demands a universe with real possibilities, real indeterminations, real beginnings, real ends, real evils, real crises, catastrophes and escapes, a real God, and a real moral life".

5. Opposed to static reality: Explaining the distinction between naturalism and pragmatism concerning the nature of reality, William James has said, "For Naturalism reality is readymade and complete from all eternity, while for Pragmatism it is still in the making, and awaits part of its complexion from the future". Thus, the Pragmatists believe that our aim is not so much to know the world as to make it. The life should not be rigid or static but dynamic and flexible. It is clear that the pragmatist explanation of reality is nearer to modern human consciousness.

6. Value of moral ideals: The moral values have no place in the naturalist world-view. The pragmatist, on the other hand, considers moral values to be very important in human life. While the naturalist makes moral and aesthetic aims secondary, the pragmatist considers them primary.

PRAGMATISM AND IDEALISM

As has been already pointed out, in comparison to naturalism Pragmatism is nearer to idealism. However, the two differ in the following respects:

1. Explanation of the world: The idealists explain nature, man and God in terms of one spiritual element. This has led to pragmatists' reaction in metaphysics. According to the pragmatists the world is neutral, neither spiritual nor physical. The presence of an eternal unchanging spiritual substance at the basis of the world is not admissible by logic or experience.

2. Number of reality: As regards the number of reality the idealists are monists while the pragmatists are pluralists. This pluralism is characteristic of pragmatists' explanation not only in philosophy but also in ethics, religion and other fields of life.

3. Change and status: The values, ideals and truths; according to idealists, are eternal and unchanging. According to Pragmatists, on the other hand, there is nothing eternal or unchanging. The world is a constant flux. The truths, values, ideals and postulates change according to space and time.

4. Value of reason: The idealist philosophers consider reason to be most valuable and interest as the source of moral dictates and cultural expressions. According to the pragmatists, on the other hand, reason is and ought to be the slave of passions. It has no other business but to follow will. Man's future depends on his will and his intellect and the will is based upon natural tendencies and not reasoning. Thus, reasoning has got the secondary place in pragmatist psychology.

5. Ends end means: While the idealists emphasise ends, the pragmatists give importance to means in education. This difference makes for the distinction in their contribution to education. While the idealists present aims and ideals, the pragmatists explain important means. However, even in the field of aims and ideals, while the idealists emphasise spiritual values, the pragmatists hold human values in highest regard.

6. Role of concept and action: The idealists are conceptualists. Idea is most important in their philosophy. To the pragmatists, on the other hand, action is more important than idea. This difference makes so much distinction among the two types of thinking concerning teaching methods, and curriculum.

7. Value of the world: Most of the idealist philosophies consider the objective world to be less real than the world of ideas. This has sometimes led to world negating attitude. On the other hand, according to the pragmatists, the physical world and mundane life are the ultimate valuable.

8. Static versus dynamic approach: Thus the idealist thinking is static while the pragmatist thinking is dynamic. The pragmatists present a progressive and evolutionary approach in education.

In spite of the above distinction between the idealism and the pragmatism, the two are nearer than pragmatism and naturalism.

JOHN DEWEY

John Dewey (1859-1952), greatest of the pragmatists and generally recognized as the most outstanding philosopher his country has yet produced, made significant contributions to virtually every field of philosophy as well as to such other areas of inquiry as education and psychology. Active for 70 years as a scholar, he was a prolific writer publishing approximately fifty books and more than eight hundred articles. Many of these have been translated into various foreign languages. New volumes are still coming out with more Dewey material, mainly correspondence; and books and articles on him are appearing at a rapidly increasing rate.

Some Dewey material is at present available only in Chinese. In February and March of 1919 he lectured at the Imperial University of Tokyo, and these lectures were published as *Reconstruction in Philosophy*. While in Japan he was invited to lecture in China also, he spent from May 1, 1919 to July 1921 there, finding the developments there of extremely great interest. He lectured extensively in Peking, Nanking, and Shanghai, speaking in English from brief lecture notes; and his lectures were translated and recorded in full on the spot in Chinese by his former students. Dr. Hu Shih, for example, translated his Peking lectures. According to Dr. Shih's account in "John Dewey in China",[1] Dewey provided the translators and recorders with his typed lecture notes in advance of each lecture so that they could study them and think out suitable Chinese words and phrases before the lecture and its translation. The translation was checked against his notes before publication in newspapers and periodicals or later publication in book form. What was known as "Dewey's Five Major Series of Lectures" in Peking, some 58 lectures on Modern Tendencies in Education, Social and Political Philosophy, of Education, Ethics, and Types of Thinking, according to Hu Shih, went through ten large reprintings in book

1. Charles A. Moore, ed., *Philosophy and Culture—East and West* (Honoulului, University of Hawaii Press, 1962), pp. 762-769.

form before Dewey left China and continued to be reprinted for at least three decades before government authorities on the mainland put a stop to them. There were also series on such other topics as Democratic Developments in America, Experimental Logic, History of Philosophy, and (as an introduction to Russell's lectures there in 1920), Three Philosophers of the Modern Period: James, Bergson, and Russell.

Fortunately, the Institute for Advanced Projects, East-West Center, University of Hawaii, with Professor Robert W. Clopton as special consultant, had undertaken to translate these materials, and in the fall of 1964 Dr. Tsuin Chen Ou as the first of a team of translators began the work of translation. When this material was available it shed significant new light on various areas of Dewey's thought.

The Southern Illinois University Co-operative Research Project on Dewey Publications has discovered a number of previously unlisted publications by Dewey, and it has assembled the most complete collection in existence of works by and about him. Under the direction of its Editorial Board—Professors George E. Axtelle, Jo Ann Boydston, Joe R. Burnett (University of Illinois), S. Morris Eames, and Lewis E. Hahn-the project, with the cooperation of a number of other leading Dewey scholars, planned a definitive edition in forty or more volumes of all his published writings (books and articles).[1] The materials were to be arranged chronologically with careful textual editing but with a minimum of interpretive comment. The editorial and textual work connected with this pioneering venture for a major American philosopher extended over many years, but it was hoped that the first volume would be ready from the Southern Illinois University Press in 1967. Accompanying *The Work* was a one-volume *Readers' Guide* with interpretive essays by eminent Dewey scholars on the main subject areas of his thought and writings. It was expected that this volume should be completed by 1967 so that it might be used throughout the publication period of *The Work*.

Further evidence of the contemporary relevance of Dewey, especially in education broadly conceived, may be had in

1. The Editorial Board had the assistance of a larger Advisory Committee under the chairmanship of Professor Willis More, Chairman of the Philosophy Department Southern Illinois University.

connection with the activities of the John Dewey Society for the Study of the Education and Culture. Organised at Atlantic City in February 1935, it existed to promote the study of the educational aims and educative methods of a democratic society. Regular meetings were scheduled in connection with the annual meetings of the National Society of College Teachers of Education. Much of the work of the society was carried on through its Commissions on Meetings and Communications, Monographs in Educational Theory, and Annual John Dewey Lectures. It helped launch the journal, Educational Theory, and it had a distinguished series of year-books going back to 1937 when William H. Kilpatrick edited the first one on *The Teacher and Society.* Among the other editors for this series were Harold D. Alberty, Christian O. Arndt. George E. Axtelle, Harold Benjamin, Theodore Brameld, Boyd H. Bode, John S. Brubacher, Samuel Everett, Hollis L. Caswell, H. Gordon Hullfish, Virgil Clift, Archibald Anderson, Ernest O. Melby, Harold Rugg, William Van Til, Harold G. Shane, Lindly J. Stiles and William W. Wattenberg. The Annual Dewey Lectures have included Ordway Tead, Oscar Handlin, Seymour Harris, Gardner Murphy, Loren Eiseley, R. Freeman Butts, and Huston Smith. Arthur G. Wirth was the current Chairman of the Society's Commission on Publications.

For one who has written so voluminously and who has made major contributions in so many different areas, no brief summary can be fully adequate. Selecting a few emphases, moreover, is especially dangerous in connection with the thought of one who commonly transcended conventional categories and boundaries and who habitually saw special topics in terms of larger contexts. And yet if one is to discuss this complex thinker as well as a group of others in a single chapter, a high degree of selectivity is required. One can only hope that many readers will be led to turn to extensive reading in his works to supplement this review.

1. Analysis of reflective inquiry: Perhaps the most important single emphasis of John Dewey is his insistence upon applying reflective or critical inquiry to problems or indeterminate situations. What is involved in problem solving or thinking through a problem? What is critical inquiry? How does one apply intelligence to human affairs? Dewey's answer to these questions is set forth in its simplest terms in *How We Thinks* and a more sophisticated version is given in *Logic; The Theory of Inquiry.* In a sense the phases or steps in a complete act of reflective thinking afford an outline for each of his major works; and he had a lifelong concern with what is involved in reflective thinking.

(*i*) The first step in a complete act of reflective thinking is the appearance of the problem. This may be marked by a, more or less, vague sense of something having gone wrong, a breakdown in habitual responses or modes of action. One of our beliefs is questioned, or acting upon it leads to a conflict or perplexity, (*ii*) The second step or phase is clarification of the problem. Through analysis and observation we gather sufficient data to formulate the difficulty or define the problem. If, for example, a belief is disputed questioning or analysis may indicate what precisely is in dispute, (*iii*) With the problem clearly stated we pass to the stage of appearance of suggested solutions or hypotheses as to how to solve the problem. Various ideas occur to us as to how it may be solved, (*iv*) The fourth stage is that of deductive elaboration. We reason out the implications of the various hypotheses. If we take the first hypothesis, we may expect such and such consequences; or we need to make additional observations or gather more information to see what may be expected. If we take the second one, we may expect such and such other consequences; and so on. On the basis of a survey of the implications of the various proposed solutions we decide which to test in action, (*v*) The fifth step is that of verification. Through observation or experiment we check out the hypotheses or hypotheses which looked most promising to us. If one of the hypotheses works out, the indeterminate situation is replaced by a determinate one in which stable lines of action are possible; instead of the problematic situation or perplexity we have a resolved or clarified one.

These steps or stages do not necessarily come one right after another in the sequence in which these have been listed here. For example, the first three stages may be telescoped in such a fashion that we do not get a clear indication of the stages, but in general, the more difficult the problem, the more likely the stages are to be clearly outlined before it is solved. Or, again, after we have reached the stage of deductive elaboration, we may discover that we need to go back and further clarify the problem or think of additional ways of trying to solve it.

Though this pattern is somewhat oversimplified, in fundamentals it is basically accurate. This is what is involved in problem solving activity whether it is a personal problem, an important social conflict, or a weighty scientific problem. When we solve a problem in this way, moreover, we have not merely a solution to our difficulty but also some descriptive or explanatory statements about how it was solved.

2. View of experience: Experience is one of the central concepts in Dewey's thought, occurring and recurring throughout his writing. Though he finally concluded that he might have done better to use another term, many of his most important works are concerned with clarifying it—for example, his Casus Lectures: *Experience and Nature:* or his *Art as Experience* or *Experience and Education.* For him experience constitutes the entire range of men's relations to, or transactions with the universe. We experience nature and things interacting in certain ways made up of experience.

A brief presentation of Dewey's views can perhaps best be summarized in terms of a contrast with what he calls the orthodox view of experience, that is accepted by both the traditional empiricists and their opponents.[1] Whereas the orthodox view treats experience primarily as a knowledge affair, Dewey speaks of it as intercourse between a living being and its physical and social environment. The traditionalists regard it as a subjective inner affair, separate and distinct from objective reality; but Dewey has always thought of experience as being of a piece with the objective world, which enters into the actions and sufferings of man and which, in turn, may be modified through human response. Instead of a gulf between disparate inner and outer realms of being, one may move freely from experience to that which surrounds, supports, and maintains it. The proponents of the orthodox view have been preoccupied with what is "given" in a bare present, whereas Dewey was more concerned with what might be done to change what is given or taken, in furtherance of human purposes. The older empiricists thought in terms of what has been or is given, looking toward the past if they passed beyond the present. For Dewey the salient trait of experience is its connection with a future. If change is what we are interested in, we look primarily toward the future, and not recollection but anticipation is central for the experimental form of experience.

---

1. See "The Need for a Recovery of Philosophy" in John Dewey and others, *Creative Intelligence, Essays in the Pragmatic Attitude* (New York Henry Holt and Co., 1117), pp. 3-69.

One of the main differences between Dewey's and the orthodox view of experience, however, turns about the latter's particularism, its concern with sense data to the neglect of connections and continuities, and its supposition that relations and continuities are either foreign to experience or are dubious by-products of it. Dewey, like James, emphasized the relations. The contextual, situational, transactional, or field character of experience stands out in his account. The traditional view opposed experience thought in the sense of inference, but for Dewey experience is full of inference, as might be expected for one who sees the directional and relational character of experience. Where one seeks to control what is to come through employing present environmental supports to effect changes which would not otherwise occur, inference is of vital importance. From the standpoint of the future life-activity of the organism, environmental incidents are favourable or hostile; and if one is to eliminate the latter and insure the former, an imaginative forecast of the future is essential for guidance in this process.

The structure of experience, however, comes out most clearly on Dewey's view in aesthetic experience. There we have experience in full, vivified, clarified and intensified.

3. View of knowledge: Dewey rejects the traditional epistemology which sets up a knower outside the world and then asks about the possibility, extent and validity of knowledge in general. He laughingly suggests that we might equally well have a problem of digestion in general—its possibility, extent, and genuineness—by assuming that the stomach and the food-materials were inhabitants of different worlds. The significant problem is not how such a knower is somehow to mirror the antecedently real out but rather one how one set of experienced events is to be used as signs of what we shall experience under another set of conditions. The important distinction, moreover, is not between the knower as subject and the world known as object. Instead it is between different ways of being in the movement of things, between an unreflective physical way and a purposive, intelligent one.

On Dewey's view knowledge needs to be placed in the context of the problematic or indeterminate situation and reflective inquiry. Knowledge is more than immediate awareness or the presence of a set of sense data. Having qualities before us does not constitute knowing. Knowledge is always inferential, and the problem is how the processes of inference are to be guided to trustworthy or warranted conclusions. It involves operations of controlled observation, testing, and experimentation. It is a product of inquiry—the steps in a complete act of reflective thinking. Dewey liked Bacon's idea that knowledge is power and it may be tested by the promotion of social progress.

4. Conception of philosophy: In *"The Need for a Recovery of Philosophy"* Dewey declares that philosophy must cease to be "a device for dealing with the problems of philosophy" and become "a method, cultivated by philosophers, for dealing with the problems of men". But the problems of man as he sees them cover a range broad enough to include in one way or another most of the traditional problems as well as many others. The method involves treating philosophy as vision, imagination and reflection; and though the clarifying process may show that certain epistemological problems are pseudo-problems, the fact that they are raised may point to genuine cultural crises. If action at all levels needs to be informed with vision, imagination and reflection to bring clearly to mind future possibilities with reference to attaining the better and averting the worse, there is more than enough for philosophy to do.

Developing an adequate conception of the place of intelligence in human affairs is one important task for philosophy. How can intelligence which is a creation of a culture also be a creator or forming influence on that culture? How can it define the larger patterns of continuity between a stubborn past and an insistent future? How can philosophy adjust the body of traditional beliefs to scientific tendencies and political aspirations which are novel and incompatible? These are tasks which involve the application of reflective inquiry on the broadest scale possible, and in applying it we need to remember. Dewey reminds us in the little essay on *Philosophy and Civilization,* that in philosophy we are occupied with meaning rather than truth.

This, of course, is not to deny either the crucial importance of truths as a sub-class of meanings or the relevance of existence to meanings. It is rather to suggest that imaginative sweep, values and significance are our primary concern.

In *Reconstruction in Philosophy* Dewey stresses the social function of philosophy, holding there that the task of philosophy is to clarify men's minds as to the social and moral issues of their day, to enlighten the moral forces which move mankind, and to contribute to the aspirations of men to attain a more ordered and intelligent happiness.

For Dewey, in general, philosophy is both a product of human culture and a process of criticizing or clarifying it, distinguishing meanings within and helping give it direction and form. In *Experience and Nature* he speaks of philosophy as criticism or criticism of criticism; as the "critical operation and function becomes aware of itself and its implications". It becomes a kind of theory of criticism—a consideration of alternating ways of critically evaluating values and beliefs. Meaning and values are focal in Dewey's conception of philosophy, and this aspect is not lost when he treats philosophy as general theory of criticism. For him we criticize for the sake of instituting and perpetuating more enduring and extensive values; and each of the various philosophical disciplines, metaphysics no less than the others, makes its distinctive contribution to this end.

5. Biologism: What is sometimes referred to as Dewey's biologism reflects: (*a*) his emphasis on the genetic point of view, and (*b*) his conviction that inquiry has a biological matrix. He was interested in how ideas originate and become more complex, in the parallels between human responses and lower levels, and in the continuity of different species of organic life from the lowest forms to man. To understand the present situation, he held, we inquire into its specific conditions as well as into its probable consequences.

Darwin and James helped Dewey to see the focal importance of the living creature adjusting or adapting to its environment and to view intelligence as a distinctive form of behaviour—one concerned with choosing appropriate means for the attainment of future ends. Whatever else mind may be, it is at least a means of controlling the environment in relation to ends of the life process. Within this framework the senses are not primarily gateways to knowledge but stimuli to action, and sensations are not so many pellets of knowledge but signals to redirect action, or signs of problems to be solved. In *The Influence of Darwin on Philosophy* Dewey suggests that the philosophic lesson of Darwin is that philosophy itself becomes a method of locating and interpreting the most serious of the conflicts that occur in life and a method of projecting ways of dealing with them.

6. Experimentalism: Dewey's experimentalism relates to his analysis of reflective inquiry for which hypotheses, prediction and experimentation are central. An experiment is a programme of action to determine consequences. It is a way of introducing intelligence into a situation. It is an intelligently guided procedure for discovering what adjustments an organism must make to its environment to ward off ill or secure goods. Experimentation for Dewey is relevant not merely on the individual biological level, but wherever planned reconstruction of a situation may help effect desired transformation, for example, in social planning or in education. The more important the issue at stake, the more clearly is experimentation seen to be preferable to such alternatives as authoritarianism, simple guesswork or merely waiting for events to run their course.

In some ways the best contrast with Dewey's experimentalism is the quest for certainty. Whereas Desecrates sought demonstrable proof or certainty through reason and Berkeley took sensory awareness as the bedrock of certainty, Dewey argued that what we are really after is not certainty of any sort but security in the face of a hostile environment. We are trying to stabilize responses or adjust successfully to a hostile environment.

7. Instrumentalism: Dewey's instrumentalism also stems from his analysis of reflective inquiry. Ideas are not copies, images or visions of external objects but rather tools or instruments to facilitate an organism's behaviour. They are instruments for operating on things or on stimuli. Things or objects are what we can do with them, and we can distinguish among them by the behaviour reactions they make possible.

Truth, accordingly, is adverbial. It is a way ideas work out in practice. It is a matter of whether hypotheses lead to predicted consequences, an affair of verified predictions or warranted assertions.

Dewey's instrumentalism encourages a new respect for instruments or means. The more we value ends or goals, on his view, the greater is our attention to the means which may bring them about. The separation of goods into natural and moral or into instrumental and intrinsic may have the harmful consequence of making moral and intrinsic goods more remote from daily living besides encouraging us to think that we can have the intrinsic without having to concern ourselves with the instrumental.

Viewing any good as merely instrumental, moreover, is fairly sure not to do it justice.

8. Relativism: Dewey's relativism is to be opposed to absolutism and is a way of stressing the importance of context, situation, relationships. To take things out of relations is to deprive them of value and meaning. Absolutes are ruled out on his view, and unqualified generalisations are likely to be misleading. An economic policy or a plan of action is a good relative to a specific situation which makes it desirable. A knife may be good for sharpening pencil and bad for cutting a rope; but to speak of it without qualifications as good or bad is quite misleading.

9. Meliorism: In ethics, according to Dewey's account in *Reconstruction in Philosophy,* the emphasis should be placed on improving or bettering our present situation rather than upon good or bad in some absolute sense. The good, if one is to speak of the good rather than the better, is what will enable us to solve the problem or difficulty. Thus what is usually referred to as a moral end or standard becomes on this view a hypothesis as to how to overcome a moral problem. Since every problematic situation is unique, values are also unique; but if one is to specify an end, then growth, education, or problem solving would be that end. Instead of treating acquisition of skill and attainment of culture as ends, we should see them as marks of growth and means to its continuing difficulties or furthering growth.

In the *Quest for Certainty,* Dewey's Gifford Lectures, we find a somewhat different approach, stressing the construction of the good; and in this construction, it is argued, we have to test our likings, enjoyments and desires. We do this by checking on the conditions and the results of certain forms of enjoyment of liking; and this involves running through the steps in a complete act of reflective thinking. It is not simply a question of whether as a matter of fact we do or do not enjoy or like something but whether this enjoyment or liking meets the test of reflection. It is not merely enjoyed or desired but also desirable or enjoyable in the sense of being worthy of being desired or enjoyed? When we say that something is desirable we are claiming that future consequences will be such as to meet the test of reflection.

Further discussion of Dewey's views on valuation and some of the questions growing out of his view may be found in the

Theory of Valuation[1] and in Ray Lepley, Editor, *Value: A Cooperative Inquiry*[2] in which Dewey, H. D. Aiken, C.E. Ayres, A.C. Garnett, G. R. Geiger, L. E. Hahn. B. E. Jessup, H. N. Lee, Ray Lepley, E. T. Mitchell, Charles Morris, D. H. Parkar, S. C. Pepper, and P.B. Rice re-examine fundamental issue of value.

10. Humanism: Dewey's humanism stems from his acceptance of the Beconian view that knowledge is tested by promotion of human intelligence based in good part on the experience of modern science for the sake of bettering the human situation. Supernaturalism and the usual dogmas of revealed religion have no place in Dewey's view. As he tells us in *A Common Faith,* the things of greatest value in civilization exist by the grace of the continuous human community in which we are a link and we have the responsibility of conserving, transmitting, rectifying and expanding our heritage of values in order that those who come after us may share it more generously and more securely. Our common faith draws its main stand from our attempt to carry out his responsibility.

Dewey's humanism is expressed also in his democratic outlook. As he saw it, democracy as a way of life is controlled by a working faith in the possibilities of human nature. Granted proper conditions, and Dewey devoted a lifetime to working for them, human intelligence can work out aims and methods by which experience can grow in richness. His faith in discussion, persuasion, education and conference techniques as opposed to force or coercion as a way of resolving differences was at one with his democracy or his faith in human nature. With free inquiry, free assembly and free communication of ideas, he was convinced, reflective inquiry is self-corrective.

11. Art as experience: On Dewey's view, as set forth in *Art as Experience,* there is an aesthetic quality to all experience and not merely to works of art. His account stresses the continuity between everyday experience and art. Wherever experience is vivified, clarified, intensified and unified, we have an aesthetic experience more meaningfully more coherently, and with greater vividness, clarity, and intensity, than daily life ordinarily manifests. The humdrum and the routine are the chief enemies of the aesthetic.

1. In *International Encyclopaedia of Unified Science* (Chicago: University of Chicago Press, 1939), II. No. 4.
2. *Op. Cit.* New York, University Press, 1949.

Ordinarily, we simply recognise objects for this use, but if we can have full perception of them, take in their full quality for its own sake, then we have an experience in a distinctive sense.

If any experience has the potentiality of becoming something appreciated for its own quality, moreover, human intelligence has the responsibility of applying aesthetic principles, not merely in art, but to our houses, our machine products, our cities, our highways and our general environment.

12. Education and experience: Most of the major theses in Dewey's general philosophy find expression in his philosophy of education. Reflective inquiry is as central for education, on his view, as for any other phase of life or experience. Indeed, for him education is a problem solving process, and we learn by doing, by having an opportunity to react in real life situation. In education not indoctrination, but inquiry is focal. Not simply amassing facts but learning to apply intelligence to problem solving has top priority. Education must be experimental without being simply improvisation.

The reconstructive purpose is as much at work in education as anywhere else in experience. As he says in *Democracy and Education*, "Education is a constant reorganising and reconstructing of experience". Present experiences must be so guided as to make future experiences more meaningful and worthwhile. Though the values and the knowledge of the past are transmitted, this must be done in such a fashion as to broaden, deepen and otherwise improve them. Criticism and not simply passive acceptance is demanded.

Dewey equates education and growth. As teachers we start with the child where he now is, with his present stock of interests and knowledge and seek to help him expand and enrich both his interests and his knowledge and grow as a person in his community and his society. He learns to work responsibly for his own development and for social conditions which will encourage a similar development for all other members of his society. Education must not be simply a means to something else. It should not be merely preparation for the future. As a process of growth it should have its own enjoyable and intrinsically rewarding features at the same time that it helps further continued education, and, on Dewey's view, the test of our social institutions may be found in their effect in furthering continued education or growth.

Dewey himself had considerable reservations over some features of "progressive education", but he continued to emphasize some of the strengths of the newer education as compared with the traditional outlook. His humanism and meliorism are richly examplified in his account of the theory and practice of education. His philosophy of education stresses the social nature of education, its intimate and multiple relations to democracy, and its cultural significance.

AIMS OF EDUCATION

According to Dewey the aim of education is the development of child's powers and abilities. It is impossible to lay down any definite principle for a particular kind of development, because this development will differ from one child to the next, in conformity with the unique abilities of the individual. The educator should guide the child according to the abilities and powers he observes in it. It is better, in Dewey's opinion, to leave the question of educational objectives unanswered. If a definite aim is ascribed to education, it may do very great harm by compelling the teacher to guide the educand in a particular direction, not in keeping with the innate abilities of the child. In general, the aim of education is to create an atmosphere in which the child gets an opportunity to be active in and contribute to the social awakening of the human race. From the pragmatic standpoint, education aims at creating social efficiency in the child. Man is a social being who must develop within the confines of society, outside which he cannot develop at all. For this reason, education must aim at creating social efficiency and skill.

Pragmatic education aims at instilling democratic values and ideals in the individual, at creating a democratic society in which there is no distinction between one individual and another, each individual is completely independent and willing to co-operate with others. Every individual must be given the freedom to develop his own desires and achieve his ambitions. Every individual must be equal to every other member of society. Such a society can be created only when there is no fundamental difference between the individual and collective interest. Hence, education should create co-operation and harmony among individuals, instilling democratic values in school-going children. In fact, the school itself is a miniature form of a democratic society in which the child undergoes various forms of development, of which moral education and development is the most important. Morality can be developed through active participation, because such participation in the activities of the school trains the child in shouldering responsibility. This develops the individual's character and grants him social skill. Equality of opportunity in the school helps to develop boys and girls according to their own individual traits and inclinations.

Pragmatic education is basically practical inasmuch as it aims at preparing the individual for future life in such a manner that he can fulfil his requirements and achieve contentment. Future life in the pragmatic sense implies not merely individual life but also social life. Dewey was critical of the contemporary modes of education because they tend to drive the child away from democratic life by giving advantages to a small section of society. It also lays more stress on book or formal teaching than is really desirable. This mode of teaching compels the educand to listen long lectures which blunt his own mental powers. Hence, Dewey laid the foundations of a progressive education in the form of a Progressive School which aimed at establishing democratic values and developing the child's personality.

CURRICULUM

Dewey believed that the educational process has two aspects—psychological and social.

(*a*) Psychological: The curriculum and the method of education should be determined by the child's instincts and abilities. The child should be educated according to his interest and inclination. Education should be attempted only after discovering the interests of the child, and these should be used as the basis for determining the curricula for the various stages of education.

(*b*) Social: All education has its beginnings in the individual's participation in the social consciousness of the race. Hence it is necessary to create an atmosphere in the school which will allow the child to take an active part in the social awakening of his group. This improves his conduct and develops his personality and abilities.

Dewey has stressed the following four principles as underlying the formation of educational curricula:

1. Utility: The curriculum imposed on the child must have some utility, meaning thereby that the curriculum should be based on the child's interests and inclinations during various stages of his development. In general, the child evinces four major interests—the desire to talk and exchange ideas, discovery, creation and artistic expression. The curriculum should be conditioned by these four elements, and designed to include the teaching of reading and writing, counting, manual skill, science, music and other arts. It is not desirable to introduce the child to all these subjects at once, but to teach a subject only when it is desired at a particular stage of mental development.

2. Flexibility: It is better for the curriculum to be flexible and not predetermined and rigid. It must be capable of accommodating the changes in the child's interests and inclinations.

3. Experiential: The curriculum should be related to the child's contemporary experiences, and these can be multiplied and reinforced by presenting different kinds of activities in the guise of problems which inspire the child to attempt a solution. In this way, the variety of his experiences can be increased. As far as possible, the teaching of each subject should be related to the content of the child's experiences.

4. Close to life: As far as possible, the curriculum should include only those subjects which can be related to the child's pattern of life at that particular stage. This proximity to life can help in creating a distinctive unity in the knowledge imparted to him and thereby some harmony can be created in the teaching of history, geography, mathematics and language, etc. Dewey was very critical of the contemporary method of dividing knowledge into separate compartments, because he felt that such fragmentation of knowledge was unnatural. As far as possible the various subjects in the curriculum should be harmonized.

EDUCATIONAL METHOD

Dewey, himself a successful educational psychologist, has presented many novels and useful ideas on educational methods in his two books, '*How We Think*' and *Interest and Efforts in Education*'. The most well-known principle enunciated by him is the theory of learning by doing, in which the child learns best when he himself performs actions related to particular subjects. The educator is not to stuff the child's mind with information he himself has gathered throughout his life, but to guide the child to those activities by which the child can develop his own natural abilities and qualities. The child should be acquainted with facts while he is engaged in activity relating to those facts. Besides, the child should be confronted with practical difficulties and problems which he should try to solve. Problem solving is a good technique because it adds to the child's experience.

Dewey is of the opinion that there should be integration between the child's life his activities and the subjects he studies. All subjects to be taught to the child should be arranged around his activities in such a manner that he acquires knowledge in the process of doing activities to which he is accustomed. Dewey's principle was later on adopted by Mahatma Gandhi in his plan of basic education.

The next question that arises is that of designing the method of teaching according to the child's interests. Dewey considers interest and effort to be of supreme importance in the process of education. The educator must understand the child's interest before organising the activities which are useful for the child. Given the opportunity to formulate programmes on their own, children will be able to make programmes according to their own interests. It is better if this effort is free of any fear or compulsion, because only then can the children make a programme independently. Once this is done, all school activity takes on the form of self willed activity. Dewey's ideas on educational methods later on led to the evolution of the project method in which the child was made to indulge in those activities which helped in the development of enthusiasm, self-confidence, self-reliance and originality.

In a democratic educational pattern, the child should be made to participate in collective activity which can help in evolving a cooperative and social spirit.

This method of education is apparently very suitable inasmuch as it meets the requirement of educational psychology. But in fact it has one inherent shortcoming that if the education of the child is fashioned exclusively according to the child's natural inclination he will remain ignorant of many subjects. Besides, even his knowledge of other subjects will remain disorganised, objections which are accepted by Dewey himself.

SCHOOL ORGANISATION

Dewey has commented in detail upon the organisation of schools as follows:

Role of the Educator

Pragmatic education grants considerable importance to the educator, who is conceived as a servant of society. His task is to create in the school an environment which will help in the development of the child's social personality and enable the child to become a responsible democratic citizen. Dewey considers the educator to be so important that he goes so far as to call him God's representative on earth.

In determining the educator's own behaviour in the school, Dewey accepts democratic principles and educational psychology as suitable guides for shaping the educator's conduct. In order to realise the values of equality and independence in the school, the educator should not treat himself as superior to the children. He must also consciously abstain from imposing his own ideas, interests, views and tendencies on the children. He must confine his own activity to an observation of the child's own natural inclinations and personality traits, to engaging the child in suitable activities which will help in developing these traits. Hence, it is essential for the educator to pay constant attention to the individual differences of the children. If this is done, administration of the school becomes easier. The educator must also try and engage the children in activities which compel them to think and reason out things for themselves.

Discipline

If the educator conducts himself on the lines suggested above, discipline in the school becomes easy. Difficulties arise only when discipline takes the form of an external force employed to restrain the child from expressing his natural desires. This is the traditional concept of discipline, which was severely criticised by Dewey. He argued that discipline depends not only upon the child's own personality but also upon the social environment in which he is placed. True discipline takes the form of social control and this is evolved when the child engages in collective activity in the school. It is therefore desirable to create an atmosphere in the school which encourages the children to live in mutual harmony and cooperation. Discipline and regularity of habit can be induced in children by making them act in consonance with each other in trying to achieve a single objective. This objective may be social, moral, intellectual or purely physical. School programmes go a long way in creating the child's character. It is therefore better to provide the child with a social environment and a mode which inspire him to self-discipline rather than to subject him to long lectures. By methods such as these the child can be turned into a really social being. A peaceful atmosphere is undoubtedly conducive to good and rapid work, but peace is only a means, not an end in itself. The educator's real task is to engage the children in work which suits their natural inclination. If, in the process, the children come into conflict with each other, it is not desirable to scold them and compel them to be peaceful Self-discipline is a better weapon, and this can be taught through responsibility. When the educand is faced with the responsibility of looking after most of the work of the college or school he automatically evolves self-discipline.

Participation in social activity is an essential part of educational training, in Dewey's opinion. The school itself is a rudimentary form of society. If the child is encouraged to take part in all collective activities in the school, he will not only be able to maintain discipline in the school, he will also be simultaneously trained for many activities he must perform in social life. Thus he will also learn to lead a disciplined life as an adult.

CRITICISM

Although Dewey's views on educational principles were enthusiastically received, they were also subjected to criticism on the following grounds:

1. Difficulties of not accepting truth to be permanent: Pragmatist philosophy does not treat truth as permanent and objective. Instead, as Dewey explains, all truth is relative to time and space. No philosophy is always true or correct. It has its utility only in a particular set of circumstances. And utility is the final criterion of truth. In actual practice, of course, Dewey's philosophy is fairly useful, but when his own principles are applied to his own theories, the latter also become relative to time and space and thus have only a limited utility. Hence, the principle of pragmatism itself becomes only relatively true because it does not accept truth as something permanent.

2. Materialistic bias: Pragmatism was born out of reaction to idealism, and consequently it manifests a distinctly materialistic bias, in contradiction of the spiritual bias of idealist philosophy. At the same time, Dewey wants to realize democratic ideals of freedom, equality and fraternity through education. But it is difficult to understand how this can be done unless he accepts an idealistic basis for his system of education. If worldly success is the only criterion of truth, few if any people will concern themselves with moral superiority, since the latter has no obvious relationship with material success.

3. Absence of any aim of education: The achievement of democratic ideals through education seems to be implicit in Dewey's educational philosophy, because he rarely ascribes particular aim to education in explicit terms. For him, education is life itself, and it is not possible to determine any objective for it. Most scholars disagree with this opinion because they believe that education can progress only when it has some definite aim and objective. There is always some definite purpose in sending the educand to school. And even though school resembles society in many ways, it has a distinct existence within the larger framework of society. Hence, the aims of education must be defined.

4. Excessive emphasis upon individual differences: Modern educational psychology accepts in principle that the curriculum of education must take into account the individual differences of children and that children must be educated according to their individual and unique interests and inclinations both in respect of curriculum and also of the method of teaching. While in theory this is quite acceptable, any attempts to apply it in practice lead to immediate complications. It is almost, if not completely impossible to provide a separate educational plan for every individual child in a school. It is for this reason that all schools now-a-days provide a uniform pattern of education imparted in the same manner. Besides, the teacher may have to educate the educand in a subject in which the latter is not all interested. Thus, it is not possible to eliminate many complex and difficult subjects from the curriculum only because the student is not interested in them.

5. Limitations in learning through doing: There is no doubt that the child should learn by actually doing things, as Dewey suggested yet the theory has its limitations. Many facts known to an individual are acquired from another person. It is almost impossible for one individual to experience every fact known to him. Thus, the educand should also try to benefit from the experience of his teacher, educator and colleagues. The educator must also supplement the educand's efforts at self-education with guidance and communication of his own experience.

DEWEY'S INFLUENCE ON MODERN EDUCATION

Many of Dewey's ideas have had great impact on modern education. Some important facts in this connection are:

1. Impact on the aims of education: Now-a-days, one of the important aims of education is the teaching of democratic values. Dewey insisted on developing social qualities in the child. In modern schools these aims of education have been accepted as valid.

2. Impact on educational methods: The greatest impact of Dewey's ideas is seen in the methods of education in more recent times. Dewey suggested that education should be based on the child's own experience, and also that the method of teaching should vary according to the interests and inclinations of each individual child. These ideas influenced modern teaching techniques and led to active teaching in schools. One such school is the Activity School. The project method is also a result of Dewey's ideas. Even in the other schools, attention is paid to the principles of child psychology which guide the educator in creating an atmosphere suitable for developing social consciousness in the educand.

3. Impact on curriculum: The impact of Dewey's ideas on the subject of curriculum led to the introduction of manual skill subjects into modern curricula. Special importance is now being attached to various kinds of games, objects, the use of certain tools and implements, etc. In selecting the subjects to be taught, attention is now paid to the individual interests and abilities of the child.

4. Impact on discipline: As a result of Dewey's theorising on the subject of discipline, now the educand is entrusted with much of the work done in the school. In this manner the educand is trained in self-control and democratic citizenship. Apart from this, once the educand has to face responsibility, he is compelled to think scientifically and reason out things for himself.

5. Universal education: Dewey's thinking and ideal also led to faith in universal and compulsory education. Education aims at the development of personality. Hence every individual must be given the opportunity to develop his personality through education. The current stress on the scientific and social tendency owes much to Dewey's influence. He pointed out that education was social necessity, in that it was not merely a preparation for life, but life itself. It aimed at the development of both the individual as well as society. This leads to the comprehensive development of the individual.

BERTRAND RUSSELL (1872-1970)

In contemporary times the philosophy of education of Bertrand Russell is a fine example of pragmatic approach to education. Among his most important works may be mentioned:

(1) *Principles of Social Reconstruction,* 1916.
(2) *The A.B.C. of Atoms,* 1923.
(3) *The A.B.C. of Relativity,* 1925.
(4) *On Education,* 1926.
(5) *The Analysis of Matter.*
(6) *Principia Mathematica,* 1927.
(7) *The Outlines of Philosophy,* 1928.
(8) *Skeptical Essays,* 1928.
(9) *Marriage and Morals,* 1929.
(10) *The Conquest of Happiness,* 1930.
(11) *The Scientific Outlook,* 1931.
(12) *Education and the Social Order,* 1932.
(13) *Freedom and Organisation,* 1934.
(14) *Power*: A new Social Analysis, 1928.
(15) *An Enquiry into Meaning and Truth,* 1940.
(16) *A History of Western Philosophy,* 1946.
(17) *Human Knowledge, Its Scope and Limits,* 1948.
(18) *Authority and Individual,* 1949.
(19) *Now Hopes for a Changing World,* 1951.
(20) *The Impact of Science on Society,* 1952.

Philosophical Ideas

Russell's philosophy has been called *Logical Atomism*. For the first time Russell propounded his mature views on Logical Atomism in a series of Lectures, delivered in London, in the year 1918. Later on, the University of Minnesotta published them under the title, *The Philosophy of Logical Atomism.* Russell was an eminent mathematician. He developed his philosophy of Logical Atomism as a consequence of his deep and penetrating studies in the philosophy of mathematics. By atom Russell meant that point in analysis where further analysis is not possible. In other words, logical atom is the irreducible element of logical analysis. Thus, Russell tries to find irreducible elements through logical analysis instead of physical or chemical analyses. Explaining the reasons for naming his philosophy Logical Atomism, Russell writes, "The reson that I call my doctrine logical atomism is because the atoms that I wish to arrive at as the sort of last residue in analysis are logical atoms and not physical atoms".

The philosophers subscribing to the viewpoint of Logical Atomism believe that logical analysis is a method of discovery. According to Bertrand Russell, we can learn about the fundamental elements of the universe by using the technique of logical analysis. The fundamental task before philosophy is the discovery of the basic elements of the universe and this is possible through analysis of the gross objects. The philosophers like Hegel, F.H. Bradley and B. Bosanquet do not accept the technique of logical analysis to be valid. According to them an object upon analysis ceases to be what it originally was; it is transformed into something else. For example, if we analyze man into his limbs, this would be distortion. The man can exist as a totality only; his limbs have no existence apart from this totality. Therefore, according to them, we can understand things as a unity; apart from this unity they are not real but merely appearance. Russell, however, rejects this line of argument and firmly believes in the efficacy of the logical analysis to reveal reality. It is, according to him, a most appropriate means of discovery. It may not be practically a very fertile method in philosophic inquiry; but undoubtedly, there is no theoretic difficulty or problem in its application to philosophy. The logical analysis is different from the physical or chemical analysis. David Hume also used the analytic method in his philosophy, but his method was psychological and not logical. In psychological analysis we analyze memories, thoughts, emotions and such psychological processes, whereas in logical analysis the objects of analysis are concepts and propositions. The main object of logical analysis is the discovery of the fundamental elements of the universe and from this it follows that logical atomist philosophy postulates the reality of the universe and the existence of facts therein.

After the First World War Russell published his famous work *Principles of Social Reconstruction* in 1916. In this book he maintained that expression of creative tendencies of the individual and society is the aim of human life. Creativity can be expressed in a democracy and free atmosphere. It is the opposite of possessive tendencies which are the major source of evil in social institutions. Russell maintained that family, marriage, education, religion, state and other human institutions should be guided by creative tendencies and not possessive tendencies. Happiness is the result of expression of creativity. Therefore, Russell suggested reconstruction of social institutions and social organisation in such a way as to realise maximum expression of creativity.

Aim of Education

The aim of education, according to Russell, is to create individuals who are creative and may realise a creative society. Such a system will be democratic. According to Russell, one cannot progress without education. Therefore, with Dewey and other American educationists, Russell supported democratic system of education. He appreciated American system of education as an ideal system. The aim of education is to develop the child in such a way as to express his creative tendencies. In this process the educand should develop vitality, courage, sensitiveness and intelligence. The educated persons must have openness of mind. Observation, patience, industry and faith in the possibility of knowledge are necessary for everyone who wants to learn. The above-mentioned four qualities are necessary for the development of character and personality.

General Principles of Education

The child's education should start at the age of six years. At this stage the aim of education should be to satisfy curiosity and to develop the natural skills of the child. The most important traits required for the educand are curiosity, freedom from prejudice, faith in the possibility of knowledge, perservance, intense, durable and voluntary' attention, patience and realism in ideas, words and action. Education must be interesting according to the educands stage of development. The teacher should act as a friend, philosopher and guide.

Nursery Schools

The responsibility of the early development of the child may be entrusted to nursery schools. Nursery education must be free and compulsory. The teacher at this stage should be well versed in psychology and medicine so that he may help in the physical development of the child. Kindergarten and Montessori schools are ideal for nursery education.

Pre-Primary Education

At this stage care should be taken to provide education according to the individual peculiarities of the children. The children should develop the ability of reading and writing. This should be creative during the first five years. Mental exercises such as the study of mathematics may be postponed up to the age of seven years. Before it a knowledge of geography and history and general knowledge may be given. The teaching of history and geography should start at the age of five years. Children may be allowed to develop skill in art and languages. Teaching of science and mathematics should start between the age of 12 and 14.

Arithmetic, Algebra, Geometry, Physics, Chemistry and Biology may form part of the curriculum during this period. Classical languages should be taught between 12 and 11 years of age.

Education between 14 and 18 years

Russell has classified curriculum into:

1. Classical languages,
2. Mathematics and Science,
3. Modern Humanities.

Science and Mathematics are correlative, however, they may be taught separately. By the age of 18 the child must learn at least one of these special groups.

Teaching Method

The teaching method should be based upon interest of the child. Educational standards must be maintained. The teacher should himself have sound knowledge of the subject. He should be well prepared and motivate students to learn. Along with interesting subjects the students must learn uninteresting subjects in science and mathematics. The teacher should try to make these subjects interesting. The educand should actively participate in the learning process. Learning by doing is an important method. Individual work should be given more importance than class work. The students may be given guidance and opportunities for developing their individual potentialities. Academic, physical and social development should go together. The school should be treated as a miniature society and the students may be asked to develop interest in all sorts of subjects, social, political, religious and secular. They should be taught to think independently. Their aim should be the search of truth. Free exchange of ideas should be developed.

School Organisation

There may be day schools and residential schools, since both have their own merits and demerits. These schools should be organised on democratic basis. Either of these two type of schools may be selected for the child on the basis of his circumstances, health, age, household conditions, nature and interests. The parents should select a suitable school for the child after careful consideration.

University Education

University education should be allowed only to the able and willing students. The aim of university education is firstly to expand knowledge and research and secondly to prepare trained men and women for various vocations. Admissions to the universities may be given according to merit. The teachers should encourage the students to study books giving necessary knowledge and also catering individual tastes, interests and abilities. The teacher should guide the students in their studies and evaluate their abilities. The teachers themselves should be free from financial worries. They should get sufficient leave for enrichment of their knowledge. Research work is an important aim of universities. The universities are research workshops. The research work should aim at welfare of humanity and progress of the world.

FUNDAMENTAL PRINCIPLES OF PRAGMATISM

The following are the fundamental principles of pragmatism in the field of education:

1. Pluralism: Philosophically, the pragmatists are pluralists. According to them there are as many worlds as human beings. The ultimate reality is not one but many. Everyone searches truth and aim of life according to his experiences. The truth changes according to different spatio-temporal circumstances.

2. Emphasis on change: The pragmatists emphasise change. The world is a process, a constant flux. Truth is always in the making. The world is ever progressing and evolving. Therefore, everything here is changing.

3. Utilitarianism: Pragmatists are utilitarians. Utility is the test of all truth and reality. A useful principle is true. Utility means fulfilment of human purposes. The results decide the good and evil of anything, idea, beliefs and acts. If the results are good, these are good, if bad these are evil. Beliefs and theories are detennined by circumstances. Utility means satisfaction of human needs.

4. Changing aims and values: The aims and values of life change in different times and climes. The old aims and values, therefore, cannot be accepted as they are. Human life and the world is a laboratory in which the aims and values are developed. Everyone should seek aims and values according to his tendencies and abilities.

5. Individualism: Pragmatists are individualists. They put maximum premium upon freedom in human life. Liberty goes with equality and fraternity. Everyone should adjust to his environment.

6. Emphasis on social aspects: Since man is a social animal, therefore, he develops in social circumstances. His success is success in society. The aim of education is make him successful by developing his social personality.

7. Experimentalism: Pragmatists are experimentalists. They give more importance to action than ideas. Activity is the means to attain the end of knowledge. Therefore, one should learn by doing constant experimentation which is required in every field of life. According to William James, "Pragmatism is a temper of mind, an attitude; it is also a theory of the nature of ideas and truth, and finally it is a theory about reality".

FORMS OF PRAGMATISM

According to H. H. Horne, "The main principle of pragmatism is that the theories that work are true". As E. S. Brightman maintains, "Primarily, pragmatism is a criterion of truth." According to them everyone should discover his truth according to his experience and commonsense. The following four types of pragmatism are distinguished according to emphasis:

1. Humanistic pragmatism: This type of pragmatism is particularly found in social sciences. According to it the satisfaction of human nature is the criterion of utility. All truths are human truths. As the British humanist philosopher F.C.S. Schiller pointed out, "Some London squires are circular". Contradiction in this statement disappears when we know that the term squire here means the meeting of roads and not the geometrical figure known by this name. Similar instances may be multiplied in different social sciences. In philosophy, in religion and even in science man is the aim of all thinking and everything else is a means to achieve human satisfaction.

2. Experimental pragmatism: Modern science is based upon experimental method. The fact which can be ascertained by experiment is true. In other words, whatever works in the real world is the truth. The truth of a theory in science can be ascertained by its workability. No truth is final, truth is known only to the extent it is useful in practice. The pragmatists use this criterion of truth in every field of life. The field of experiment, however, is widest in the field of science. In science, experiment is the only basis for arriving at conclusion in a controversial matter. The human problems can be solved only through experiment. This is true even in the field of religion. In his famous book *Varieties of Religious Experience* William James has advised that everyone should discover his God, mode of worship and man-God relationship by experiments in his own life. No other proof is required for a belief. By experiment in a field of life, one may know what to believe and what not to believe, what to do and what not to do. Whatever is proved by experience is true.

3. Nominalistic pragmatism: When we make any experiment we attend to the result. Our aim is examination of the material. Some hypothesis about the results invariably precedes every experiment. According to nominalistic pragmatism, the results of an experiment are always particular and concrete, never general and abstract. According to medieval European nominalistic philosophy, a universal is only a name. While only particulars are existing, the universals have no concrete existence. For example, while we find existing human individuals, we do not find humanity outside these individuals. In the words of E. S. Brightman, "This kind of pragmatism is closely affiliated with sense experience as criterion for the particulars that we meet are mostly sense data, including their relations". In the field of education emphasis is laid on concrete particular things and their experiences in comparison to verbal knowledge.

4. Biological pragmatism: According to John Dewey, "The pragmatic test is found in the function of thought in adapting the human organism to its environment". Experimentalism of John Dewey is based upon this biological pragmatism according to which the ultimate aim of all knowledge is harmony of the man with the environment. Education develops social skill which facilitates one's life. The school is a miniature society which prepares the child for future life. From the biological point of view, man is a psycho-somatic being. Everyday we begin our work by means of set habits. Suppose some day we receive a letter which raises a problem requiring immediate decision the success of thinking in this function depends upon the best answer to the problem.

PRAGMATISM IN EDUCATION

Pragmatism emerged as the twentieth century revolution against the nineteenth century rationalism, dogmatism, universalism and monism, etc. On the basis of their philosophy, pragmatists refuted the doctrines of other thinkers in the sphere of education and presented their own novel propositions. Some of the more important pragmatic concepts are the following:

1. Importance of human effort: Pragmatists believe that education depends upon the active participation of the child. The entire form of the universe is based on human effort and man is the architect of his own destiny.

2. Faith in the future: The pragmatic thinker is convinced of the brilliant and prosperous future of the human race. He believes that by making continuous and dedicated effort in the sphere of education, man can create a better adjusted and more powerful generation.

3. Empiricism: It is suggested that, at every stage of education, the educator and the educand should refer every fact to his own experience and interpret it in that light. Only then can the new piece of information become a part of his life. Hence, only vocal or verbal education is not enough. It cannot be sufficient until it is based on and related to experience. For this reason, pragmatists believe that the child should be given oral instruction, but this instruction should be supplemented by experience in the fields related to each particular subject.

4. Experimentation: Pragmatic philosophy believes in continuous experimentation in every aspect of the educator-educand relationship and in every sphere of education. These experiments will reveal many new facts which can be useful in modifying the curricula, educational methods, aims of education, etc. Seen from this viewpoint, the school itself is a laboratory in which the educator is continuously experimenting. This approach of the pragmatic thinkers has given immense encouragement to educational psychology and child psychology, both of which have experienced remarkable progress.

5. Dualism: Concerning the aims, methods, curricula, etc., of education, pragmatism adopts a dualistic approach. It demands that every educator is to base his education on his own experience and philosophy, while every educand is required to acquire an education in keeping with his own specific inclinations, interests and abilities.

6. Stress on practical success: The only criterion of the propriety of teaching methods, aims and curricula is the individual's success in later life. Only those principles of education are correct which take the educand to success. Our only aim is to satisfy our natural desires and to develop life. All that assists in this process is true and good, and knowledge of this truth can be obtained only through experience and experimentation.

7. Humanitarianism: Pragmatism aims to create humanitarian values in every sphere of education, the methods of teaching, aims, curricula, etc. Education of all kinds should aim at evolving human values.

8. Democracy: Pragmatists are fundamentally democratic because democratic society is the best means of achieving humanitarian ideals. They want to utilise education to create democratic values and ideals in educands, so that they can be trained to occupy a responsible place in a democratic society.

9. Emphasis on human personality: Pragmatists attach the greatest importance to the human personality, because they consider it the most significant element in the process of education. Education must be paidocentric, based on the natural activities and inclinations of the child. Besides, it must aim to make the child capable of adapting to the social environment.

10. Social function of education: Brubacher points out that the pragmatic conception of education is based on two basic principles, the first that education has a social function and the second that it must provide experience to the child. Knowledge for its own sake is a principle which the pragmatist does not accept. For him, knowledge must have some purpose, the purpose of adaptation which must take place in the social context. In the school the educand must be trained to become used to a democratic pattern of life. Pragmatists stress the importance of social values. Society is composed of man's social experience. One important mode of education is for the educand to participate in social experience. The school itself is only a miniature society, which should be organised on democratic principles of society. If this is done, then the child can acquire many democratic qualities in the process of his education, and these qualities will facilitate his social life later on. In such a society, these social qualities can be easily acquired because a democratic society stresses the importance of equality, liberty and fraternity. Prejudices relating to caste, language, religion, region, etc., can and should be eliminated by creating a we-feeling in the school. The organisation of the school, the administrative system, the curriculum, in fact, everything pertaining to the school should be so evolved as to prepare the educand for a democratic social life.

11. Comprehensive education: Pragmatists believe that the aim of education is a comprehensive practical education, a concept of education which is based on the philosophy of liberal education. The aim of education is to achieve the educand's intellectual, moral, aesthetic, physical and spiritual, in fact, every kind of development. Neither knowledge nor ideals, in themselves are the ends. They are only means to satisfy certain human needs, just as education is intended to facilitate human life. Not only the ideals of goodness, beauty and truth, even spirituality and religion are means of developing life. Hence, education must be comprehensive and it must aim at developing the educand's personality in order to help him achieve a better social adjustment.

THE AIMS OF EDUCATION

The various characteristics of the pragmatic concept of education clearly indicate the aims of education as conceived of by pragmatists. Pragmatic thinking is opposed to all kinds of dogmatism, blind faith, narrow mindedness, etc. It objects to imposing some particular ideal on the child against his wish. Besides, it is not prepared to accept an ideal as correct or good merely because it has been so accepted in the past and because some famous educationists have propounded it. Pragmatism favours frequent experimentation in the field of education in order to determine more modern ideals which accord with present-day social life. In the words of Brubacher, "The progressive education has no fixed aims or values in advance. Educational aims, no matter how well authenticated by the past, are not to be projected indefinitely into the future. In a world rendered precarious and contingent by a compound of the novel and the customary, educational aims must be held subject to revision as one advances into the future. If education has any general aim in the light of which their successive revisions can take place, it is only that of pupil's growth. But growth itself has no end beyond further growth. In other words, education is its own end". It is apparent, thus, that pragmatists accept growth or development as the aim of education. The various ramifications of this aim are not discussed in detail, for they are to be discovered in the future. The pragmatist refuses to lay down any aim or ideal which can be permanently valid, its validity unchallenged by changes in time and space. All the aims of education must be concerned with the present and the future, and must be subject to modification. As John Dewey puts it, "Education, as such has no aims; education is an abstract idea. Only persons have aims. And the aims of persons are indefinitely varied, differing with different children, changing as children and their teachers grow. Stated aims, such as we are about to make, will do more harm than good unless they are taken only as suggestions as to how to look ahead for consequences, to observe conditions and to choose means in the liberating and directing of children's energies". Obviously, then, the aims of education are mere suggestions, not to be taken literally. They are to be taken as guides by the educator so that he is assisted in his task of educating the child. He is primarily concerned with training the educand in facing those situations which are likely to arise in his future life. In providing such a training, the educator is to take advantage of any aim that helps his effort. John Dewey believes that in fact these aims are to be determined by the educator himself. Despite this, he points out, that the educational aim must possess the following three elements in order to be a good or proper aim:

1. Such aims are based on the educand's actions and needs.
2. They elicit the educand's co-operation.
3. They are specific and temporary, not permanent and general.

Keeping in mind the above directive principles, it is easy to arrive at the aims of education. But this does not imply that the pragmatic thinkers have not adduced any aim of education themselves. If one glances at the criterion of good educational objectives one can see that by thinking along the lines suggested by it, the pragmatist does arrive at some conclusions. Dewey points out, "Education is all one with growing even as growing is all one with living". Thus, the aim of life is growing, and hence education aims at growing. Put differently, it implies, that education aims at the comprehensive development of the educand. Despite this, such imprecision and lack of definiteness has led to confusion in educational circles in America. Commenting on this, Bode points out, "The chief defect in American education today is the lack of a programme, a sense of direction. It has no adequate mission or social gospel". Although this is one criticism of the pragmatic conception of education, it does apply in its totality because the pragmatic aims of education imply that education must aim at realizing democratic values in life. The United States of America is the representative of democratic societies in the world, and it is vigorously engaged in protecting democratic values against the constant onslaught of communist thinking. Hence, pragmatic thinking in America indicates that education aims at creating a democratic environment in society which can instill in the educand a respect for democratic institutions. Kilpatrick, the finest exponent of Dewey's philosophy of education in America, is correct in saying, "Our school rooms must become living democracies, that in a democracy it is self-directing personalities that we try to build, the kind that can carry forward life even more successfully in a developing world, and that the progressive development of a better life for all men is the basis out of which morality and moral conduct arise". It is evident that pragmatism favours the democratic ideals of education.

CURRICULUM

As has already been pointed out, pragmatists favour an educational curricula which permits the educand to develop all his qualities and obtain all knowledge that he can use fruitfully in future life. They have suggested the perusal of the following guidelines in determining a curriculum:

1. Principle of utility: Pragmatists are utilitarians who believe that utility lies in facilitating human adjustment and adaptation. The greater the satisfaction of human needs, the greater is the utility of the object achieving such satisfaction. The more it helps the child to adapt in his later life, the greater is the utility of his education. Hence the curriculum must make it easy for the child to later on take up some profession. For this reason, technical and scientific education forms an important part of the pragmatic curriculum. Pragmatists suggest that girls should be taught home science and boys trained in agriculture and the sciences. Apart from this, great stress is laid on physical training because it is essential for physical development. Putting it briefly, pragmatists favour the inclusion of all those subjects which will help the educand in adapting to his circumstances in later life. That is why it is suggested that the curriculum should include history, geography, mathematics, hygiene, etc. No useless subject which cannot assist in the child's adaptation, should be included in the curriculum. The aim of education is human progress which can be achieved through various kinds of knowledge. Only those subjects the knowledge of which can assist in this progress should be taught.

2. Principle of child's interest: The child's own interest plays a significant part in the process of learning. Generally, children evince four kinds of interests-talking, searching or discovering, creative activity and artistic manifestation. In order to shape the curriculum according to these interests, it must be made to include reading, counting, handicraft, painting, etc. As the child develops, his interests also undergo change and modification, and therefore it is desirable that the curriculum at different stages of education should accord with the interests manifested by the educand at that stage.

3. Principle of child's experience: Being empiricists, the pragmatic thinkers insist on teaching through providing the child with actual experience rather than rote learning. Thus, teaching through books should be supplemented by programmes which provide practical experience of various kinds. In this connection, Dewey has pointed out, "Abandon the notion of subject matter as something fixed and ready made in itself, outside the child's experience; create thinking of the child's experiences as something hard and fast; see it as something fluent, embryonic, vital; and we realise that the child and the curriculum are simply two limits which define a single process.... The studies represent the possibilities of development in the child's immediate crude experience". Thus, the pragmatic conception of a curriculum is dynamic. It is desirable to create such a community and environment in the school which will enable, the child to learn the technique of self-discipline and evolve qualities of citizenship in it.

4. Principle of integration: Pragmatists believe that knowledge and intelligence are same all over the world, and that is why integration is of special importance in education. In the school, the different subjects should not be completely segregated from each other, because the subjects themselves are not important. What is more important is the human activity they encourage. The educand should be encouraged to acquire knowledge of many subjects and therefore the teaching of various subjects should not be separated, but integrated into a single unit.

THE EDUCATOR

The pragmatic methodology of education is based on psychological facts, and in direct contrast to the naturalist method, it grants far greater importance to the educator. Like the idealists, the pragmatist believes the educator to be a guide and a counsellor who educates the child in self-discipline and active participation. In fact, the educator is the most important element in the school's social environment. By coming into contact with the educator, the educand can develop a set of very desirable and useful social habits, attitudes and interests. The educator can help this process by constantly observing the educand and devising new ways and means of solving the various problems that afflict the child. In this, he should also concentrate on motivating the educand himself use his intelligence to solve such problems. It is essential for the educator to present a good model in his own behaviour to create an atmosphere of co-operation and brotherhood. On the one hand, he must examine the child's habits and the characteristics of its personality, while on the other he must try to discover the conditions under which the child can be usefully influenced. The intelligent and devoted educator is forever studying the methods by which various subjects can be successfully taught to the educand. He realizes that many things unconsciously influence the educand in the school. Since this influence comes from the child's natural action and reaction to the environment in the school, the educator must aim at creating a desirable social environment and at evolving proper educational techniques.

EDUCATIONAL METHODS

The pragmatic methods of education are based on psychology and sociology, subject to the conditions that they give adequate scope for active participation by the educand and also that the method adopted must be dynamic and changeable. Both these conditions are laid down by the pragmatists because they believe in teaching through actual experience. One of the methods evolved by them is the Project method. Pragmatic thinkers point out that the success of any educational philosophy lies in its ability to raise the standard of teaching. They are critical of the traditional methods of teaching, because they believe in constant experimentation. They revolt against the traditional belief that the educand should sit at the educator's feet and learn anything that is thrown at him by the education. For the pragmatist, education lies not in learning what the educator teaches, but in developing the ability of independent cogitation. And this is possible only when the method of teaching is purposeful and is fashioned by the child's interests, desires and inclinations.

Pragmatism refuses to distinguish between theory and practice. True education lies not in knowing but in doing, and the child learns by active work, either in group activity or individual activity. This is known as the method of learning by doing. The educand has to learn not from the educator's experience but by his own experience, and this experience cannot be replaced by books, schools or any other institution. The first element in any educational method is the educand's own effort. Once he motivates himself to learn something, he needs no encouragement to gain knowledge. This does not imply that verbal teaching is meaningless. All that is implied is that the teacher must create a set of circumstances in which the child is inspired to face the situation. The educator must also provide the child with the means of facing the situation and solving any problems inherent in it.

The principle of integration is of major importance in pragmatic theory. It is believed that knowledge should not be fragmented. The process of learning should be an integrated one, because it is natural for human beings to create a unity in their experience. Man forever tries to create a unity in the myriad impressions which impinge upon him. The educator must take care that the child achieves a synthesis of all the information that he gathers in the process of education. One of the methods of achieving this is purposeful teaching. All these qualities can be seen in the Project method invented by Kilpatrick, Dewey's follower. In Kilpatrick's own words, "A project is a whole-hearted purposeful activity proceeding in a social environment". In the project method the educand is presented with a problem in the form of a project. He makes his best effort to try to put this project into practice. And, because it is posed in the form of a problem, the child is inspired to solve the problem. Most of the problems of day-to-day life, and the solution of such problems requires more than mere mental activity. The educand is compelled to bring into play all his other faculties, in order to solve the problem. During the task the environment is entirely natural. As far as possible the educand is made aware of the importance of the project. As the problem changes, the form of the project also changes. In the early stages of growth the child is faced with simpler problems, which grow more complex as he grows older and improves his ability to face it. Some of these educational projects relate to handicrafts, linguistic difficulties, problems concerning scientific subjects, problems of history and geography, trade and industry, etc. The first step in the project method is to determine the objective, and then to consider the various ways in which it can be achieved. The next step is to formulate a project for achieving it. Following this the project is put into actual practice and finally the success or failure of the project is evaluated. All that remains is to prepare a complete detailed report of the project. The merits of this method lie in the fact that it involves active participation and hence it takes the educand along the path of self-development and self-discipline. Being psychological in nature, it helps to evolve social and civic qualities in the individual and thus leads to success in adult life. The project method has been particularly successful in the case of curricular programmes. On the whole, this method of education is natural, purposeful and highly motivating.

DISCIPLINE

Even in general, discipline is an important factor in school life and administration, but under the pragmatic pattern of education it assumes special importance. Pragmatists believe that the child must benefit from his social environment, and this he obviously cannot do, in the absence of discipline. According to the pragmatist theory, discipline is primarily social, and it emerges through active participation in group activity and purposeful activity. In the words of Dewey, "Out of doing things that are to produce results and out of doing in a social and cooperative way, there is born a discipline of its own kind and type". This is self-discipline, the foundation of the educand's character. In the school, the educand must be permitted to perform those activities which help him to develop such qualities as self-reliance, independence, sociability, co-operation, sympathy, etc.

Freedom is an important element in the pragmatist conception of discipline, for it is assumed that the aim of education is to generate democratic qualities in the educand. Of these democratic qualities, the first and most important is liberty. Consequently, it is only desirable that the educand be given as much freedom as is possible. In democratic countries, educators try to protect this freedom as much as they can. They realise that if this freedom is taken away from them, schools and colleges will never be used as the means of social progress. This freedom is the root of all true discipline, because this discipline is never imposed from outside. It is self-discipline. That is why the pragmatist believes in an intimate relationship between freedom and discipline. The aim of discipline is to create in the educand a social consciousness which will prevent him from indulging in anti-social activity. He is also inspired by this self-discipline to engage in those activities which lead to the fulfilment of his social obligations. The school's only responsibility is to equip the educand with all those qualities, such as responsibility, inspiration, insight, etc., by the use of which he can assume the role of a responsible democratic citizen. Discipline certainly does not mean a simple obedience of rules or commands imposed from outside. When such commands issue from the individual's own mind, the obedience of them amounts to self-discipline. Blind obedience is, in fact, a negation of democracy. All that the educator has to do to create discipline is to evoke a sense of social responsibility in the child, not to compel the child to submit to external pressure. Social responsibility helps the educand to become disciplined and this discipline helps him in successfully performing all personal and social tasks. This is the psychological justification of discipline. The pragmatic educationist constantly experiments in order to discover new ways to creating real discipline in the school. As a result of such untiring effort, many new methods have been evolved.

CRITICAL EVALUATION

Though the contribution of pragmatism in the field of education is undeniable, the following criticisms have been levelled against it:

1. Biological bias: The pragmatist philosophy of education suffers from biological bias. As reason has been subordinated to passions, there is a likelihood of uncontrolled expression of passions.

2. Limitation of the theory of truth: According to the pragmatist expression, that idea is true which explains our problem. The truth of any idea does not depend on the fact of its conformity with reality. The true ideas, according to the pragmatist, are workable. According to the realist, on the other hand, the true is that which correctly represents the facts. For example, the proposition that the sun shines is true as it is a fact. Thus the criterion of a concept is its factuality. It should correspond to facts. What the pragmatists call truth is the impact of truth according to the realists. Now, if the criterion of truth supported by pragmatists is applied to their philosophy, it will be held true only if its followers succeed. However, success may also be found in the case of idealist and realist. Again, the pragmatist's theory of truth is not accepted everywhere and this failure is an argument against its truth.

Now, if some one points out that it may be true in future, this criterion will not be pragmatist since it will have to be submitted that the present success is not a necessary attribute of truth. John Dewey has admitted the influence of circumstances. Then, the pragmatist theory will also change. Such a view will fail to provide any theory of truth. As H.H. Horne has pointed out, "The truth that does not change is so because it correctly represents a situation". Thus pragmatist theory of truth is self-contradictory. It will lead to conflicting theories and criteria everywhere. So many examples confirming this truth may be cited in different fields of knowledge. While pragmatist approach may encourage original thinking about so many problems in a brilliant student, it will confuse the average and below average student since he wants a definite answer to his question. Again, sometimes even wrong theories succeed at least for the time being. In such cases, they may be taken as right and correct.

3. Eternity and permanence: Pragmatist denies any eternity and permanence to anything. He rejects the idealist worldview and everything eternal along with it. At least in the field of aims and ideals of education some sort of permanence is necessary.

4. Lack of purpose: Basing everything upon individual experimentation will result in lack of purpose everywhere. Most of the persons cannot derive any principle as they do not succeed much in any field of life. The pragmatic ideal may be more conducive to the creative persons but not to the average students.

5. Neglect of cultural ideals: The pragmatist's emphasis upon the physical and mundane world may sometimes lead to neglect of cultural ideals which is not acceptable in the field of education.

The above criticisms show that in order to arrive at an integral philosophy of education, the pragmatist philosophy should be synthesised with idealism, naturalism and realism.

8

Existentialism

Ever since the inception of reflective thought, the problem of Being and Existence has loomed large in the minds of philosophers, saints and seers. In ancient Upanishads we find direct reference to this question in the form of an inquiry into the quintessence or the element in man which survives death and destruction, that is, which is unaffected by becoming or change. The philosophers of East as well as West, of the ancient as well as modern times have all been seriously preoccupied by the problem of Existence. In short, no philosopher can avoid considering the ontological problems and thus all philosophies are at bottom existentialists. Then, how is the modern existentialist different and why do we not call other philosophies existentialism? The reason is that modern existentialism is concerned, unlike other philosophies, more with the problem of becoming than the problem of being; more with particulars than universals; more with existence than essence. As the father of modern existentialism, S. Kierkegaard puts it, the chief concern of an existentialist Christian is not the knowledge of rules and principles of Christianity but "how am I to become a Christian". The non-Christian or atheist existentialists substitute the word "Authentic Being" for the term Christian. Thus the extentialists have emphasized "Action" and "Choice" instead of usual emphasis on knowledge and explanation, and replaced the question of what by how.

Attempts have been made to trace the beginning of existentialism in the Greek philosophy; in particular, the philosophy of Socrates. According to Dr. Radha Krishnan, "Existentialism is a new name for an ancient method". And, according to J. Blackham, Existentialism "appears to be re-affirming in modern idiom the protestant or the stoic form of individualism, which stands over against the empirical individualism of the Renaissance or of the modern or of Epicurus as well as over against the universal system of Rome, or of Moscow or of Plato.... It is a contemporary renewal of one of the necessary phases of human experience in a conflict in ideals which history has not yet resolved".

THE CHIEF CHARACTERISTICS OF EXISTENTIALISM

It is clear from the above account that in existentialism, human person and his freedom are given great importance. In it the ancient personal value stressed by Stoics and Epicureans and exemplified in Socrates' hemlock drinking have been reinterpreted. According to existentialism personal growth and development can take place through individual's own efforts and none can help him in this regard. Thus the practical problems of living are attached great value and importance. Briefly, the chief characteristics of existentialism are the following:

1. Criticism of Idealism: Existentialism has emerged and developed as a reaction against idealism. Existentialist philosophers are highly critical of idealism and conceptualism.

According to idealism human person is essentially an expression of some underlying spiritual or psychic element which is of universal character: that is all men are fundamentally same and share with each other the universal character. It is this common character which truly defines the man. Therefore, the human freedom is subject to the good of humanity in general. There is no arbitrariness or individual will accounting for human freedom. But the existentialists criticize idealist's contention about universal element and man's good being subject to general good. They regard the search for essence a mistaken pursuit and according to them it is not the essence but existence which is real.

2. Criticism of naturalism: The existentialist philosophers are also critical of the philosophy of Naturalism. According to naturalists, life is subject to physico-bio-chemical laws, which, in turn, are subject to the universal law of causation. According to the law of causation whatever happens is due to antecedent causes and there is no event which can appear suddenly without some or the other cause. Thus, if the law of causation is universally operative there can be no human freedom of action. Human acts are as mechanical as the actions of an animal. This, however, is anathema to the existentialists and they stoutly defend the freedom of man. As a matter of fact, man is so free, according to J. P. Sartre, that he is fearful of his freedom.

3. Criticism of the scientific philosophy: Besides being critical of idealism and naturalism, the existentialist philosophers are also critical of scientific conceptualism. Science abstracts from the immediate data and brings them under some universal law or general rule, whereas, according to existentialists, all abstraction is false, reality is in the immediate data only. Furthermore, with the tremendous progress in science and technology, rapid industrialization and urbanization have taken place. This has given rise to crowded towns in which an individual is lost. Everything is done or happens on a large-scale and all personal values, individual likes and dislikes are altogether lost sight of. Today it is not the individual who chooses his end; rather all decisions are made by computers or statistical laws and data. Thus, science has made the value of man negligible. This is why the existentialists are opposed to scientific philosophy and culture. Indeed, the appeal of existentialist philosophy for artists and litterateurs is due mainly to the stout opposition to science by existentialism. It is the basic belief of existentialism that any true philosophy must be grounded in axiology or theory of values and not in epistemology or theory of knowledge.

4. Born of despair: As has been indicated above, on account of an unparalleled progress of science and technology, huge, industrial complexes and townships have sprung. Everywhere man is losing touch of nature. In big towns the problems and inner conflicts of man have multiplied phenomenally. The two world wars have completely shaken man's faith in world's future and philosophy. With the growing application of technology and consequent increase in the mechanisation of life, there is a growing despair in the minds and hearts of men. The worth of human efforts is decreasing and the life is becoming like a raft on the open sea which is carried hither and thither without any definite direction. Under these circumstances a sensitive mind finds himself lost and forlorn. The existentialists try to analyze and describe these human predicaments and find a way out of these. The existentialist is attacked on this count as indulging in gross exaggeration and raising false alarms. While it is very true that modern life is infested with hydra-headed problems and that intricacies of life overwhelm the spirit of man, giving up struggle in despair and cry in stiflement is no sensible solution of the current human predicament. Rather, any intensification of the feeling of despair and hopelessness would further complicate the matters. What is needed is an intelligent and sensible compromise with the hard and harsh facts of life. If man allows himself to be overwhelmed by misery, pain and apparent hopelessness of the situation, he would sink into apathy and cynicism. Thus he would not be able to improve his situation, on the contrary, every hope of any possible way out will recede. Psychologically, such an attitude is symptomatic of hypersensitiveness and hypochondria. Moreover, by advising man to feel fully unremittingly responsible for his life-situation, the sense of responsibility becomes abnormal and pathological. Such a man feels so intensely that he is led to commit suicide for small acts of omission and commission. As it is true elsewhere, it is true in this context that too much of anything is bad. The sense of responsibility and duty and the respect for human person are good things; but an exaggerated version of these can produce abnormal and pathological personality.

5. Value of human personality: From the observations made above about existentialism, it is obvious that existentialism recognizes the paramountcy of the human personality. As a matter of fact, for an existentialist "man" is the centre of the universe and nothing else is equal to it. Even Brahman, God, universe, etc., are subsidiary to "man". The basic feature of human person is his freedom—unfettered and unrestrained. Society and social institutions are for the sake of man and not vice versa, as is believed by idealists and others. There is no "general will" to which the "individual will" is subject. If any social law or principle is restrictive of human freedom it is invalid and unjust. Anything which obstructs the growth and development of the individual must be discarded. With this aim in view, existentialist writers, artists and thinkers have expressed their views uncompromisingly and waged great battles for securing these freedoms for man.

6. Importance of subjectivity: The Danish philosopher S. Kierkegaard has said that truth is subjective, truth is subjectivity: objectivity and abstraction are hallucinations. While scientists lay so exclusive a stress on the objectivity and consider any intrusions by subjective elements as wholly unwarranted and vicious, the existentialists are extremists who believe that only the immediate feeling or apprehension reveals the truth and that abstraction in any form or manners vitiates the truth and reality. The immediate experience or feeling about which existentialists talk is the direct experience by individuals of things like conflict, divisiveness, pain, anguish, anxiety, suffocation, etc. It is these conflicts and pains that tell a person the quality of his life and the business of philosophy is to analyze and describe these conflicts and trace their causes. Usually these conflicts are moral in nature and are indicative of inauthentic existence. The various existentialists have tried to describe in minute details the experiences like spiritual crisis, sexual crisis, marital crisis, etc. The existentialist thinking is beyond thinking and reasoning and is rooted in direct experiences and their ungarbled descriptions. A biographical account, if honest sincere and frank, usually helps in appreciating and understanding the truth of one's own situation. F or example, a marital discord may be due to lack of respect for the other spouse and too much expectation of him or her. An honest account of such an experience may help relieve tensions in many perusers of this account by providing them insight into their own problems. Everyone by probing into the depths of one's subjectivity can discover the truth of one's being and discover his authentic role in life. This is a creative process which gives rise to fresh insights. The man, when he encounters his existence first hand, stands alone. It is only when one is alone that one comes to grips with his true self. This ability to be alone, to stand by oneself, is the true freedom and this again is the basis of all morality. According to existentialists the origin of values is not in the social situation but in the personal insight.

7. No construction of philosophical system: From the ancient times philosophers have cogitated and pondered over problems of God, Soul, Space, Time, physical world, its origin and evolution, etc. They have tried to present philosophies which embraced all these problems and developed a theoretical system. However, the existentialists distrust system making and theorization. According to them, the true aim of philosophy is action and not theory. Therefore they do not cogitate over traditional problems.

8. Emphasis on the problem of the relation of individual and world: Lastly, a problem which is thought to be crucial by the existentialists is the relation between individual and world. The traditional explanations to this problem are not satisfactory according to existentialists. If we, after Hegel, believe in the one universal element called Absolute whose manifestation everything is, the individual has no value *per se* and is not free. According to Hegel the acceptance of necessity is the true freedom. This robs individual of all freedom and his unique quality. Such a view is repugnant to the existentialists; they, therefore, are consistently and consensusly anti-Hegelian. According to existentialists man cannot be considered subject to any law, rule or principle, be it a universal natural, social or political law. They are uncompromising free-willists and are extremely wary of any external encroachment upon human freedom. The rule does not verify and authenticate the case; on the contrary, the case does verify the rule. The validity of art is in the artistic impulse and expression and not in any aesthetic theory. The worth of man is underivable from any universal element. The existentialist's account of man is neither mystical nor philosophical. Man and world both are unbound and free. Briefly, the existentialists consider man to be the centre of all value and activity. That is why their view is also called anthropocentrism.

9. Emphasis on the problem of inner conflict: The central problem of the modern highly complex world is not ideological but practical. It is neither relevant nor important today to win followers for a particular ideology or theory but to inspire in men a sense of responsibility and freedom. If there is this sense, the process of communication is facilitated. The world peace cannot be accomplished by raising slogans. We require for this purpose individuals who are free, who communicate freely and, above all, who respect theirs as well as other's personalities. A *fortiori* the peace is possible if and only if there is peace in each heart; if each man is free from inner conflicts, if each can be free from the desire to subject others to his will. That is why existentialists attach so great importance to the problem of inner conflict. The traditional philosophies do not consider these problems philosophically worthwhile; but for existentialists these are extremely crucial and fundamental. The source of modern philosophical issues is the feeling of alienation from world, society as well as self. If we regard the existence and thought disparate, the problems arising out of this severance between reason and existence cannot be rationally solved. These can be resolved in practice only.

A true harmony is not a harmony of ideas or thoughts but a harmony of desires. A true philosophy is not a philosophy of substance but rather a philosophy of existents, a philosophy of immediate experiences. The true nature of this philosophy is not thinking about the being but participating in its movement, that is, commitment. The existentialist philosophy does not have any definite aim because, life being movement and flow which is not mere mechanical change but a creative advance, it is not possible to tie down life to any particular aim. Life cannot be aimless or having an aim but only inauthentic and authentic. An authentic existence is the only aim that life has but this is not some future state but a present quality of life. An authentic life can be personal only. The existentialism condemns both historicism and the scientific philosophy. With the exception of Karl Jaspers no other existentialist philosopher attaches much importance to history or science.

The existentialist philosophy is not a creation of any single philosopher. We find the existentialist writings scattered in the works of many philosophers, the important ones of which are Friedrich Nietzsche, Soren Kierkegaard, Gabriel Marcel, Martin Heidegger, Jean Paul Sartre, Karl Jaspers, Abbagnamo, Bardyaev and Albert Camus, etc. These philosophers have elaborated various themes and cardinal features of existentialist philosophy. There is of course no consensus among existentialists as to what is the essential nature of existentialism. J. P. Sartre calls his philosophy existentialist in a peculiar sense, while G. Marcel and K. Jaspers do not at all consider Sartre an existentialist philosopher. Kierkegaard and Marcel are both religious and subjectivist whereas the philosophy of Heidegger is objectivist. Some existentialist thinkers are theist while others are atheist. Whereas Kierkegaard, Jaspers and Marcel are theist, Heidegger, Sartre and Nietzsche are atheist. Nietzsche is severely critical of Christianity and considers the morality of Christianity to be the morality of slaves.

THE AIM OF EDUCATION

The aim of education, according to existentialism, is the realisation of inner truth. Contemporary mechanical and industrial life has alienated modern man. He is full of anexities, frustrations, fears and guilts. He is lonely though in the crowd. His individuality is being corrupt. The education should make him realise his subjective consciousness. The existential aim of education is humanitarian and humanist. It aims at self-realisation. It provides knowledge of self-existence.

CHILD-CENTRED EDUCATION

Existential education is child-centred. It gives full freedom to the child. The teacher should help the child to know himself and recognise his being. Freedom is required for natural development. Education should convert imperfection into perfection. Education should be according to the individual's needs and abilities of the child. The relation of the child to himself should be strengthened by education.

CURRICULUM

Existentialist's approach to education is almost an inversion of the realist approach. In the field of curriculum while the realists exclusively emphasise science, the existentialists find out that science and objective education severes our relation with ourselves. Science cannot help in inner realisation and achievement of peace. This, however, does not mean that science education should be ignored. It only means that besides science the curriculum must include humanities, ethics and religion. In keeping with this viewpoint contemporary engineering colleges have included some philosophy, ethics and social studies, in their curriculum. Without this synthetic approach to curriculum the aim of character formation and personality development will be defeated.

THE TEACHER

According to the existentialists the teacher creates an educational situation in which the student may establish contact with himself, become conscious of it and achieve self-realisation. This requires existential approach in the teacher himself. He should also have an experience of self-realisation so that he may be capable of guiding the students m this process.

RELIGIOUS AND MORAL EDUCATION

The existentialists particularly lay emphasis upon religious and moral education. Religion allows a person to develop himself. Religious education gives him an understanding of his existence in the cosmos. It shows the religious path of self-realisation. It also makes him capable of utilising faith in self-development. Moral education is closely related to religious education.

Both develop the inner self and help in the realisation of the infinite with the finite.

CRITICAL EVALUATION

Existentialism developed as a reaction against the contemporary social, economic and political situation in which man has lost his self. This philosophy has widely influenced art and literature. In politics it has stood against war. Its followers are active pacifists. In the field of education the contribution of existentialism is as follows:

1. Total development: The existentialists have aimed at total development of personality through education. Education should aim at the whole man. It should aim at character formation and self-realisation.

2. Subjective knowledge: The present age of science has made too much of objective knowledge, so much so that the term subjective has come to mean unreal, non-sense, ignorant and irrelevant. The existentialists rightly point out that subjective knowledge is even more important than objective knowledge. They rightly hold that truth is subjectivity. It is a human value and values are not facts. Reduction of values to facts has led to widespread loss of faith in values. Therefore, along with the teaching of science and mathematics, the humanities, art and literature should also be given suitable place in curriculum at every stage of education. Most of the ills of the modern man are due to over-objective attitude. This requires a subjectivist correction in the light of existentialist ideas.

3. Importance of environment: The present industrial, economic, political and social environment is valueless. Therefore, it helps confusion and corruption, tensions and conflicts. The existentialists seek to provide an environment proper to self-development and self-consciousness. This environment in the school requires contribution from humanities, arts and literature. These will help in the development of individuality in the educand so that he may cease to become a cog in the social wheel. Rather he should develop to be a self-conscious and sensitive individual.

In spite of the above mentioned contribution of existentialism its disadvantages are obvious since, as a philosophy also it has never provided a balanced thought. Some of the existentialist theories, in spite of all their genius, verge upon pathological symptoms. Such is the philosophy of Kierkegaard, the father of modern existentialism. If truth is not objective, it is not merely subjective. Existentialist revolt against intellectualism has its merits but also its serious limitations. Existential methods may be useful in moral and religious education but it cannot work in the education of science and technology. Therefore, the following limitations of existential philosophy of education may be noted:

1. Existential aim of education is as much one-sided as that of any others 'ism'.
2. Exclusive emphasis on humanities, art and literature is as much one-sided as emphasis upon science.
3. In their enthusiasm for self-realisation, the existentialists forget that a very important aim of education is earning a living. For that purpose the utilitarian aim of education has its advantages.
4. The existentialist method of teaching may be useful in moral and religious education but it will not work in the teaching of science and technology.
5. From a perusal of the advantages and limitations of existential approach in the field of education, it is clear that it serves as a corrective to contemporary gaps of education. However, it is far from being satisfactory as a complete philosophy of education.

9

Logical Positivism

Logical Positivism is the most recent trend in philosophy. Though its parallels may be found in all times and ages in philosophy in the form of anti-speculation tendencies, it is only in the 20th Century that this philosophy has been fully elaborated and has come to dominate the philosophic scene. In the 20th Century, logical positivism came into existence with the establishment of Vienna Circle. The Vienna Circle was a group of philosophers or scientists with philosophic inkling who met off and on under the Chairmanship of Moritz Schlick, who, at that time, was holding the chair of philosophy in the University of Vienna. The common thread binding this group together was a thorough dissatisfaction with the current philosophy, which, according to them, was non-scientific, speculative and non-empirical. They wanted to cry halt to all speculation and give a new turn to the philosophy by basing it upon science and experience. G. Weinberg in his book *An Examination of Logical Positivism* has said that "the official programme on which the Viennese Circle was first organised had two principal aims: to provide secure foundation for sciences and to demonstrate the meaninglessness of metaphysics". Thus the aim of the founders of Vienna Circle was to show that only a philosophy based on experience and scientific methodology has any validity and that the speculative philosophy of the past was merely will-of-the-wisp and lacked all validity and veracity. They wanted to usher in a new era in philosophy wherein all speculation would be abandoned.

In the beginning, the activities of the Vienna Circle amounted to the activities of a private club and were not like an open movement, that is, during the incipient stages the philosophers of

Viennese Circle debated and discussed the various issues amongst them and had not as yet formulated any positive philosophic programme. In order to propagate and disseminate their views, the members of the Vienna Circle published a pamphlet *"The Vienna Circle, Its Scientific Outlook:"* wherein they put forward their point of view and programme. Indeed, it was the manifesto of the logical positivism. In the early twenties, the logical positivism has had most impact on the philosophers of Vienna and Cambridge universities; but soon the movement of logical positivism swept the whole world. The philosopher whose views had maximum impact on the Vienna Circle philosophers in turning them away from metaphysics and formulating a philosophy sans Metaphysics was Ludwig Wittgenstein. Wittgenstein's *Tractatus Logico Philosophicus* had paved way for anti-speculation philosophy. He had asserted that the traditional philosophical problems were merely verbal tricks and that philosophy must fight this "bewitchment of intelligence". The period between 1930 and 1939 was a golden age of Vienna Circle; during this period logical positivism was riding the high crest of philosophic tidal wave. It was a young movement and had all the enthusiasm and zeal of the youth. Many top intellectuals of the world joined the movement in these years. In 1930, the eminent Polish logician Alfred Tarske was invited to deliver his discourses on mathematics. Rudolf Carnap was greatly impressed by these lectures and he propounded his logical principles on these lines. Though logical positivism has made sufficient progress since then, the Vienna Circle had begun disintegrating during Second World War. In 1934, Professor H. Hahn died of heart failure. In 1936, Professor Schlick was murdered by his student. After Schlick the mainstay of the Vienna Circle was gone. The best known members of this group were M. Schlick, R. Carnap, F. Weismann, O. Neurath, Feigl, F. Kaufmann, H. Hahn, K. Menger and Kurt Godel.

THE AIMS OF LOGICAL POSITIVISTS

If we make a close examination of logical positivism, we find in it two strains; one positivist and the other negativist. On the positivist side, the aim of these philosophers was to make the foundations of the science, to rid it of the pseudo concepts of metaphysics and to lay its foundations on strictly empirical principles. On the negativist side their aim was to prove the futility and barrenness of the traditional philosophy and condemn metaphysics as meaningless, invalid and misleading.

According to logical positivists, it is sheer waste of time and energy to indulge in speculation because that which transcends experience has no meaning, no sense. Only those statements, theories or principles have meaning and relevance which are about something within our experience and which can be validated or invalidated by reference to the facts of experience. And inasmuch as the theories and principles of Metaphysics are not based upon any experience, they are meaningless. Metaphysics, which literally means after-experience, is *exhypothesis* concerned with something that transcends experience. And as only empirical facts can be the subject matter of science and can have any validity or meaning, the subject-matter of Metaphysics, if any, is therefore, beyond the realm of sense or meaning. That is why, the logical positivists are so fond of debunking Metaphysics as "nonsense". What they mean is not that Metaphysics is a folly or foolish but that it has no relevance because it is nonsense (non-experiential or not about sense experience). If philosophy cannot deal with transcendental spheres without losing sense and with regard to facts of experience it stands nowhere before science, then what can be the proper function of philosophers. Some thinkers are of the opinion that the proper business of philosophy is to harmonize or synthesize the scientific knowledge. The science deals with particular aspects of the Reality. In order to gain a general or total viewpoint, we need philosophy. Thus, philosophy is the science of sciences. However, this view is unacceptable to logical positivists. According to them, the conceptions of harmony, synthesis, totality, etc., belong to the sphere of literature and poetry.

Explaining the proper function of philosophy Rudolf Carnap writes: "The proper function of philosophy is to analyze the statements asserted by scientists and study their kinds and relations". Thus the logical positivists deprived philosophy of its traditional function of being surveyor of all knowledge and determiner of what should constitute valid knowledge and to reveal to man the hidden laws of the universe. They have restricted philosophy to a narrow and technical function of evaluating the scientific assertions. According to logical positivists philosophy is to science what grammar is to language. As the knowledge of grammar does not enable us to create the language but equips us only with the rules which any linguistic expression must follow, similarly, philosophy frames the rules whereby it can be determined if a particular scientific assertion is correct or incorrect.

THE CONCEPTION OF MEANING

In his first book *Tractatus Logico Philosophicus,* Wittgenstein developed his conception of meaning through the logical analysis of language and experience.

According to Wittgenstein philosophy is nothing but analysis and discussion of language. The language is nothing but a symbolic expression of the facts of experience. The language is comprised of two types of expressions or statements: the simple and compound. The entire fabric of language is analyzable in compound statements, which, in turn, are analyzable in simple statements. Thus, language is nothing but "the totality of propositions". A simple or atomic proposition is a mirror or reflection of the reality. According to Wittgenstein, "A proposition is a picture of reality". Since language represents the facts of experience, the relationship between facts and the linguistic expressions thereof must indeed be very close. It is the fact which makes a proposition true or false. If the proposition is correspondent to the facts it is true; otherwise false. Wittgenstein is here reviving the correspondence theory of truth, according to which a proposition is true if and only if it asserts what the facts indeed are. For example, if we say that a ripe Dusseri mango is sweet, what we are asserting is according to the nature of Dusseri, that is, our statement of Dusseri mango corresponds to the fact. On the contrary if we say "King of Nepal is a Moslem" our statement is untrue because King of Nepal happens to be a Hindu.

Thus, we learn that a compound proposition can be so translated or analyzed as to give us simple proposition and that each simple proposition is a symbolic expression for a single fact. Since a simple proposition stands for some simple fact, the truth of the proposition can be determined by comparing the two. A momentous and crucial fact which follows from this analysis is that each linguistic expression is, directly or indirectly, overtly or covertly, connected with some or the other fact of experience. Therefore, if there is any linguistic expression which masquerades as a proposition but on analysis fails to show any connection with any fact of experience, then that linguistic expression is not a proposition but a pseudo-proposition. A pseudo-proposition is not merely not connected with any fact but it is impossible to think that it can be so connected. This is the basic difference between pseudo-propositions and false-propositions. This difference can be best explained by examples. Let us have two following propositions: (1) "Aspirin causes headache" and (2) "God exists". Now (1) is false because aspirin is a pain remover but aspirin and headache are facts, whereas (2) is neither true nor false but meaningless because there is and cannot be a fact which will answer to or correspond with our idea of god. Thus a pseua-proposition is neither true nor false because the criterion of truth has no relevance to it.

The precise and scientific explanation of Wittgenstein's conception of the meaning is in the following words: "The sense of a proposition is the method of its verification". That is, a proposition is a proposition if and only if some empirical facts are to be found which may confirm or disconfirm the proposition in question. Those propositions which can neither be confirmed nor discontinued by the empirical evidence are meaningless. It is a mistake to call them propositions.

ELIMINATION OF METAPHYSICS

It was the British philosopher David Hume who was the first philosopher to have maintained that Metaphysics was impossible because its principles were neither tautologies nor were based on experience. Taking the empirical foundations laid by Locke and Berkeley to their logical conclusion Hume had argued that there can be no basis for inferring something unseen from the seen. If we observed no causal necessity or regularity in nature, we could not be justified in believing it to be there. Thus, Metaphysics is unwarranted because it has no basis in experience. Kant had also declared that the science of Metaphysics is impossible. However, it was left to logical positivists to lead an organised revolt against Metaphysics and to make their viewpoint heard and respected in philosophical circles. According to A.J. Ayer the futility of metaphysics becomes transparent if we remember that "The fundamental postulate of metaphysics is that there is super-phenomenal reality". And whatsoever the super-phenomenal reality may or may not be, one thing is quite clear; namely, that the statements pertaining to "this reality" cannot be analyzed into simple propositions or protocol statements. Such being these are unverifiable. Being unverifiable they make no sense. Like couplets, stanzas or cantos of poetry they may have great impact upon our feelings; they may be highly edifiable, but seen on the touchstone of meaningful propositions they lack credibility. Thus, metaphysics has no relevance to knowledge.

Though in his *Philosophical Investigations* Wittgenstein is not uncompromisingly critical of metaphysics, in his earlier work referred to above he is vehemently opposed to metaphysics. According to him the metaphysical language is confusing and its problems unreal. The metaphysical problems are due to conscious or unconscious abuse of the language. According to him it is the business of philosophy to remove the veil of secrecy and show that metaphysical problems are unreal. As a phobic, if one understands the irrationality of his fear, he immediately gets rid of his phobia, in the same way if we see through the subterfuges of linguistic manipulation in the creation of metaphysical problems we would instantly cease to regard them as problems, Wittgenstein believes that word is invariably linked with some or the other sense-experimental fact. Therefore, if we find that there are certain alleged linguistic expressions which have no connection with empirical facts, then these expressions must be pseudo. Therefore, Wittgenstein refuses to consider metaphysical statements to be propositions, because, these, by definition, transcend experience and hence cannot be verified. Though since ages philosophers have been making metaphysical assertions, none of them has ever tried to offer any empirical evidence in their favour. As they cannot be subjected to either logical or empirical proof, these must be rejected as meaningless expressions.

The metaphysicians claim that though metaphysics is not based upon any external experience, it is nonetheless based upon internal experience. Wittgenstein does recognize that there are internal experiences but these cannot be known unless we express them. When we express them they are linked with some objective reality and should, therefore, be verifiable. But the statements of metaphysicians are unverifiable, therefore they cannot be claimed to be based upon any experience whatever.

The basic contention of Wittgenstein is that all logical propositions are correspondent to facts, that is, these stand for some or the other objective fact. The metaphysical statements, on the other hand, are devoid of all objective reference and are, therefore, logically sterile. These propositions are not made up of simple propositions but are supposedly based on spiritual experiences and facts; therefore these are unanalyzable and consequently unverifiable.

LANGUAGE

As has been earlier referred to there was some change in the viewpoint when Wittgenstein wrote his second book—The *Philosophical Investigations.* Unlike Tractatus, in which he had defined meaning as the mode of verification, now he defines meaning in terms of a game or play. To imagine a language; according to him, is to imagine a form of life. Thus, language is a style of life and the activity of man is a game. The terms used in a language have some special meaning. If a word has no special meaning it is senseless. For example, the words "sky" and "flower" each has meaning and refers to some thing particular; but the word "sky flower" is devoid of meaning because no special meaning is inherent in it. It refers to nothing.

Applying the analogy of "sky flower" to the philosophical problems, Wittgenstein asserts that though sky and flower each has meaning, yet the syntax of two "Sky flower" fails to convey any meaning. In the same manner, the words used in asserting metaphysical problem may each have meaning but the assertion taken as a whole may be syntactically defective and therefore has no meaning. A simple example would explain the point. The metaphysical assertion: "All reality is ideal" has no meaning though each word in it is meaningful. We can only talk of this or that real object or fact but to say "All reality" makes no sense because there is nothing corresponding to all reality as we have objects corresponding to a red rose, a philosophy book, etc. In order to resolve metaphysical puzzles the philosophical usages should be, according to Wittgenstein, re-interpreted as commonsense usages of daily life. "What we do is to bring words back from their metaphysical to their every day use." In an ideal language, according to Wittgenstein, only the words which are symbols for some real state of affairs are used. The philosophical problems crop up when we deviate from this principle and use words having no referents. The philosophical language usually is immaturish and imperfect. This is the reason for the lack of clarity in the philosophic assertions. Wittgenstein disregards grammar. The grammar sometimes misleads and systematically misleading expressions produce in us illusion of a problem and we feel restless. Once we let reality juncture and dispel the illusion our problem vanishes into thin air. The one-sidedness of philosophy is responsible for the puzzles of philosophy. In *Philosophical Investigations,* Wittgenstein says that "philosophy is a battle against the bewitchment of intelligence by language". The role of philosophy is to protect us against falling into illusions due to grammatical similarities. For example, a noun is a name of something and it follows that to every name there must correspond an objective fact. This may lead us to believe that since God is a noun, there must be some person, place or thing which is called God. By avoiding these errors we find almost all metaphysical problems disappear. They are dissolved like a dream dissolving on waking.

Though the writings of Wittgenstein had great impact on the logical positivists and linguistic philosophers, the conclusions drawn by him through rigorous analysis are not universally acceptable. Indeed, they have been severely criticized. Undoubtedly the views of Wittgenstein brought about a revolutionary change in philosophical thinking and his theories proved very fertile in as much as through their criticism new insights were achieved. The verification theory of meaning propounded by Wittgenstein has been shown to be built upon the foundations of shifting sand. Among its numerous criticisms the most crucial is that the criterion by which the meaning is to be tested is itself untested. For example, "This is a table" can be verified by visual, tactual and other means but there is no way to verify that to verify the meaning by these means is a meaningful proposition. To this criticism, Wittgenstein replies that "My propositions are elucidatory in this way; he who understands me finally recognizes them as senseless, when he has climbed through them, on them, over them. (He must, so to speak, throw away the ladder, after he has climbed upon it.) He must surmount these propositions, then he sees the word rightly". The principle of verification, if strictly adopted as a criterion of meaning, would render many a scientific proposition meaningless. For example, "There are atoms" is not verifiable in the ordinary sense. We know the existence of atoms inferentially and direct observation of these is as yet not possible.

Therefore, adherence to the strict verification criterion would rule out science as senseless.

The crucial errors into which Wittgenstein slipped was that he failed to make distinction between science and philosophy and treated them as similar, whereas science and philosophy are unlike both in subject matter and methodology.

Wittgenstein greatly under-valued philosophy. He accorded to the physical world the status of ultimately as real, but, as a matter of fact, the world of values is as much real as the physical world. The values are not capable of analysis. Philosophy has made significant contribution towards understanding and development of values. Wittgenstein utterly ignored this aspect of philosophy. He did so on account of his over-reliance on the physical world as being ultimately real.

THE NEW ROLE OF PHILOSOPHY

The elimination of Metaphysics is not the only task before logical positivists. In fact, they are equally, if not more, interested in filling up the vacuum created by the rejection of metaphysics by a new role (the logic of science). According to Carnap, it is "to analyze the statements asserted by scientists, study the kinds and relations and analyze terms as components of those statements and theories as ordered systems of those statements". The linguistic analysis of the scientific statement has been called "logic of science" by Carnap. According to him only sciences can give us the knowledge about facts. Philosophy has no technique and methodology to assess and determine the facts. Philosophy, therefore, must not try to evaluate facts but accept them on the basis of scientific knowledge. This is why Philosophy should address itself exclusively to the task of analyzing the language of science. The logic of science performs two following functions:

1. Logical syntax
2. Semantics.

1. Logical Syntax

In logical syntax we study the forms of linguistic expressions. Inasmuch as logical syntax is concerned with the forms and not the contents of linguistic expressions or propositions, it is also called formal logic. In the study of the logical syntax we are not concerned with the content or meaning of the propositions but with the reduction of complex forms into elementary forms and the elementary forms into their constituents. It also inquires into the logical relations of consistency and inconsistency, dependence and independence among different propositions. Logical syntax helps us to reach the basic statements of various sciences and realize the logical relations among these.

In his book *Logical Syntax of the Language*, Carnap has split up language in two divisions: the primary and the secondary. He has separately treated the rules of the two.

Primary Language or Language I

Defining Language I, Carnap says, "Language I is restricted so as to admit only the definition of those concepts and the formulation of those propositions which fulfil some requirements of constructivism ".

Although the scope of Language I is limited it does not follow that it has definite sentences. The real reason for the limitation of Language I is that it "consists primarily in the fact that only definite number of properties occur in it". On account of this limitation it is called definite language. Language I has been classified into two categories by Carnap:

1. Universal and
2. Existential.

Besides, there are five types of preliminary statements:

1. Sentential Calculus;
2. Sentential Operators;
3. Identity;
4. Arithmetic;
5. K-Operator.

As there are two sentences, there are two types of operators as well viz.:

1. Universal and
2. Existential.

These can be limited or unlimited. They are expressed with the help of symbols which may be defined or undefined.

Besides, in Language I there is reference to the rules of inference and judgement. The logical syntax of Language I is formulated on the basis of these rules.

Language II

Contrary to language I the scope of Language II is wide. According to Carnap, "Language II is very comprehensive, it makes available sufficient sentential forms for the formulation of everything that occurs in classical mathematics and in classical physics. Whereas Language I is limited in scope, the Language II is comprehensive in scope. Language I is, however, employed in Language II as a sub-class. Though the Language II is more clear and accurate than the Language I, the Language I's sentences and symbols are appropriate to the Language II. Inasmuch as it is comprehensive, the Language II "contains indefinite concepts".

The General Syntax

Besides linguistic syntaxes, Carnap has also referred to the rules of general syntax. Whereas the rules of linguistic syntax are applicable to a particular language, the rules of general syntax refer to all languages, oral as well as gestural. Carnap has related the general syntax with the philosophical discourse. According to him, in theory there are two types of questions:

1. Questions relating to Subject matter.
2. Questions relating to Logic.

The contextual questions pertain to metaphysical, ontological and physical inquiries and the logical questions pertain to Epistemology and Logic.

2. Semantics

Rudolf Carnap has propounded his view on Semantics in his three books: *Introduction to Semantics, Formalization of Logic* and *Meaning and Necessity*. In semantics the concepts of meaning and truth are studied and the various theories thereof examined. Semantics considers the relation of linguistic expressions to objects designated by them. The Semantical analysis of the scientific language reveals that a word may represent a particular object (*e.g.*, table) or a certain property (*e.g.*, sweetness) or a relation between two things (*e.g.*, friendship) or a physical function (*e.g.*, breathing). It also reveals the fact of synonymity, that is, two words may stand for the same object or same property.

In language there are three distinct elements:

1. The speaker;

2. The expression uttered and

3. The designation.

And a language system makes use of three types of rules: (*i*) Syntactical rules; (*ii*) Semantical rules; and (*iii*) Pragmatic rules. The science dealing with these rules is called Semiotic.

In Semantics, Carnap splits language in two parts; the object Language and the Metalanguage. The object language is that which is the subject matter of our discussion and analysis. In Metalanguage we say something about the object language. For example, if the teaching of Hindi is done through the medium of English, Hindi is the object Language and English the Metalanguage. The simple most unit of a language is sign. A series of signs is known as expression. Furthermore, signs are also of two types: sign event and sign-design. The semantics, too, is of two types: descriptive semantics and pure syntax. The descriptive semantics studies the historical changes in the forms of semantical signs and expressions. The pure syntax analyzes the methods and techniques of Semantics. A concatenation of signs results in a formula. A concatenation is the serial order of the signs. The different patterns of concatenation give rise to different forms of sentential syntax. The various syntactic arrangements or systems have their peculiar logic. If we know the pattern of arrangement in any concatenation, we can formulate the rules of its syntax. The peculiar concatenation of signs determines the terms, operators, sequence and sentential calculus and the techniques thereof. The pure syntax examines the techniques of semantics and this is known as calculus. The semantic technique frames rules for determining the necessary and sufficient truth of every type of sentence. Besides formulating the semantical rules, Carnap has also developed a number of metalanguage systems. He has shown that a metalanguage has four elements: (*i*) The Logical; (*ii*) The Sentential Syntax; (*iii*) Translation; and (*iv*) Semantical. These elements in a metalanguage are interdependent. The semantics is not a science, according to Carnap, because it does not help us to gather facts about the physical world. It is only an instrument for acquisition of knowledge. It determines and regulates modern logic. The modern logic has two chief constituents—the sentential syntax and semantics. According to Carnap the apparatus of modern logic is applicable to and useful not only in philosophy but sciences as well.

The views given above have been propounded in *Formalization of Logic* and *Introduction to Semantics* two of the three books mentioned above. In his third book *Meaning and Necessity* Carnap has analyzed in depth and detail the semantic aspects of meaning. The other feature of this work is the theory of forms. In it the concepts of necessity, chance, possibility and impossibility have been examined in detail. This part is known as Logic.

In his book *Logical Foundation of Probability* Carnap has considered the problems of probability and induction. According to him there is a close relationship between the two. Indeed, the inductive logic is the logic of probability. The probability is a type of relationship obtaining betwixt two propositions. The concept of probability plays crucial role in statistical science.

THE VALUES

According to Rudolf Carnap it is not possible to present any comprehensive theory of values. This is so because values depend upon human interests and desires. Carnap divides values in two classes—(1) The Relative values and (2) The Absolute values.

The Relative values are born of experience. They are the outcome of desires, interests, likes and dislikes. A man acts according to his values because these help him achieve the desired ends or goals. The acts done in accordance with absolute values are automatically good. They are not derived from experience.

According to Carnap all values are meaningless. All statements regarding values are incomplete because they have neither logical non-scientific evidence in support of these. The belief of certain philosophers that values are universal is mistaken. The values are nothing but the outcome of human desires and interests which, in the long run, assume the status of law. For example, the moral rule that telling lies is bad is an outcome of the experience of man that life is impossible in a society where lying is permissible, because in that event it will be impossible to believe anyone. Therefore, it is the interest of man which dictates the moral rule "Lying is bad."

Carnap has formulated three principles of morality. His ethics can be best described as Scientific Humanism. The three principles of morality proposed by Carnap are:

(1) There is no transcedental being who may be regarded to be the destroyer or the preserver of man. It follows, therefore,

that for the development and progress of man the self-help or personal efforts by man are indispensable.

(2) Man can effect such modifications in the changing circumstances of man that he can gain freedom from pain and disease. These constructive efforts can bring about definite improvement in personal and social life of man.

(3) The science is the best instrument for the betterment of human life.

Carnap has made definitive contribution to the realm of knowledge by his linguistic analysis and logical studies. Besides, he has also purged philosophy of many redundancies. However, like other logical positivists Carnap has been more successful in condemning philosophy than in presenting a positive philosophy.

The view of Carnap that philosophy has no independent status and that it is dependent upon science is utterly false. As a matter of fact, it has an independent status and is in no way dependent upon science. Without the foundations provided by philosophy it is impossible to raise the structure of science, therefore it is science which is subject to philosophy and not vice versa. The dictum "Philosophy is science of sciences", expresses a fundamental truth.

The explanation of values by Carnap is based on a misconception. As a matter of fact values are not just the expression of human desires and interests. The values are the fundamental principles underlying the facts. In order to know the bases of a fact we should know its values.

Carnap has gone into very fine details of logical principles but has, in the process, rendered them extremely intricate and complex. He has made his logical and linguistic theories too complicated to be of value.

EDUCATIONAL IMPLICATIONS

Logical positivism is a philosophical system and not a theory of education. In philosophy its contribution is particularly notable in the field of epistemology. Therefore, its implications are particularly important in teaching methods and the methods of communicating knowledge in education. The following are the important implications of logical positivism in the field of education.

1. Aims of education: Logical positivists insist upon meaningful propositions so that some meaning may be conveyed. Therefore, according to them, the aim of education is to distinguish between sense and nonsense, knowledge and ignorance, meaningful and meaningless propositions. It aims at propagation of scientific knowledge. It seeks to base the entire educational process on intelligence and reasoning. It lays emphasis upon objective knowledge as against subjectivity. Thus, its aim is precisely the opposite of existentialism. Knowledge, according to it, is empirical. The educational system should be based upon reliable and verified knowledge. Verification is through the practical consequences. Thus, logical positivists advise the use of utilitarian criterion in knowledge. Education aims at creating critical and scientific attitude. This is possible by training in language.

2. Educational method: The educational method, particularly emphasised by logical positivism, is both logical and positive. The teacher should himself analyse propositions in knowledge and check their verification. His approach should be strictly scientific and objective. He should adopt educational methods verified by educationists. He should test hypotheses and assumptions in every field of knowledge. He should develop the power of reasoning. He should train the student in logical thinking. He should have a sense of purpose everywhere and reject everything which cannot be verified.

3. Curriculum: The logical positivist rejects metaphysics, religion and all such knowledge which may not be verified. Language and grammar, besides logic, find central place in logical positivist curriculum. The training in analysis of language is necessary for every student. It is only analysis which leads to clarity of thought. Religious, moral and spiritual education have no place in positivist curriculum. Sciences occupy a prestigious place in it. It rejects self criticism everywhere. All criticism must be objective. Science and scientific research, both theoretical and practical, should be encouraged by the universities. The students should develop constructive imagination.

4. School organisation: Logical positivists believe in scientific humanism. The school should be managed by the students as much as by the teachers. The school organisation should be based upon functional efficiency, utilitarianism and humanism. Humanism considers every thing relative and nothing absolute.

So, innovations should be encouraged in place of confirmity and traditions. Educational process should be confined to the realm of knowledge. Only objective knowledge should be propagated. Only logical definitions should be accepted. Only valid interpretations should find currency.

In the final analysis the contribution of logical positivism is the evolution of philosophy of language and a principle of verification. Logical positivists develop a scientific theory of truth. They reject everything which may not be verified. The task of philosophy, according to logical positivist, is to work as a science of sciences. Thus, logical positivists act as catalysts. They down right reject all confused and unverified beliefs, hypotheses and propositions.

Logical positivist's method is not only useful in the field of philosophy but also in the field of sciences. The scientists present a theory after prolonged observation and experimentation, gathering the data, classification, generalisation and verification. The presentation of theory, however, should be strictly according to the rules laid down by logic and grammar. Without this method scientific knowledge will not be valid and no valid implications may be deduced from it. This training is necessary for all the students. This is also necessary for all the teachers and researchers, Thus, logical positivists have sought to remove confusions and indefiniteness in every field of knowledge. They are against all verbosity and verbal tricks. The movement started as an examination of empirical principles. It condemned the traditional role of philosophy and allotted new functions to it. It made philosophy concur to science. According to it what grammar is to language that philosophy is to science.

10

Socialism, Fascism, Marxism and Communism

SOCIALISM

Characteristics of Socialism

(1) *Social Justice*: Socialism aims at social justice.

(2) *Equality*: Socialism aims at equality.

(3) *Classless Society*: Socialism aims at establishing a classless society, free from exploitation, oppression and disparity.

(4) *Fellow Feeling*: Socialism aims at establishing a society based on mutual co-operation and fellow feeling.

(5) *Public Ownership*: Socialism pre-supposes public ownership of the means of production.

(6) *Abolition of Capitalism*: Socialism aims at abolishing the capitalist system.

(7) *Abolition of Class Conflict*: Socialism aims at abolishing conflicting classes in the society.

(8) *Active Participation*: Socialism aims at the active participation of the individual in the productive process of society.

(9) *Developing Necessary Attitude*: Socialism aims at developing necessary skills and favourable attitude towards work.

(10) *State Control*: Socialism stands for total state control in affairs of life.

Impact on Education

Various Committees and Commissions in India have suggested educational measures conforming to Socialist Pattern of Society.

The Kothari Commission has observed, "One of the important social objectives of education is to equalise opportunity, enabling the backward or under-privileged classes and individuals to use education as a lever for the improvement of their condition. Every society that values social justice and is anxious to improve the lot of common man and cultivate all available talent, must ensure progressive equality of opportunity to all sections of population. This is the only guarantee for the building up of an egalitarian and human society in which the exploitation of the weak will be minimised". The impact of socialism on education is as follows:

1. Teaching of socialism: It is the responsibility of educational institutions to bring about adequate awareness regarding socialism among the teachers and students. Such knowledge will enable the young people to chart the course of nation towards the goal of socialism. A school can convey positive attitudes and values regarding socialism to students through the following:

(1) Direct teaching of socialism.

(2) Living the values and attitudes to be learned through the organisation of various activities.

(3) Teachers becoming models embodying the desired values and attitudes.

2. Common school system: The so-called public schools provide good education only to microscopic minority of rich children. It goes against the principles of socialism. The Kothari Commission advocated the abolition of this system and suggested a system of common schools throughout the country which will be open to all children, irrespective of caste, creed, community, religion, economic conditions or social status. It observed, "On grounds of social justice as well as for the furtherance of democracy it is essential to make special efforts to equalise educational opportunities between these groups". However, due to various reasons this has not been possible in India. The public school system of education still thrives in our country. In fact, it is becoming popular day-by-day.

3. Nationalisation of textbooks: Textbooks at the school stage have been nationalised as an impact of socialism. Their contents are oriented and regulated according to the national policy and ethos. Efforts are being made to keep price range of textbooks within the easy reach of the parents.

Means of Providing Equality of Opportunity in Education

(1) *Tuition Free Education*: School education should be completely free from tuition fee.

(2) *Free Textbooks at the Primary Stage*: At the primary stage, a programme of providing free textbooks should be given high priority and introduced immediately.

(3) *Book Banks*: A programme of book-banks should be developed in secondary schools and in institutions of higher education.

(4) *Grants for Purchase of Books*: The top 10 per cent of the students in educational institutions should be given small grants annually for the purchase of books which need not necessarily be textbooks.

4. Adequate scholarships: The Education Commission has suggested the following programme of scholarships at different stages:

(*i*) *Scholarships at the Primary Stage*: At the end of the lower primary stage, no 'promising' child should be prevented from continuing his studies. The target should be to provide scholarships for 25 per cent of the enrolment at the higher primary stage.

(*ii*) *Scholarships at the Secondary Stage*: The target should be to provide scholarships for 10 per cent of the enrolment.

(*iii*) *Scholarships at the University Stage*: Scholarships should be available to at least 25 per cent of enrolment at the undergraduate stage. Scholarships should cover at least 50 per cent of the enrolment at the post-graduate stage.

5. Kinds of scholarships

(*i*) *Scholarships for those who have to Stay in Hostels*: These should cover all direct and indirect costs of education, *i.e.*, tuition fees, books, supplies, etc., and living costs.

(*ii*) *National Scholarships*: As against the present provision of one per cent, the target to be reached should be to cover 10 per cent of such students.

(*iii*) *Scholarships for Study Abroad*: A national programme for award of scholarship is needed to enable some of our talented persons to go abroad for further education or training in research.

(*iv*) *Loan Scholarships*: A comprehensive programme of National Loan Scholarship should be undertaken. A National Loan

Scholarship Board may be set up for administering this programme.

6. Transport facilities: Adequate transport facilities may be provided in the rural areas so that students are encouraged to attend educational institutions.

7. Day-study centres and lodging houses: At the secondary and university stages a large number of day-study centres should be provided for students who do not have adequate facilities for study at home. Lodging houses may also be provided where students can stay throughout the day, and even at night, but go home for food.

8. 'Earn while learn' facilities: Facilities for students to earn and pay a part of their expenses should be provided on as large-scale as possible.

9. Special facilities for girls: Special facilities may be provided to the girls.

10. Education of the backward sections of society: Special investigations may be carried out, regarding important aspects of spread of education amongst the tribals and their effects. The Education Commission recommends, "The education of the backward classes in general and of the tribal people in particular is major programme of equalization and of social and national integration. No expenditure is too great for the purpose".

11. Egalitarian admission policy: There is a great need to introduce an egalitarian element in admissions to institutions so that students coming from rural areas are not handicapped due to language or some other factors.

12. Special assistance to backward areas or states: At the national level, it should be regarded the responsibility of the Government of India to secure equalization of educational development in the different states. The necessary programmes for this, include special assistance to the less advanced states.

13. Meeting the needs of slow learners: In the ordinary classes, where instruction is traditionally geared to the need of the average child, the dull children have to work under a great hardship. They need individual attention, special, remedial help and a modified curriculum to suit their rate of learning. In some educationally advanced countries, special schools have been established for this category of children. Such a feasibility may be explored in India in big cities. Special classes in ordinary schools can also be held very profitably. Such a treatment is likely to be better for their emotional and social development also. Guidance and counselling services have an important role to play in the education of such children.

14. Common school system: A common school system of public education should be evolved in place of the present system which divides the management of school between a large number of agencies whose functioning is inadequately co-ordinated. An adequate level of quality and efficiency should be maintained so that no parent would ordinarily feel any need to send his child to the institutions outside the system. Such a step will be helpful towards eliminating the segregation that now takes place between the schools for the poor and the underprivileged classes and those for the rich and the privileged ones.

15. State schools: The state should itself open a large number of state schools for the spread of education.

16. Suitable legislation: The state should take suitable steps to exercise control on private enterprise which thrives on high fees charged from the students. The public schools run by such organisations should not be allowed to perpetuate class differences.

FASCISM

Meaning

Derived from the Italian word Fascio (a bundle of wood), fascism expresses unity, discipline and strength. This term was applied to the regimes of Mussolini and Hitler which were established in 1922 and 1933 in Italy and Germany respectively. Aggressive nationalist, undemocratic, communal, anti-communist regimes, movements and parties are usually called fascist. Fascism is a reactionary and counter-revolutionary theory. Its object is to safeguard the crisis-ridden capitalist socio-economic and political order. It is opposed to democracy, human rights, socialism and any kind of revolutionary change.

Fascism In Europe

The first Fascist state was established on the 28th October, 1922, when aimed members of Fascist party, dressed in black, held a 'March on Rome' in Italy under the leadership of Mussolini.

Fascism in Germany

German Fascism evolved under the leadership of Nazi Party, led by Hitler, formed in 1920 on the basis of an attractive and radical 25-point programme.

Educational Implications

1. Objectives: The primary objective of fascism is to cultivate in the young an emotional and intellectual commitment to the racial superiority. The individual's education must develop in him an intense spirit of nationalism. My country, right or wrong, should be the dominating factor and slogan guiding all educational activities including the aims and objectives of education.

2. Curriculum: Fascism attaches great importance to the inclusion of subjects relating to physical education. Hitler held the view that as a certain racial quality is the pre-supposition of the intellectual efficiency, so all education must first of all develop physical health. The Fascists decry physical weakness as crime against the state. They believe that the genetic constitution of the body owes much from physical education.

3. Methods of teaching: Fascism discourages questioning and independent thinking on the part of the students. Students are required to listen to their teachers passively.

4. Discipline: There are rigid and strict rules and regulations to be followed by the students. They are treated like dumb-driven cattle. They are required to sacrifice their individuality for the sake of state.

5. Teachers: The primary duty of a teacher under fascism is to prepare children in such a manner that they would profess faith in the service of their nation.

MARXISM

What is Marxism?

Marxism has been regarded as a body of social doctrine worked out by Karl Marx (1818-1883), a revolutionary author, thinker and philosopher of his age. He was assisted by his colleague and friend Frederick Engles.

Main Characteristics of Marxism

1. Revolutionary programme: In the contemporary world, Marxism makes its claims as a scientific philosophy, revolutionary programme, progressive movement, and the socio-economic, political, cultural and moral basis of the social systems of more than a thousand million people. During the course of its history of 130 years or so, Marxism had to face many challenges from within and without, guided many revolutionary movements and aroused hopes in millions of people. It provided a scientific outlook towards the universe, society, history, man, etc. The revolutionary power of this ideology and of the revolutionary mass movements based on it, has divided the world into two blocks the capitalist or liberal block, and the socialist block.

2. Anti-capitalism: Marx did not appeal to the conscience of the capitalists to improve the conditions of the working class. He did not appeal to the reason of the capitalist class. He did not entrust the state with the welfare functions to improve the conditions of working class. On the contrary, he gave a revolutionary message of changing the society— "Workers of the world unite, you have nothing to lose but your chains and you have a world to win".

3. Philosophy of socio-political change: The most important aspect of the development of Marxism is its philosophy of socio-political change.

4. Materialistic concept of history: Marx found the paradigm of actual social and human development and translated it into materialist terms. Materialistic conception of history was the Hegelian idealistic conception turned upside down or back upon its feet. Marx rejected idealism and replaced it with materialism. His method is known as dialectic materialism and it is the philosophical basis of Marxism. It is called dialectical materialism because its approach to the phenomena of Nature, its method of studying and apprehending them is dialectical, while its interpretations of the phenomena of Nature, its conceptions of these phenomena, its theory is materialistic.

5. Proletarian revolution: Marx wrote in *Communist Manifesto,* "All previous historical movements were movements of minorities, or in the interest of minorities. The proletarian movement is the self-conscious independent movement of the immense majority, in the interests of the immense majority. The proletariat, the lowest stratum of our present society, cannot stir, cannot raise itself up, without the whole super-incumbent strata of official society being sprang into the air. The proletariat revolution will be social revolution, as the proletariat represent the interests of the society as a whole. Thus, Marxism is a theory of revolutionary change. Capture of political power by the working class is a beginning and, after it, the dictatorship of proletariat should be established and massive task of social and economic transformation should start, so that the way for a classless society may be paved.

Criticism of Marxism

1. Revolutionary: Development and change in society can be brought through reforms rather than through revolution.

2. Destructive: Revolution is destructive and it implies violence.

3. Dictatorship: After the revolution, instead of the dictatorship of the proletariat, dictatorship over proletariat is established and it destroys the liberties available in an open society, and gives birth to a closed society.

4. Class conflict: Classes are not abolished by revolution and even after the revolution class-struggle continues.

5. National loss: During the revolution, one generation has to pay a very heavy price and it is illogical that a generation should sacrifice itself for the sake of the coming generation.

6. No withering away of state: In socialist societies there are no chances of the withering away of the state.

Implications of Marxism in Education

1. Formation of character: According to Marxism, the character formation of the child should be guided by the objectives of the classless society which was the ultimate end or objective of communism.

2. Production-oriented education: According to Marx, education should be combined with productive work. He appreciated the work of a British factory owner, Robert Owen, for initiating this idea in his factory at New Lanark, Scotland in 1799. He observed, "From the factory system budded, as Robert Owen has shown us in detail, the germ of education of the future, an education that will, in the case of every child over a given age, combine productive labour with instruction and gymnastics, not only as one of the methods of adding to the efficiency of production, but as the only method of producing fully developed human beings".

About "socially useful work" the views of Gandhi and Marx are quite similar. Brubacher has stated in this context "Gandhi not only strongly opposed a purely literary education because it unfitted youth for the manual work in which most of them would be engaged during rest of their lives, but he believed education through economic work to be a great moral source as well". According to Marx, the teaching of practical life activities is essential and these activities must be social as well as useful.

3. Study of history: Marx stressed the importance of studying history scientifically. It is not to be confined to any particular region, but it must have a universal appeal. History is not a catalogue of past events but useful for the present flowing into the future.

4. Study of economics: Marx emphasized the study of social sciences including economics for understanding the social and economic conditions of life. The significance and importance of "class struggle" may be fully understood through the study of social sciences.

5. Stress on group work: Marxian education mitigates competition and substitutes it by group activities of different kinds. In Russian schools as well as in daily life, competition is eliminated and a cooperative spirit is promoted. Marxism insists that man will develop his full nature by participation in social life. The child is made to feel that he is a unit in society and has a duty to the society.

Marx has made an important contribution in propounding a philosophy of great significance. Moreover, it is very difficult to give a concrete shape to his ideas in the field of education. As C.E.M. Joad said, "Marx's writings, despite the great influence they have exercised over the working classes, are by no means free from difficulty, and there is considerable controversy as to the correct interpretation which should be placed upon them".

COMMUNISM

Meaning

According to Websters *New World Dictionary*, communism means, "1. a theory or system based on the ownership of all property by the community as a whole. 2. (*a*) a hypothetical stage of socialism, as formulated by Marx, Engels, Lenin, etc., to be characterised by a classless and stateless society and the equal distribution of economic groups, (*b*) the form of government in the USSR, China, etc., professing to be working toward this state, 3. (*a*) a political movement for establishing a communist system, (*b*) the doctrines, methods, etc., of the communist parties". From this definition of communism its following characteristics may be derived:

(1) Communism is a theory based on community ownership of property. Therefore, it is against the capitalist system of individual ownership of property.

(2) Communism envisages a classless and stateless society.

(3) Communism asks for an equal distribution of economic goods.

The Communist Manifesto

In the above mentioned definition of communism it has been pointed out that it is a philosophy propounded by Karl Marx and Engels and later own developed by Lenin. Therefore, it will be only in the fitness of things to go through the fundamentals of communism as laid down in *The Manifesto of the Communist Party,* published first in German language in 1872. It was written by Karl Marx and Frederick Engels. Its Russian Edition was published in 1882 and English Edition was published in 1888. Distinguishing the programme of the communist party from the programme of other political parties Marx and Engles wrote, "The Communists are distinguished from the other working class parties by this only:

(1) In the national struggles of the proletarians of the different countries, they point out and bring to the front the common interests of the entire proletariat, independently of all nationality.
(2) In the various stages of development which the struggles of the working class against the bourgeoisie has to pass through, they always and everywhere represent the interests of the movements as a whole. In the words of C.E.M. Joad, "Communism seeks to lay down principles upon which transition from capitalism to socialism is to be accomplished and its two essential doctrines are class war and the revolutionary, that is the absolute transference of power to the proletariat". According to Gettel, communism is a philosophy of history based upon the materialistic theory of human development. The following characteristics of communism were

laid down by Marx and Engels in *The Manifesto of the Communist Party:*

1. Progressive ideal: Laying down the outline of the progressive political ideal of the communist party, Marx and Engels wrote, "The Communists, therefore, are on the one hand, practically, the most advanced and resolute section of the working-class parties of every country, that section which pushes forward all others; on the other hand, theoretically, they have over the great mass of the proletariat the advantage of clearly understanding the line of march, the conditions, and the ultimate general results of the proletarian movement".

2. Immediate aim: According to Marx and Engels, "The immediate aim of the communists is the same as that of all the other proletarian parties: formation of the proletariat into a class, overthrow of the bourgeois supremacy, conquest of political power by the proletariat".

3. Abolition of private property: According to Karl Marx and Engels, capital is not a personal but social power. Therefore, it should be converted into common property. In the words of Karl Marx and Engels, "We Communists have been reproached with the desire of abolishing the right of personally acquiring property as the fruit of a man's own labour, which property is alleged to be the groundwork of all personal freedom, activity and independence..." When, therefore, capital is converted into common property, into the property of all members of society, personal property is not thereby transformed into social property. The social distinguishing feature of communism is not the abolition of property generally, but the abolition of bourgeois property. Modern bourgeois private property is the final and most complete expression of the system of producing and appropriating products, that is based on class antagonism, on the exploitation of the many by the few.

4. Abolition of exploitation: Therefore, communism deprives no man of the power to appropriate the products of society; all that it does is to deprive him of the power to subjugate the labour of others by means of such appropriation. This has been called expropriation of expropriators.

5. Abolition of the family: The most important charge against the communist view of human society is their concept of abolition of the family. Explaining this idea, Marx and Engels have written,

"On what foundation is the present family, the bourgeois family, based on capital, on private gain"? In its completely developed form this family exists only among the bourgeois. But this state of things finds its complement in the practical absence of the family among the proletarians and in public prostitution. The bourgeois family will vanish as a matter of course when its complement vanishes, and both will vanish with the vanishing of capital. Do you charge us with wanting to stop the exploitation of children by their parents? To this crime we plead guilty. But, you will say, we destroy the most hallowed of relations, when we replace home education by social.

6. Role of education: The communists do not approve the present capitalist system of education. They advocate their own system of education which is free from the influence of the ruling class. Criticising the current capitalist system of education Marx and Engels wrote, "The bourgeois clap-trap about the family and education, about the hallowed co-relation of parent and child, becomes all the more disgusting, the more, by the action of modern industry, all family ties among the proletarians are torn asunder, and their children transformed into simple articles of commerce and instruments of labour".

7. Ideal of human unity: Marx and Engels rejected nationalism and called for a unity of the working men of all countries which will gradually abolish the boundaries of nations and establish one human world. Explaining his ideal Karl Marx and Frederick Engels wrote, "The working men have no country. We cannot take from them what they have not got. Since the proletariat must first of all acquire political supremacy, must rise to be the leading class of the nation, must constitute itself the nation, it is, so far, itself national, though not in the bourgeois sense of the word".

National differences and antagonisms between peoples are daily more and more vanishing, owing to the development of the bourgeoisie, the freedom of commerce, to the world-market, to uniformity in the mode of production and in the conditions of life corresponding thereto.

The supremacy of the proletariat will cause them to vanish still faster. United action of the leading civilised countries at least, is one of the first condition for the emancipation of the proletariat.

In proportion as the exploitation of one individual by another is put to an end the exploitation of one nation by another will also be put to an end. In proportion as the antagonism between classes within the nation vanishes, the hostility of one nation to another will come to an end.

8. Revolution: For the total change and transformation of society from the capitalist society to communist society Marx and Engels have suggested communist revolution. This revolution will be developed according to local circumstances in every country but Marx and Engels have also laid down some fundamental characteristics which will be common in communist revolution in every country. As they put it, Nevertheless in the most advanced countries, the following will be pretty generally applicable:

(1) Abolition of property in land and application of all rents of land to public purposes.

(2) A heavy progressive or graduated income tax.

(3) Abolition of all right of inheritance.

(4) Confiscation of the property of all emigrants and rebels.

(5) Centralization of credit in the hands of the state, by means of a national bank with state capital and an exclusive monopoly.

(6) Centralization of the means of communication and transport in the hands of the state.

(7) Extension of factories and instruments of production owned by the state; the bringing into cultivation of wastelands, and the improvement of the society generally in accordance with a common plan.

(8) Equal liability of all to labour. Establishment of industrial armies, especially for agriculture.

(9) Combination of agriculture with manufacturing industries, gradual abolition of the distinction between town and country by a more equable distribution of the population over the country.

(10) Free education for all children in public schools. Abolition of children's factory labour in its present form. Combination of education with industrial production, etc.

9. Classless society: The most significant characteristic of communist society is that it is a classless society. In the absence of classes, the state will also wither away. As Marx and Engels put it, "When, in the course of development, class distinctions have disappeared, and all production has been concentrated in the hands of a vast association of the whole nation, the public power will lose its political character. Political power, properly so-called, is merely the organised power of one class for oppressing another. If the proletariat during its contest with the bourgeoisie is compelled by the force of circumstances, to organise itself as a class, as such, sweeps away by force the old conditions of production, then it will, along with these conditions, have swept away the conditions for the existence of class antagonisms and of classes generally, and will thereby have abolished its own supremacy as a class".

11

Humanism

Humanism is the philosophy according to which man is central in the scheme of things. Man is the only worthy object of knowledge. Humanism is the criterion to solve the controversies arising in human life. Ever since reason dawned in man, thoughtful persons have been in search of some one or the other criterion of reality to solve the controversies arising in human life. Such have been the attempts of Socrates, Plato, Aristotle and other ancient Greek philosophers. Philosophical thinking in ancient times everywhere was not distinguished from the religious thought. But gradually philosophers extricated themselves from religious dogmas and established philosophical thinking on independent grounds. Such were the rationalists, the empiricists, the realists and the idealists and other modern philosophers. In contemporary world of philosophy, philosophical thought was very much influenced by the developments in physical and social sciences with the result that new criteria of reality were accepted by the philosophers. The unprecedented progress in the means of transport and communication have today made the world small and brought human beings very near to each other. Human problems, therefore, have become central in all serious thinking. This has created a favourable climate for the rise of humanism.

Like other trends of thought the roots of humanism can be traced in the old Greek philosophy and in the ancient thought of India. In the West, Protegoras of Greece declared that man is the measure of all things. After Protegoras, the humanist idea could be seen in the thought of sophist philosophers and the ideas of Plato and Socrates. But this humanist trend received maximum encouragement by the Naturalist and Materialist philosophies.

Charles Darwin's *Theory of Evolution* established that there is no deep gulf between man and animal in Nature. After Darwin, the idea of evolution was utilised in almost every field of human thinking and so many theories were established. Today, it has been generally accepted that animal and man are two different stages in the same process of evolution.

Humanism: Its Meaning and Implications

The English word humanism has been derived from the Latin term 'Homo' which means human being. Thus, literally speaking, humanism is the philosophy in which man occupies a central place. Etymological meaning, however, is not the sufficient meaning of a term, it includes its historical usage as well. The use of a term in the historical tradition gradually unveils the different aspects of its meaning. Thus, in order to understand the full implication of the term humanism one must take into account its historical evolution. In this historical evolution whatever has been found to be useful for human welfare has been attached with the concept of humanism such as the idea of social welfare, scientific attitude, progress of democratic institutions, etc.

Essentials of Humanism

The above discussion makes it clear that humanism is obviously against all types of super naturalism or super-humanism. It cannot consider any man to be essentially greater than other human beings. In it the term human welfare means the welfare of ordinary human beings. It does not aim at superman but only at man. Its central standpoint is faith in the dignity of man. Since man is the creature of this earth, humanism is this—worldly and against all types of other—worldly theories. The humanist ethics is not governed by any religious faith other than faith in human dignity. So far as human welfare has been advanced by science, the humanist respects science but if science becomes an impediment in his progress he would not hesitate in criticising it and fixing its limitations. The Western humanists have been lagging behind in this particular function though today many Western thinkers have started pointing out to the evils and dangers of a cult of science. Since each human being is important for the humanist, humanism is against all distinctions among human beings on the basis of country, nation, race, class, caste, sex, religion, economic status, scholarship and abilities. As a human being no human being is lower than the other. Thus humanism supports the idea of world citizenship. But as has been already pointed out, the concept of humanism does not negate other human loyalties but fulfils them because unity in diversity is the basis of the richness of the human culture.

Every philosophy holds some particular concepts in metaphysics, epistemology and axiology. As the philosophy differs so do its conceptions in these fields. According to humanism, man is the essence of reality. There is no other super human ontological reality beyond him. He is the proper object of knowledge and whatever human faculties help us in knowing any thing are faculties of knowledge. All truth is human truth and there is no truth beyond man. In axiology humanism seeks to realize a world in which the human values may be achieved to their maximum limit. For this purpose we will have to, first of all, satisfy the physical needs because in their absence no mental or spiritual development is possible. But since man is more than the animal, the bread and butter, clothes and house are not sufficient for his welfare. After the satisfaction of the physical needs the humanist, should plan for mental and spiritual progress. Man is an animal, but he is a cultural animal. Without the cultural evolution he cannot realize his humanity. Therefore, after the satisfaction of the basic physical needs, the humanist seeks to achieve progress in the fields of literature, art, thinking and other fields of cultural evolution.

Humanist Sociology

In the field of sociology the humanist approach has led to the thinking that every where the social scientist has to find social factors governing human behaviour aiming at the reform and welfare of the human individual. For example, in the field of criminology, an important branch of sociology, the social scientists have been busy in finding out the causes of crime and the possible ways of reforming the criminal. Thus, the humanist trend has led to the search for social reforms in the field of different social institutions.

Humanist Psychology

In the field of psychology the humanist trend is particularly clear in the branches known as fields of applied psychology. Thus, in industrial psychology, the psychologist aims at finding out the of all-round welfare of the human beings working under industrial conditions. His aim is not only search into conditions for realising maximum production but achieving circumstances where the worker may develop as a human being. Thus, the psychologists help him in labour welfare, a branch of human welfare in general. Similarly, in the fields of abnormal psychology and psychiatry the psychologists aim at the understanding of human beings suffering from psychological ailments and finding out ways to cure them so that they might enjoy their normal life and behave as normal human beings. Thus, the aim here is not merely curative but seeks welfare. The application of psychology, consequently, is growing gradually in different fields of industry, law, medicine and above all in education. In the field of education the psychologist is everywhere in search of ways and means to improve educands as human beings. Thus, in the field of education today the humanist approach is the guiding principle.

Aims and Ideals of Education

According to humanism education aims at man-making. It should be secular, rational and scientific. It should aim at the realisation of humanist values in the individual and society. According to it the education aims at complete development of human personality. It enables man to solve individual and social problems. Its purpose is to increase efficiency and happiness of human beings. It supports democratic philosophy of education since the values of liberty, equality and fraternity are fundamental human values. Thus, the educational institutions should be based upon democratic principles. It seeks to realise peace upon the earth. The humanist tendency is rationalist and integral. It is positivist since it supports meliorism. Science alone can provide more leisure for cultural development. The individual and society are intimately related, Therefore, the children should develop team spirit and co-operation through play-way method. Community programmes should make community living easy and spontaneous. The society should be made conductive to all-round human progress.

The humanist trend integrates psychological, sociological and eclectic tendencies in education. It makes human nature the basis of education. It emphasises the value of individual differences in education. It makes education child centred. While on the one hand the aim of education is the propagation of knowledge, social control, social development and preservation of social heritage, it also seeks to integrate all these. Thus, it is an integral approach to education. Its aim of education is integral.

This aim of education is based upon integral psychology. Man, according to the humanists, is a self having body as well as intellect. All these should be integrated.

1. Curriculum: The humanist curriculum is liberal and extensive. Along with science it has arts and humanities and also moral, religious and spiritual subjects. In fact, all types of knowledge are included in humanist curriculum.

Method of Teaching

The humanist method of teaching is based on psychology. The teacher educates according to the principles of child psychology, developmental psychology and educational psychology. Besides, the theoretical instruction methods for development of social virtues are emphasised.

Education is provided through the mother-tongue since it encourages originality and creativity. National and international languages are also taught at higher stages since the humanist seeks to encourage human communications on national and international stage.

School Organisation

The school organisation should be democratic in which the management, the teachers and the students should together govern all the activities. The school should be organised in such a way as to encourage responsibility, liberty, equality and fraternity. The school administration should be liberal and democratic. Discipline should be self-discipline. Peaceful relations should be encouraged so that the boys and girls may help in the establishment of peace upon earth. The rules and regulations should be rational and secular. Humanism is against narrow nationalism. It synthesises nationalism and internationalism. Of these it even subordinates nationalism to internationalism. Humanists believe in the principle of unity through diversity. The universities should encourage development of all the aspects of culture. Regional universities should encourage preservation of regional culture but also its synthesis in the national culture. Again, national universities should not only help in the preservation of national culture, but also encourage mixing of students from different nations and thus create an international humanist cultural atmosphere. Examples of humanist universities in India are Santiniketan of Rabindra Nath and Sri Aurobindo International University at Pondicherry.

The above educational implications of humanism reveal that it is the best blue print for the planning of future education. It is the solid basis for development of values and culture. It is an integral approach to aims and ideals, means, curriculum and organisation of education. In fact, humanism may be called the future philosophy of education acceptable and required everywhere.

12

Secularism

DEFINITION OF SECULARISM

The word 'secularism' was first used in the nineteenth century by George Jacob Holydake. He derived it from the Latin word 'Seculum' meaning "this present age". He used it in the context of social and ethical values or systems. Thus, secularism came to be known as a social and ethical system. The following principles were evolved by Holydake to mark this system:

(*i*) Primary emphasis on the material and cultural improvement of human beings.

(*ii*) Respect for and search for all truth, whatever be its source, which can be tested in experience leading to human betterment.

(*iii*) Concern for this age or world and its improvement.

(*iv*) An independent rational morality, which does not base itself on faith in divine commandment.

Bradlaugh observed that secularism was hostile to religion and maintained that either secularism or religion should survive.

1. Chambers Dictionary: According to Chambers Dictionary secularism is, "the belief that the state, moral, education, etc., should be independent of religion."

2. Oxford Dictionary: Oxford Dictionary defines secularism as, "the doctrine that the morality should be based solely in regard to the well-being of mankind in the present life, to the exclusion of all considerations drawn from belief in God."

3. Webster's Dictionary: Webster's Dictionary states that secularism is, "the belief that religion and ecclesiastical affairs should not enter into the functions of the state".

The limited sense of the word secularism is often placed in contrast with religion. Thus Webster gives us an alternative definition of secularism: "A system of doctrines and practices that rejects any form of religious faith and worship".

4. Brubacher: Secularism has "no religious point of view while it has a theory of moral education". "If the secularist has any religion at all it is likely that scientific doctrine constitutes the presuppositions of that religion and that scientists are its high priests".

EDUCATION COMMISSION (1964-1966)

The adoption of a secularist policy means that no religious community will be favoured or discriminated against. The instruction in religious dogmas will not be provided in state schools. But the secularist policy is not an irreligious or anti-religious policy. It does not belittle the importance of religions. It gives to every citizen the fullest freedom of religious belief and worship. It promotes not only religious toleration but also an active reverence for all religions. We have to make a distinction between 'religious education' and 'education about religions'. The former is largely concerned with the teaching of tenets and practices of a particular religion in a particular form, and it would not be practicable to provide this type of religious education in respect of any religion to pupils belonging to different faiths. But it is necessary for a multi-religious democratic State to promote a tolerant study of all religions so that its citizens can understand each other better and live amicably together.

The Education Commission (1964-66) has recommended: "We suggest that a syllabus giving well chosen information about each of the major religions should be included as a part of the course in citizenship or as a part of general education to be introduced in schools and colleges up to the first degree. It should highlight the fundamental similarities in the great religions of the world and the emphasis they place on the cultivation of certain broadly comparable moral and spiritual values". The Commission further observed: "There will be natural points of correlation between the moral values sought to be inculcated and the teachings of the great religions. All religions stress certain fundamental qualities of character, such as honesty and truthfulness, consideration for others, reverence for old age, kindness to animals, and the compassion for the needy and the suffering. In the literature of every religion, the story of parable figures prominently as a means of impressing an ethical value on the followers. The narration of such stories by the teachers at the right moment in the programme of moral education would be most effective, particularly in the lower classes. At a later stage, accounts of the lives of great religious and spiritual leaders will find a natural place.... Similarly, the celebration of festivals and different religions will afford opportunity for the narration of incidents from the life history of the leaders of these religions. In the last two years of the secondary school, a place should be found for the study of the essential teachings of the great religions".

CONSTITUTIONAL PROVISIONS

After obtaining her independence India adopted secularism as a way of life. Our Constitution guarantees the fullest freedom of religious belief and worship. It has laid down the following provisions in connection with religious and moral education in educational institutions.

Article 19 (1): "Subject to public order, morality and health and to other provisions of this part, all persons are equally entitled to freedom to conscience and the right freely to profess, practise and propagate religion."

Article 21: "No person may be compelled to pay any taxes, the proceeds of which are specifically appropriated in payment of expenses for the promotion or maintenance of any particular religion or religious denomination."

Article 22 (1): "No religious instructions shall be provided in any educational institution wholly maintained out of State funds."

Provided that nothing in this clause shall apply to an educational institution which is administered but has been established under an endowment or trust which requires that religious instructions shall be imparted in such institutions.

(2) "No person attending any educational institution recognised by the State or receiving aid out of State funds shall be required to take part in any religious institution or to attend any religious worship that may be conducted in such institution or in any premises attached thereto unless such person, or if such person is a minor his guardian has given his consent thereto."

Article 30 (1): "All minorities whether based on religion or language, shall have the right to establish and administer educational institutions of their choice."

(2) "The State shall not, in granting aid to educational institutions, discriminate against any educational institution on the ground that it is under the management of a minority, whether based on religion or language."

RECOMMENDATIONS OF THE SECONDARY EDUCATION COMMISSION

The Secondary Education Commission (1949) observed that healthy trends in regard to religion or moral behaviour spring from three sources: (1) The influence of the home, (2) the influence of the school, through the conduct and behaviour of the teachers themselves and life in the school community as a whole, and (3) the influence exercised by the public of the locality. No amount of instruction can supersede or supplant these three essential factors.

The following steps were suggested:

(1) Morning assembly with all teachers and students present should be utilized for this purpose. A general non-denominational prayer may be offered.

(2) Inspiring talks on moral instruction may be given by suitable persons selected by headmaster. Such talks should dwell on the lives of the great personages of all times and of all climes.

(3) In view of the provision of the Constitution of the Secular State, religious instructions cannot be given in schools except on a voluntary basis and outside the regular school hours; such instructions should be given to the children of the particular faith and with the consent of the parents and the management concerned. In making this recommendation we wish to emphasize that all unhealthy trends of disunity, rancour, religious hatred and bigotry should be discouraged in schools.

CHARACTERISTICS OF SECULAR EDUCATION

Secular education is identified because of the following characteristics:

1. Moral outlook: Secular education results in development of moral outlook. It is the foundation for development of character and moral development. It inculcates in students humanity, truthfulness, tolerance, honesty, courtesy, sympathy, spirit of service and sacrifice which form a noble character of man and develop his personality.

2. Development of wider attitude: Secular education makes a man dynamic and enlightened. It develops in him a wider attitude towards life, and he takes interest in social service by sacrificing his selfish motives. Education makes him courageous enough to face the problems of life and solve them to the best of his efforts and intelligence.

3. Pluralistic outlook: Secular education leads to the emergence of a healthy pluralistic outlook which fosters the growth of science, art, philosophy and even religion. A pluralistic outlook is the very essence of democracy.

4. Democratic value: Secular education helps man in developing democratic qualities like liberty, equality, fraternity and co-operative living. True secularism stresses the dignity of the individual and the sacredness of human personality. Secular education helps to establish and incorporate democratic process. Every person is treated as an end and never as means only.

5. Cultural development: Secular education helps in promotion of cultural development. It preserves and reinforces culture. Secularism and culture go hand in hand and influence each other. Secularism is the dynamic aspect of culture.

6. Scientific spirit: Secular education helps in fostering scientific spirit. It releases the individual from the bonds of blind faith. Scientific spirit implies a spirit of free enquiry, a spirit of looking at things objectively and rationally, freedom from an obsession with the past, and a more humble attitude towards our own history and achievements. Secular education promotes scientific values of rationality, objectivity and open-mindedness.

7. Synthesis of spiritual and material: Secular education glorifies material needs and promotes reverence for earthly life, without rejecting spiritual values. Secularism is based on fundamental human values. It looks upon science not merely as a means of material progress but as a quest for truth and a search for harmony with nature. It helps to strike a healthy balance between the spiritual and the material.

8. Humanitarianism: Secular education leads to humanitarianism. It stands for peace, good-will and understanding. It helps in fostering the brotherhood of man and the unity of the world.

Absence of secular education causes exploitation, corruption, disaster, selfishness, aggression and hatred, chaos and disorder. Betterment of society depends upon secular based education. It raises man to a high level. It encourages the policy of 'live and let live'. It provides the basis for true humanitarianism. It helps in replacing hatred by love, selfishness by self-sacrifice and violence by non-violence. Secular education leads to happiness, order and contentment in the society by cultivating faith in truth, beauty and goodness.

EDUCATION FOR SECULARISM IN INDIA

India's present educational system promotes secular attitudes and values through its broad-based aims, curricula, enlightened teachers and appropriate activities, all emphasizing open-mindedness, progressivism, rationality, freedom from bigotry and superstition, and equal respect for all religions. The following traits characterise education for secularism in India:

1. Alms: The aims and objectives of such a system are secular. They seek to develop India as a rational, democratic, progressive and modern welfare state. The philosophy of humanism guides such educational objectives. The well-being of all the citizens of the country is the goal towards which India's educational energies are directed.

2. Organisation of educational institutions: The organisation of most of Indian educational institutions is based on secular principles. It is necessary to observe secular, democratic, rational criteria in appointments, promotions, admissions, and all such matters.

3. Curricula: The educational curricula at all levels in India lay special emphasis on the promotion of secular values. Lessons in textbooks are free from religious bigotry and prejudice while the good ideas and values emphasized in different religions are presented in appropriate forms. The co-curricular activities aim at promoting harmony and co-operation among different groups and respect for each other's culture in the students. It is not permitted to condemn or unduly praise any one particular religion or cultural system or institution. It is the usual practice in all schools, colleges and universities to celebrate fairs, festivals, birth anniversaries, etc., relating to different religions. While imparting moral education equal importance is given to different faiths.

4. Science teaching: Secularism stands for scientific rationalism. It stresses logical thinking and abhors superstitions and irrational things. Therefore, Indian education today puts much emphasis upon science teaching. Science is taught in a practical manner at all levels of schooling, so that it might influence the attitudes and values of the pupils. The spirit of science with emphasis on inquiry, experimentation, proof and critical outlook, permeates the teaching of other subjects also.

5. Teachers: In the education for secularism in India the teachers today are expected to treat their pupils in an impartial manner. They eschew all caste, community and class considerations in dealing with students and colleagues. Equal respect is given to all students and to all religious groups. Every conscientious teacher behaves in a truly democratic and fair manner.

Thus, the present Indian secular educational system is trying to create a social climate in the country in which secular values are sought to be promoted effectively and enthusiastically.

DIFFICULTIES IN SECULAR EDUCATIONAL SYSTEM

In a country like India, in which traditional institutions like religion, caste, untouchability, and dowry have been prevailing for thousands of years, the building up of a secular state is a very challenging task. Despite the best intentions of our Constitution makers and great leaders, it is difficult to establish and promote a really functional climate of secularism in India. The main difficulties in secular educational system are as follow:

1. Traditional bias and narrow outlook: In our country today denominational schools are allowed to function with a lot of freedom. There are D.A.V. Schools, lain Schools, Vaish Schools, Ahir Schools, Kayastha Pathshalas, Shia Schools, Catholic Schools, Rajput Schools, etc. In these institutions the children of the respective communities or castes are admitted on preferential basis, and also the teachers of the same communities are preferred. This creates a serious difficulty in the functioning of Indian education as an integrative and secular force in Indian society.

2. Too much emphasis on theoretical learning: Our educational system presents many things only in theory. Very little effort is made to change the values and attitudes of education. Many highly educated people do not hesitate to demand big dowries. They are too much fastidious about gotras and sub-castes in deciding marriage. They ill-treat women-folk and do not show respect to other religions. The lack of tolerance and courtesy on the part of educated persons towards villagers, women, poor people, minority community members, old people, etc., in buses, trains and at other public places reveals that our present education has failed to change our values system in a desired manner.

3. Neglect of religious and cultural celebrations: Schools and colleges observe holidays on the days of important religious fairs, festivals and birthdays. The result is that the students do not get enough opportunities to understand or imbibe secular values.

4. Neglect of group activities: Educational institutions do not encourage group activities. Group activities and group methods of teaching and learning are neglected. This is a serious difficulty in the promotion of secular and free ideas and values.

13

Ancient Indian Philosophy of Education

The aim of Indian education was initially laid down by the Vedas. According to Vedic worldview the world is pervaded by divinity and the aim of every living being is to achieve liberation. This is possible by following one's own dharma. Thus, according to the Vedas the aim of education is liberation. According to a famous statement, 'That is knowledge which gives liberation', therefore, A.S. Altekar has rightly pointed out, "The knowledge, is a third eye of man, which gives him insight into all affairs and teaches him how to act. In the spiritual sphere it leads to our salvation, in the mundane sphere it leads to all-round progress and prosperity. The illumination given to us by the education shatters illusions, removes difficulties and enables us to realize the true values of life".

PHILOSOPHY OF VEDIC AND UPANISHADIC EDUCATION

The cause of liberation and bondage, according to Vedic thinker, is the mind or chitta. Therefore, liberation is possible only through the control of the mind. This was known as the technique of chitta-vratti nirodh. The Indian philosophers developed a whole technique for the control of the mind. Equanimity of the mind leads to self-realization. This self is neither individual nor social self but Brahman which is the essence of the individual and the society. The Vedic axiology does not distinguish between the social and the individual values since according to it both are part of the fundamental universal values.

The ancient Indian education was even more developed by the Upanishads. While in the field of religion the Upanishads were more introvert and monistic, they continued the tradition of the Vedas. This tradition was oral. In the words of Radha Kumud Mukerjee, "For thousands of years, even up to the time of Kumarila (8th century A.D.) it was considered a sacrilege to reduce the Veda to writing, for learning was not reading but realization, and knowledge was to be in the blood, as an organic part of one's self. Another point to be noted in this connection is that sabda or sound by itself has its own potency and value, apart from its sense, and its intrinsic attributes, its rhythm, and vibrations should be captured. Sabda is Brahma."

According to ancient Indian philosophy knowledge may be gained by three steps, Shravan or hearing, Manan or meditation and Nididhyasan or realization. Shravan or hearing was further categorised into six types—(*i*) *upakrama,* a formal ceremony performed preceding the study, of Veda, (*ii*) *abhyasa,* recitation of the texts, (*iii*) *apurvata,* a ready grasp of the meaning, (*iv*) *phala,* a comprehension of the outcome, (*v*) *arthavada,* the reading of elucidatory books, and (vi) *upapatti,* attainment of final conclusion.

TYPES OF EDUCATIONAL INSTITUTIONS

Describing the condition of education in ancient India, P.N. Prabhu has said, "Education in ancient India was free from any external control like that of the State or Government or any party politics. It was one of the king's duties to see that the learned pundits pursued their studies and their duty of imparting knowledge without interference from any source whatever. So also education did not suffer from any communal interest or prejudices in India". There were three types of educational institutions:

1. Gurukula: This, as the name indicates, was the family of the teacher and his residence where the students used to stay during the period of study. Gradually, the Gurukula were extended to include a number of buildings. However, the institution was built up around the family of teacher. The primary duty of the student was to serve the teacher and his family. The students were like sons of the teacher and the whole institution lived like a family.

2. Parishad: These were bigger educational institutions where several teachers used to teach different subjects. This may be compared to a college.

3. Sammelan: Sammelan literally means getting together for a particular purpose. In this type of educational institutions scholars gathered at one place for discussions and competitions, generally on the invitation of the king.

DISCIPLINE

The Vedic system of education very much emphasized the importance of discipline in the attainment of knowledge. This, however, was self-discipline. In fact, it was self-control which was realized by observance of rules of the Brahmacharya Ashrama. These rules will be discussed in details in sequence. The Parishads or the local academies were initiated by the king. Therefore, the scholars and aspirants of knowledge gathered at the Parishad with perfect academic order. There was hardly any need for insisting upon rules and regulations as these were laid down by scriptures. No one questioned the scripture's command concerning discipline. Therefore, discipline was self imposed as a part of self-culture.

EDUCATION IN THE ASHRAMA SYSTEM

Education, according to Vedic system, is the sole aim of Brahmacharya Ashrama. All the details concerning education have been given in the context of Brahmacharya Ashrama.

Meaning of Ashrama

According to *Sanskrit Hindi Dictionary* of V.S. Apte the term ashrama means stages, monastery, duties, etc. Writing in *Encyclopaedia of Religion and Ethics,* the German scholar Paul Deussen gives two meanings to the word ashram: (1) That place where people labour or make efforts, (2) To labour or make efforts. The word ashrama comes from the Sanskrit root srama giving the meaning of making an effort. In this way Ashrama literally means a step in the journey of life. In the words of P.V. Kane, "The word ashrama is derived from srama, to exert, to labour and etymologically means a stage in which one exerts oneself'. According to Hindu ethics, the final aim of life is liberation. And every ashrama is a step in the long journey to that aim. "The whole of the life of a human individual is for the Hindu," says P.H. Valvalker, "a kind of schooling and self-discipline". In the Shanti Parva of *Mahabharata,* Saint Vedavyasa has described ashrama as a four rung ladder which takes one in the direction of Brahman. Vedavyasa says, *Chatushpadi hi nihsreni brahman yesha Pratishthita, etamaruhya nihshreni brahmaloke mahiyate.*

In this way, in each ashrama the person prepares himself for every succeeding ashrama state. Literally, an ashrama is a halting place. The ashrama system is a means of systematic development for the better life. Dr. P.M. Modi has tried to prove that in the beginning there were only three ashramas and that Vanprastha and Sanyasa were considered as one ashrama. He has cited instances in his favour from *Chhandogya Upanishad and Manu Smriti.* It is in *Jabala Upanishad* that one finds the mention of four ashramas for the first time. This scheme of the stages of life during the period preceding Dharmashastras was rather indefinite. They were made definite for the first time by Dharmashastras. The Dharmashastras maintained clearly that each individual should normally pass through the four stages of life known as ashramas. In the second chapter of *Manu Smriti*, the author has described in details the characteristics and the activities of Brahmacharaya Ashrama. The third chapter describes the duties of Grihastha Ashrama. The fourth chapter describes this ashrama in four varnas. The Vanprastha Ashrama has been discussed in chapter sixth. This chapter also discusses the last ashrama known as Sanyasa. Thus, according to Dharmashastras, the stages of human individual's life are four: *Brahmacharya, Grihastha, Vanprastha and Sanyasa.* Of these, at last three have been described by Upanishads before Dharmashastras. According to P. V. Kane, "The word ashrama does not occur in the Samhitas or Brahmanas. But this cannot be stretched to mean that the stages of life denoted by this word in the Sutras were unknown throughout the Vedic period".

Number of Ashramas

From the times of the most ancient Dharmasutras the number of ashramas has been four, though there are slight differences in the nomenclature and in their sequence. According to *Ap. Dh. Sutra,* "There are four ashramas, *viz.* (staying in) the teacher's house, the stage of householder, stage of being a muni, the stage of being a forest dweller". According to *Gaut. Dharmasutra,* there are four ashramas; brahmachari, grihastha, bhikshu and vaikhanasa. According to *Vas. Dh. Sutra,* there are four ashramas, brahmachari, grihastha, vanaprastha and parivrajaka. According to *Manu Smriti* there are four ashramas, the last being called Yati and also sanyasa. According *to Manu Smriti* the span of human life is 100 years though all do not live to that age. In fact, it is the maximum age one can expect to reach. This has been divided into four parts so that one may lead an all-round integral life. It is not necessary that each of these stages should be lived for 25 years it may be more or less. However, normally the span of each ashrama was prescribed as 25 years. According to *Manu Smriti* the first part of man's life is Brahmacharya in which he learns at his teacher's house and after he has finished his study, in the second part of his life he marries and becomes a householder, discharges his debts to his ancestors by begetting sons and to the Gods by performing yajnas. Then, when he sees that his head has grey hair and that there are wrinkles on his body he resorts to the forest, *i.e.*, becomes a vanaprastha. After spending the third part of his life in the forest for some time he spends the rest of his life as a sanyasin. Similar rules have been laid down by other Dharmashastras with, of course, minor differences here and there. For example, according to *Baudhayana Dhanuashastra,* the stage of sanyasa starts after the 70th year.

Interpretation of this Scheme

The abovementioned scheme of four ashramas was interpreted from three different points of view, as follows:

1. Samuchchaya (orderly co-ordination): According to this view a person can resort to the four ashramas one after another in order and that he may not drop any one or more and pass on to the next nor may he resort to the householder's life after becoming a sanyasin. This view was primarily supported by Manu. This view lays emphasis upon the householder since the other ashramas depend upon it. Most of the Dharmashastras push the last two ashramas in the background so much so that according to some of them these are forbidden in the Kali age.

2. Vikalpa (option): According to this view there is an option after Brahmacharya, *i.e.,* a man may become a parivrajaka immediately after he finishes his study or immediately after the householder's way of life. This view has been supported by *Vashistha Dharmashastra, Yajnavalkya Smriti* and other.

3. Buddha (annulment or contradiction): According to this view there is really one ashrama and that is that of the householder. The first stage is a mere preparation for this ashrama while the other last two ashramas are inferior to it. This view was supported by

Gautama and Baudhayana. According to Gautama, there is only one ashrama. According to Baudhayana the ashramas other than that of householder do not beget off-spring and are therefore not much important. It was due to the influence of this viewpoint that almost all the Dharmashastras praise the ashrama of householder as the highest. This is particularly important from the point of view of provision for social development, progress, stability and justice.

In spite of the above three views about the following of the ashrama system, the general view believes that all the four ashramas have their value and details about the activities and duties of all these ashramas have been prescribed by Dharmashastras. Some have clearly pointed out that there is no distinction due to a superiority among the four ashramas. Other maintained that the householder's life was the rule and other ashramas were for the blind and other incapable persons. This view has been vehemently opposed by others.

Brahmacharya Ashrama

The first of the four ashramas is Brahmacharya Ashrama. It starts with the *Upanayana* ceremony. Brahmacharya means the leading of the life like a Brahman. In this ashrama, the student or Brahmachari lived up to 25 years of age with his teacher studying the Vedas and leading a life of self-control. The education and control of the Brahmacharya prepared a person for future life. Certain rules and observances are prescribed for all Brahmacharins. They are of two kinds, some are prescribed for a very short time and some have to be observed for all the years of studenthood. The first kind of observances were generally concerned with studies. The second kind of observances, *i.e.*, those which have to be observed throughout this period were concerned with the daily routine and general discipline of the persons in this stage of life. Of the two the later were definitely more important. These are principally *achamana, gurususrusa, vaksamyma* (silence), *samidhadana*. The smritis have laid down detailed rules about these observances. The rules centre principally around *agniparicharya* (worshipping fire), *bhiksha* (begging for food), *sandhyopasana*, study of Veda and its methods and duration, avoidance of certain foods and drinks and other matters like singing, etc., *gurususrusa* (including honouring him and his family and other elders) and the special vratas of the

Brahmachari. The rules about different aspects of the students life also fall in the category of the rules about Brahmacharya Ashrama.

ASPECTS OF VEDIC EDUCATION

Teacher as a Pivot

The pivot of the whole educational system of ancient India was the teacher variously called acharya, gum, upaddhyaya. In *Manu* and other *Smritis* there is some divergence about the greatness of the acharya. According to *Manu Smriti* the father (Janaka) and the teacher are called father (Pita) but the father who imparts the sacred Veda is superior to the father who gives birth, since the birth in spiritual learning is for a Brahmin of eternal benefit, here and hereafter. But in another place, Manu says that an acharya is ten times superior to an upaddhyaya, the father is superior to a hundred acharyas. According to Gautama, the acharya is the highest among all gurus while according to some the mother is the highest. According to *Yajnavalkya Smriti* the mother is higher than the acharya.

The Dharmashastras define the acharya as one who performs the upanayana of the student and imparts the whole Veda to him. The nirukta defines acharya as follows: he makes the student understand the proper course of conduct, or he collects wealth from the student or gathers together the meaning of words, or he increases the intelligence of the student. According to *Ap. Dh. Sutra*, "The acharya is so-called since the student gathers his duties from him". According to *Manu Smriti*, the teacher, after performing upanayana, teaches his pupil the rules about *saucha* (bodily purity), *achara* (rules of conduct in every day life), the offering of fuel-stick in fire and *sandhya* or adoration. Though the words *acharya*, guru and upaddhyaya are very often used as synonyms, ancient writers made a distinction between them. According to *Manu Smriti*, an upaddhyaya is one who teaches to a student a portion of the Veda or the Vedangas (subsidiary lores of the Veda) as a means of his own livelihood and a guru is one who performs the samsakars and who maintains the child. This latter definition shows that guru means the father here. According to *Yajnavalkya Smriti*, the guru is one who performs the samsakars and imparts the Veda. This corroborates the statement made above that originally the father himself taught the Veda to his son.

The word guru is often used in the sense of any elderly person, male or female who is entitled to respect. According to *Manu Smriti* whoever confers on another the benefit of knowledge, whether great or small, is the latter's guru. All these praises of the guru by the Dharmashastras shows that they held knowledge as the highest value and insisted upon the sense of gratitude in every one who achieved knowledge. Faith in the teacher was a necessary qualification for the achievement of knowledge. It is undeniable that this glorification of the teacher may have left to some of them loosing their needs but in contrast to the modern western philosophy of education it has its advantages. In fact, both these extremes are unjust, the former to the educand and the latter to the educator. In a just system of education both should be given a proper place.

The Dharmashastras have not praised the teacher without any reason. They have insisted upon very high qualifications for being a teacher. They have warned about the dangers of entrusting the job of a teacher to persons not worthy of it. According to *Ap. Dh. Sutra,* he whom a teacher devoid of learning, initiates enters from darkness into darkness and he also (an acharya) who is himself unlearned (enters into darkness). It further provides that one should desire a performer of one's upanayana who is endowed with learning and whose family is hereditarily learned and who is serene in mind and that one should study Vedic lore under him up to the end (of Brahmacharya) as long as the teacher does not fall off from the path of dharma. Similar qualifications have been laid down by other Dharmashastras. The teacher had to be a Brahmana, learned in Veda, knowing Dharma, pure, coming from a good family land having an ideal character. In educational system also the Dharmashastras have insisted upon the varna hierarchy. It has been generally maintained that Brahmana should be the teacher. According to *Vayupuran,* as to acharya in upanayana must be a Brahmana; as to the study of Veda one should ordinarily learn the Veda from a Brahmana teacher; in times of difficulty (*i.e.,* when a Brahmana is not available) one may learn the Veda from a kshatriya or vaisya teacher, but in such circumstances the only service that a Brahmana student rendered to the guru would be following after the non-Brahmana teacher, he had not to render bodily service (such as shampooing or washing the feet, etc.). The *Mit.* on *Yajnavalkya Smriti* remarks that a kshatriya or vaisya should teach a Brahmana only when urged by him and not at his sweet will. Manu allowed only teaching to a kshatriya, but did not allow him to make it a means of his livelihood. In fact, the Indian thinkers prescribed a social structure with definite division of labour and permitted only exceptions in certain cases. They very much insisted upon keeping the social structure in tact and not violating it. This rigidity had obviously resulted in so many disadvantages but it also facilitated continuity, regularity and order in social system.

Method of Instruction

The method of instruction of education was generally oral. The first thing that was taught to the boy was the *pranava* and the *vyahrtis* and the *Gayatri*. Then the boy was to be taught other parts of the Veda. Detailed instructions were laid down about the method of teaching. According to *Manu Smriti*, the student should sip water (*achamana*) when about to begin Vedic study, should face the north, should fold both hands together (and place them on his knee), should wear light (pure) clothes, should at the beginning and end of Vedic study, clasp the feet of the teacher with crossed hands and should touch the right foot of the teacher with his own right and left foot with the left hand, should repeat 'om' at the beginning and at the end of Vedic study. The teacher should say to the pupil 'repeat' and should stop from teaching with the words 'let there be a pause.' The study of Veda was the first duty of every twice born person (*dvijati*). According to *Manu Smriti*, the whole Vedas together with Upanishads were to be learnt by every dvijati. According to *Yajnavalkya Smriti*, it is Veda alone that confers the highest bliss upon dvijatis by enabling them to understand and perform sacrifices, austerities and auspicious acts (like samsakars). Since the literature was very wide, concessions had to be made to the shortness of human life and the weakness of the human mind. Therefore, generally it was prescribed that one should study the Shakha of the Veda which his ancestors studied and should perform religious rites according to it. As the study of the Veda was a duty enjoined upon a Brahmana, so teaching Veda to another was a duty. This exclusive glorification of the Brahmins very much led to what N.K. Dutt describes as the "pride of scholasticism" among the professed scholars. And it has been rightly pointed out by S. Cromwell Crawford, "Compounded with racial and sacerdotal pride, the pride of scholasticism elevated barriers between Brahmins and non-Brahmins. In this way, the good effect of the strictness of Brahmacharya in specialising learning and in enforcing high moral discipline was neutralised by the increased rigidness and hauteur of caste, which is one of the many factors making India a land of contrasts".

EDUCATOR'S DUTIES

It should not be supposed that the Dharmashastras, while insisting upon educands' respect towards the educator, used less strict words while insisting upon educators' duty towards the educand. In fact, the educational relationship was a two-way relationship. It was reciprocal. According to *Apastamb Dharmasutra*, "Loving him like his own son, and full of attention, he shall teach him the sacred science, without hiding anything in the whole law. And he shall not use him for his own purpose to the detriment of his studies, except in times of distress. The pupil who, attending to (teacher), accuses his (principal and first) teacher of ignorance, remains no (longer) a pupil. A teacher also, who neglects the instruction (of his pupil), does no (longer) remain a teacher". The purport of education was the moral and intellectual growth of the students. These two elements were never separated. Indeed, the later was contingent upon the former. According to the Sacred Law, only the person who is pure may be instructed in the Veda. Neither (the study of) the Vedas, nor liberality, nor sacrifices, nor any (self-imposed) restraint, nor austerities, ever procure the attainment (of rewards) to a man whose heart is contaminated (by sensuality). Moral culture not only preceded intellectual culture, but was the weightier of the two. A Brahmana, who completely governs himself, though he knows the Savitri only, is better than he who knows the three Vedas, (but) does not control himself.

ABSENCE OF SOCIAL JUSTICE

The absence of social justice in education is particularly observed in case of partiality towards the education of all the varnas other than Brahmin and also of the women. These were given a secondary place. Literary education among women was in a languishing state. Therefore, there was no question of co-education. Not much material is available about the education of Kshatriyas, Vaishyas and Sudras. The entire education system was entrusted to Brahmanas. Summing up the state of education in Dharmashastras, P.V. Kane has written, "The salient features of the educational system outlined in the Dharmashastras works are the high and honourable position assigned to the teacher, the close personal contact of the pupil with the teacher and individual attention, the pupil's stay with the teacher as a member of his family, oral instruction and the absence of books, stern discipline and control of emotions and the will, cheapness as no fees were stipulated for".

CRITICAL EVALUATION

The institution of education as prescribed by Dharmashastras can be favourably compared with any other system of education in the West, ancient or modern. Given the high character and scholarship of the teacher, it was the most ideal system of education. However, its defects are equally obvious. Summarising these defects, P.V. Kane, has admitted, "The defects of the Indian system were that it was too literary, there was too much memorising, boys under it had hardly any instruction in useful manual arts and crafts, the studies were not brought in contact with practical life". The discipline was rigorous and joyless. Many of these defects were due to the exigencies of the caste system which assigned particular avocations to particular, castes. Kane, however, rightly adds, "We cannot and should not compare the system with the systems of education prevalent in the 20th century, when several subjects such as literature, music and the fine arts, handicrafts, mathematics, science, history and geography are taught in the schools to all boys and when it has been recognized that education is a prime concern of the State".

14

Swami Dayananda

Aims of Education

The ultimate aim of education according to Dayananda is to get liberation. In his *Satyartha Prakash,* Dayananda has written, that the individual who can realize the form of knowledge and ignorance simultaneously can win liberation by achieving freedom from ignorance, from the cycle of birth and rebirth. Being an idealist, Dayananda has laid special emphasis upon education as a means of character development. Development of character is based on achieving knowledge, because in the absence of knowledge character cannot be formed. Knowledge brings happiness in the present world as well as in the next. The aim of education is to give true knowledge to the individual and thus enable him to conduct himself properly. On this subject, Dayananda has written in *Vyavahara Bhanu* that man can never get happiness through ignorance, and therefore, in order to get salvation one must try to acquire knowledge.

Emphasis on Practice

It is clear from the foregoing account that Dayananda laid great emphasis upon the practical aspect of education also, not merely on the spiritual aspect alone. One of the chief aims of education is to develop morality and good conduct. For this, Dayananda believes that abstinence or self-denial is essential. Another objective of education is to provide real knowledge. In his *Satyartha Prakash* Dayananda has pointed out, that parents and teachers must guide their children and their educand and tell them to adopt the actions dictated by their religion and also to discard those activities exercised by the same religion. Besides, all those who gain knowledge must propagate that knowledge. Dayananda did not neglect the social aspect of education when pointing out the objectives. Education aims not merely at the development of individuals but also at the creation of individuals who can successfully fulfil their obligations in society. Dayananda was also in favour of universal education including even the most backward sections of Hindu society, even those traditionally prevented from receiving education, for religious reasons. He believed that the educated individual is a successful and useful member of society. Dayananda said that blessed are those men and women whose minds are constantly anxious to get the satisfaction of knowledge, those who are devoid of egotism and vanity, hill of gentleness, sweetness, beautiful expression, those who are engaged in destroying the pains and sufferings of others by bestowing knowledge and truth upon them, those who put an end to the darkness of others, those who are constantly in doing good and benefiting others.

Universal and Compulsory Education

Dayananda was in favour of universal and compulsory education in the country. He favoured the education of every man, woman and child, irrespective of the caste or creed to which he or she belonged. He held the state responsible for ensuring that every parent sent his or her child for education. Obviously, Dayananda was in agreement with the democratic ideal of education. He even insisted that the State must punish those who deprived their children of education. In this manner Dayananda refuted the medieval practice of denying education to certain sections of society.

Child Education

Dayananda gave it as his opinion that the child's earliest education should take place at home. His opinion is borne out by many modern educationists. In his *Satyartha Prakash,* Dayananda has commented on child education, and pointed out that parents must give the best possible education to the children so that they may progress on the path of civilization. They should never be permitted to indulge in any bad activity. When the child learns to speak, his mother should guide him in correct pronunciation so that he may enunciate his words and sentences with the correct intonation of seniors and equated people so that he may learn, apart from proper speech, how to behave correctly in the presence of revered people.

Diversified Multi-Faceted Curriculum

Expressing his opinion on the subject of a proper curriculum for the education of individuals, Dayananda suggested a more or less common pattern for everyone. He opposed the traditional bias against allowing women to study the Vedas on the ground that ignorance of Vedas would handicap their pronunciation of Sanskrit mantras and thus make it impossible for them to participate in religious ceremonies, like the yagya. In addition to a common educational programme for children of all the four castes, Dayananda paid special attention to specific education to conform to the requirements of each caste. He did not favour the principle of allowing the educand to read any and all religious texts. He felt it would be better to subject these texts to various tests prescribed in the shastras, and only those should be prescribed which pass these tests. Education should begin with the teaching of Panini's *Grammar of Sanskrit,* paying special attention to accurate and precise pronunciation. This should be followed by teaching of the mantras of *Astadhyayi.*

Contribution to Educational Philosophy

Thus, it is clear that Dayananda favoured a diversified education, combining general education with religious as well as professional training. The need for religious education is felt in the sphere of character building, because character cannot be developed without it. And for this purpose, Dayananda established a number of *Arya Samajas* and *Gurukulas* all over the country, particularly in the north. The *Arya Samaj* is an organising institution which looks after the Vedic colleges and schools. A Dayananda Anglo Vedic College was established at Lahore in 1886, and a *Gurukula* at Kangri in 1902, which has now become an independent university. In addition to these institutions, Dayananda also established *Gurukulas* at Jawalapur and Vrindavan. For girls he established gurukulas at Dehradun, Baroda, Sasni, and at other places. Now-a-days, one finds similar colleges and schools in almost every district and big town, operated by the Dayananda Anglo Vedic Trust, which seeks to propagate the ideas of Dayananda. Thus, not only did the organisation support the idea of universal education, he also established an organisation in the form of *Arya Samaj* which is trying to spread education in every part of the country.

Dayananda's educational philosophy is based on Vedic philosophy, although his interpretation of Vedic philosophy is unique. When he first preached his lesson, there was the greatest need to protect Hindu religion and philosophy from the insulates of Muslim and Christian religions. He saved Hindu society from fragmentation, and gave to women a new place in Hindu society. He protected the ancient Hindu values from the influence of Muslim and Christian cultures and tried to maintain the traditional modes of thinking. His ideas on education have great significance for contemporary educational philosophy.

15

Annie Besant

In his article *Indian Unrest* (London, 1910), Sir Valentine Chirol wrote, "No Hindu has done so much to organise and consolidate the movement of revival as Mrs. Annie Besant, who in her Central Hindu College at Banaras, and her Theosophical Institution at Adyar, Madras, has openly proclaimed her faith in the superiority of the whole Hindu system to the arrogant civilization of the West. Is it surprising that Hindus should turn their backs upon our civilization, when an Englishwoman of highly trained intellectual power comes and tells them that it is they who possess and have from all times possessed the key to supreme wisdom—that their gods, their philosophy, their morality are in a higher plane of thought than the West has ever reached "?

Thus Annie Besant had two chief lines of approach to the re-awakening of India and the achievement of Independence: (1) the Religious (2) the Educational. She gave lectures and supported the Independence movement. She criticised the British openly regarding their policies in India. The British, in India as well as in England, opposed her strongly for her critical views.

Annie Besant was the founder of the All India Women's Conference. This attracted many Indian women and became a strong force for Women's Education, Child Marriage Bill, the Sharda Act, and many other reforms affecting women and children. Annie Besant started many of the reforms that have given women the equality of status and rights which they enjoy today in India. She brought about a revival in the study and application of Hindu philosophy and culture at a time when these were fading. To quote in her own words, "I set myself toward showing the insufficiency of materialism as an answer to the problems of life and the immense superiority of Hinduism as a philosophy encasing an all-embracing reverence, and a science of Yoga. All these were an open road to the invisible, to the ancient Rishis of India and the East, to the saints of Christendom, to the wisdom which included all religions and excluded none."

Annie Besant lived and worked in India during the period when Rabindra Nath Tagore, Sri Aurobindo Ghosh and Mahatma Gandhi were carrying on their revolutionary ideas and ideals in the social, educational, religious and political fields. She supported their causes and furthered their aims by her great work and noble example. She had a great zeal and missionary endeavour for social reform, educational expansion and India's freedom.

In India her publications include the following:

(1) Education as a National Duty (Benaras, 1903)
(2) The Education of Indian Girls (Benaras, 1906)
(3) Principles of Education (Madras, 1915)
(4) Education for the New Era (London, 1919)
(5) Theosophical Education Report (Madras, 1917)
(6) Some Lessons from the Mahabharata (Benaras, 1899)
(7) Sri Ramchandra, the Ideal King (Benaras and London, 1901)
(8) Hindu Ideals (Benaras and London, 1904)
(9) Sanatan Dharma: An Advanced Textbook of Hindu Religion & Ethics (Benaras, 1904)
(10) The Universal Textbook of Religion and Morals (Adyar 1914-1915, 3 Vols.)
(11) Lectures on Political Science (Adyar, 1919)
(12) Legends and Tales (London, 1883)
(13) Civilization's Deadlock and the Keys (London, 1924)
(14) Kamala Lectures: Indian Ideals in Education and Philosophy, Religion and Art (Calcutta, 1925)
(15) World Problems of Today (London, 1924)
(16) India Bound or Free (London and New York, 1925).

Annie Besant died in 1933. She left an indelible mark on Indian education, the fight for women's rights as well as on India's aspirations for freedom.

PRINCIPLES OF THEOSOPHY

True religion, according to Annie Besant, consists not only in one's feelings towards God but also in performing duties towards our fellowmen. A morally good man who in an atheist is in a far higher state of being than the man who believes in God and is selfish, cruel and unjust.

Theosophy as a great religion has two parts—a spirit and a body (1) Knowledge of God (2) Dogma and rites. Knowledge of God is called Brahma Vidya and belongs equally to all great religions of the world—Hinduism, Christianity, Islamic Sufism, Judaism. No man is a true theosophist unless he has a direct knowledge of God. Thus he may arrive at through any religion, or by his own earnest efforts to seek the truth.

Thus, Theosophy emphasizes two principles: (*a*) The Unity of God who is the Universal source of all existence and (*b*) Universal brotherhood of man.

Ethics of Theosophy

This consists of the highest and purest teachings of world's noblest saints, prophets and founders of religions. All that is sweet and most lofty in the world's religions and all that is most inspiring and ennobling in the philosophies of all countries and religions of the world form the ethics of theosophy. If man lives by the highest principles that he can grasp, he becomes capable of appreciating the sublime. The theosophist looks up to the examples of Christ, Buddha, Rama and all great religious leaders. He strives to become like them.

IDEAS ON EDUCATION

Annie Besant's educational philosophy is based on the Theosophical Ideal of Education according to which each child should receive an education suited to develop his particular and individual faculties. He should be imparted education which will make him useful as a citizen in his community and his country.

Aims of Education

According to Annie Besant education should draw out the child's capacities, and develop and train them so that he becomes a healthy and useful member of a civilized society.

The object of theosophical education are as follows:

(*i*) To train the body in health, vigour and grace, so that it may express the emotions with beauty, and the mind with accuracy and strength.

(*ii*) To train the emotions to love all that is beautiful.

(*iii*) To sympathise with joys and sorrows of others and to inspire to serve others until we love our elders as our parents, our equals as our brothers and sisters, and youngsters as our children.

(*iv*) To find joy in sacrificing for great causes for the helpless and compassion for those who suffer.

(*v*) To train and discipline the mind in right thinking, right judgment and memory.

(*vi*) To subdue body, emotion and mind to spirit.

(*vii*) Education should make man a good citizen of free and spiritual commonwealth of humanity.

Annie Besant divided the entire period of education in life, into three parts. These are as follows:

First Period: 1-7 Years

(1) The physical height and development of the child's body should be the chief concern of parents and the teacher. The child's entire future depends on the care bestowed on the child during the first seven years of his life. In later years nothing can fully make up for insufficient food or insufficient light, exercise and sleep, during this period.

(2) This is also the period for cultivating observation, for training the senses into alertness, accuracy and grasp, for training hand and finger, skills of memory especially the word-memory which is very quick and retentive in childhood. Nursery rhymes remain in the memory for life. Rhymes and poems employing succession of events, names or dates learnt in childhood, are never forgotten.

(3) No abstract reasoning processes should be forced upon the child during this period. His attention should be directed to observation of sequences of facts but not the logical processes. The brain cells are not sufficiently interrelated to make any train of reasoning intelligible. There is no benefit in memorising logical sequences which are not understood by the child.

Second Period: 7-14 Years

During this period education should be chiefly directed to the development and training of the emotions, and thus to the building of character. Histories consisting largely of biographical stories of great men of varied types, saints, heroes, martyrs, political, artistic, literary leaders in every department of human life. These should inspire enthusiasm and shape the ideals of developing boys and girls. In this way character will be built and the channels of right emotions will be prepared. Thus the great emotional rush which follows the attainment of puberty will find channels ready to receive it, to render it uplifting and beneficent, instead of degrading and mischievous.

Third Period: 14-21 Years

This period should be the time of intellectual development of hard and strenuous mental labour. The reasoning faculty should be thoroughly trained by logic and mathematics. Specialization in some areas should prepare the youth for his future career.

Curriculum

Annie Besant prescribed the following curriculum for different periods:

(*i*) First Period: 1-7 Years. Tales of noble deeds and heroism, emphasis on health, physical dexterity and skills; nursery rhymes, cultivation of word-memory, observation of sequences of facts, love of beauty, arousing of sympathy for the poor and helpless.

(*ii*) Second Period: 7-14 Years. History and Biography, Geography, Physiology, Physics, Chemistry and Geology should be taught. Practical and laboratory work in the sciences should be included. Algebra, Geometry and Arithmetic should occupy an important place in the curriculum.

(*iii*) Third Period: 14-21 Years. This is the period of the rapid intellectual development. Therefore, Logic and Mathematics should be taught intensively. The sense of duty to one's fellowmen should be taught through Civics and Social studies. Sciences such as Biology, Philosophy and Psychology should be mastered. Literature, Philosophy, Economics should occupy an important place. Various aspects of the Arts should also be included in the curriculum. Specialization in some chosen field should prepare the student for his future career in life.

Religious Teaching should begin with easy stories in the child's early stages of education and pass on to metaphysics in the later years in all of the three stages, being adapted to the intelligence and understanding of the student.

Physical Training should be all-pervading. It should be adapted in theory and practice to the physical development and needs of the growing pupil in all the above-mentioned three stages.

All Round Education

Explaining her scheme of all-round education Annie Besant writes, "look forward to a time when every child shall receive, in the national schools, the elements of a literary, scientific, artistic and technical education. No boy or girl should leave the school ignorant of our literature, or of the wonders of science. He should delight in beauty. He should also learn some definite means of bread-winning, let it be tailoring, cookery or carpentry or any trade or profession. Every pair of hands should be able to do at least some one thing well by which an honest living may be earned".

DR. ANNIE BESANTS CONTRIBUTION TO EDUCATION

1. Patriotism: Dr. Besant loved India. Her respect and understanding of India's religions and philosophies was profound. She wrote many books and pamphlets on Hinduism, as well as text-books for students in Physics, Chemistry, Biology and stories from the Mahabharata as well as narratives of heroic deeds for children to read.

2. Nationalism: Dr. Besant's support of India's national aspirations led her to encourage and support many innovative educational efforts. She founded many schools and colleges. The Central Hindu School and College was founded by her in 1898 at Benaras. It later became the Benaras Hindu University. She also founded the Theosophical Institute at Adyar, Madras.

3. Multisided efforts: Not only did Dr. Besant start the Central Hindu School and College at Benaras, she organised its debating clubs and many sports organisations. She was an excellent teacher and educational administrator. She set high standards for other teachers and organisers around her. She was admired and loved by her students and colleagues for her dedication and efficiency in educational endeavours.

4. Against Child-Marriage: Annie Besant took a firm stand against Child-Marriage which was widely prevalent in India at that time. Students were discouraged from marrying while they were still studying. They and their parents were made to realize that the students were not mature enough to assume adult responsibilities.

5. Social reform: She gave speeches on nationalism, freedom and social reforms in schools and colleges as well as in public. This made the students realize their responsibilities to live and work for a free India.

6. Women's education: Annie Besant was an ardent promotor of women's education in India. She organised many groups to strive for the furtherance of girls' schools and colleges in many parts of India where facilities did not exist, and girls and women were neglected. She worked to raise the status of girls and women through education.

7. Growth of educational institutions: Due to Annie Besant's pioneering work in education, many communities, Parsi, Muslim, Arya Samaj, Dev Samaj, Brahmo Samaj and other started schools for their youth on modern lines. She inspired a great deal of enthusiasm for education in India at a time when the British neglected educational betterment and expansion to fit the needs of the country in their schemes.

8. Vocational education: Dr. Besant was a strong advocate of vocational education in schools. By the end of schooling, every pupil should have learnt some trade or craft: carpentry, cooking, tailoring, or any useful skill or vocation, to enable him to earn a living, at any stage in his educational career.

9. Anti racism: Annie Besant strongly believed and preached that there is no such thing as racial superiority. She maintained that the white races and the so-called higher castes of people are not in any way superior to other people. Therefore, domination by races and castes of people over other is totally unjustified. All people in the world are endowed with intelligence and ability, regardless of race or caste. All have a right to educational opportunity and the amenities of life. There should be free schools established for universal, free and compulsory education in India. No one should be denied the right to education and the right to upward mobility.

16

M. K. Gandhi

AIMS AND IDEALS OF EDUCATION

1. Drawing out the basic: Elaborating his views about the aims of education, Gandhiji has said, "By education I mean an all round drawing out of the best in child and man, body, mind and spirit. Literacy is not the end of education, not even the beginning. It is one of the means whereby man and woman can be educated. Literacy in itself is no education".

2. Livelihood: Gandhiji was highly critical of the educational policy implemented by British government. In his opinion the aim of education is self-dependence, and education must enable every girl and boy to develop the ability to depend upon himself or herself. The ability to earn one's livelihood is part of this independence or self-reliance. As he himself puts it, "This education ought to be for them a kind of insurance against unemployment". That is why Gandhiji placed so much emphasis upon industrial training in his own plan for basic education which was intended to acquaint the child with real life. He wanted the educator to become the means of producing ideal citizens. Seeing the endemic poverty of the nation, he suggested that education in India should be based on industrial training and the development of manual skill and handicrafts.

3. Character formation: Like Rousseau Gandhiji also believes in paidocentric education, that is, education which centres around the child. He impressed upon people that the cultural aspect of education was far more important than its literary aspect, because it is through the cultural aspect that the child learns conduct and, ideas and develops his character and ideals. As he puts it, "True education is that which draws out and stimulates the spiritual, intellectual and physical faculties of the children". Hence, the aim of education is the complete development of the child, its physical, mental and spiritual aspects. For him character formation was more important than literacy. He was once asked what his education would aim at after the country won its independence. He answered without hesitation that it would be designed to develop the character of the people. And, in character, Gandhiji addressed the importance of thought, word and deed, non-violence and truth. He, like many before him, felt that abstinence was an essential weapon for the educand. He was a supporter of the ancient Indian ideals of education. He in fact felt that the words educand and Brahmachari should be treated as synonymous. And for him, abstinence meant a persistent effort to reach God in the least possible time.

4. Complete development: It is clear from the foregoing account that Gandhiji viewed education from a comprehensive or broadminded standpoint. Any education that develops only one aspect of a child's personality can be dubbed narrow and one-sided. And it is just such an education which has been the bane of our culture. Education must aim at developing the child's personality instead of limiting itself to providing the child with bits and pieces of information. Not only must education guide the individual towards self-knowledge, it must instil in him all those qualities which go to the making up of a good and responsible citizen. Gandhiji has made a distinction between the immediate and long-term aims of education, suggesting that such aims as getting certificates of merits or degrees or obtaining education for livelihood should be considered the immediate aims. But the final aim of education can only be self-knowledge. Thus, Gandhiji states that education must make the individual to live and earn his daily bread, to be the means of his sustenance. As he himself puts it, "I value individual freedom, but you must not forget that man is essentially a social being. He has risen to his present status by learning to adjust his individuality to the requirements of social progress". His faith in religion is at the base of his liberal attitude to education. Realization of good is, in fact, the end or the goal of all human activity and service to humanity its finest means. It is only natural that such a faith should lead him to stress the social objectives of education more than the personal or individual ones.

5. Synthesis of individual and social aims: In this way Gandhiji synthesized the individual and social aims of education. He did not restrict education to the achievement of any one single aim. He looked to the process of education from various perspectives. Therefore, he assigned different aims to education at different times, so much so that sometimes they looked mutually contradictory and even self-defeating. A closer examination of all these statements of Gandhiji, however, shows that these aims of education are complementary to each other.

6. All round growth: In the history of education different educationists have defined the ideals of education in different ways. Most educationists have, however, felt that the aim of education is integral development of human personality. Such was also the ideal of education formulated by Gandhiji. Like Vivekananda, Gandhiji maintained that character formation and manual skill were equally important. On the one hand, he wanted the child to earn while he learns. On the other hand, he also wanted the child to develop his character. According to him the criterion of an individual's cultural development is not the width of his knowledge but his inner growth. Culture according to him is not an adjunct of the mind but a characteristic of the soul. The aim of education is the development of such a culture. Gandhiji's plan of education laid stress upon all types of education—physical, mental, moral, aesthetic and religious.

7. Self-reliance: As has been already pointed out, Gandhiji aimed at self-reliance through education. Therefore, he visualised a craft-centred education. Explaining his scheme of Basic Education as an insurance against unemployment in India, Gandhiji said, "The child at the age of 14, that is, after finishing a seven-year course should be discharged as an earning unit. Even now the poor people's children automatically lend a helping hand to their parents—the feeling at the back of their minds being what shall they give men to eat, if I do not work with them? That is an education in itself. Even so the State takes charge of the child at seven and returns it to the family as an earning unit. You impart education and simultaneously cut at the root of unemployment". Recommending this scheme of education in the report on national education the Kothari Commission declared, "We recommend that work-experience should be introduced as an integral part of all education—general or vocational. We define work-experience as participation in productive work in school, in the home, in a workshop, on a farm, in a factory or in any other productive situation".

8. Democrative ideals: Like his contemporary Indian educationists, Gandhiji aimed at the evolution of democratic ideals through education. His basic plan of education amply demonstrates this fact. He aimed at an education for ideal citizenship. Education, according to him, should make children ideal members of a democratic society. The school, according to Gandhiji, is itself a small democratic society in which such democratic values are imparted to the children as wide outlook, tolerance and good neighbourhood. In the miniature society of the school the child learns the virtues of sympathy, service, love, brotherhood, equality and liberty, etc. These qualities are transferred from one generation to another through education. The welfare of the individual and the Nation are complementary to each other. Therefore, if the country has to progress, the future generation should develop the virtues of democratic citizenship. As Gandhiji said, "A nation cannot advance without the units of which it is composed advancing, and conversely, no individual can advance without the nation of which it is a part also advancing".

9. Moral and spiritual: All knowledge is useless without a good character in his speeches to the students at various institutions. Gandhiji laid emphasis upon the moral and spiritual aims of education. Emphasising the moral aim of education, Gandhiji said, "The end of all knowledge must be the building up of character". Character building is the moral ideal of education. According to Gandhiji that is most important in a man's life. His ideals in this connection were as much in agreement with the ancient Indian thinkers as with contemporary Western thinkers like Emerson, Ruskin, etc., Gandhiji very much admired the Indian *Gurukula* system of education and the ideal of *Brahmacharya.* According to ancient Indian ideal, education aims at liberation. This was also the aim of Gujarat Vidyapeeth established by Gandhiji in 1929. Gandhiji, however, defined liberation in a very wide sense, including political, social and economic liberation of all the members of society. Real freedom is spiritual freedom. To attain this freedom is the task of education. Again, education equally aims at intellectual, economic and political uplift, though its chief aim is moral and spiritual. Condemning the widespread indiscipline among the students Gandhiji asked them to follow the ideal of *Brahmacharya.*

10. God-realization: According to Indian philosophy the ultimate end of all knowledge is God-realization. This God-realization again, is the meaning of self-realization which has been considered to be the ideal of education by most of the educational philosophers in East and West. Agreeing with this line of thinking Gandhiji maintained that a student should live a life of *Sanyasi.* God-realization and self-realization are mutually complementary, the one leads to the other. This spiritual ideal of education does not negate mundane or immediate ideals but fulfils them. In the words of Gandhiji, "Self-realization is in itself an all comprehensive ideal". This ideal includes other ideals of education. With Sri Aurobindo, Gandhiji believed that the ultimate aim of education is spiritual. He also agreed that spiritual growth includes physical and mental, individual and social development. Thus, he synthesized different ideals of education. In this scheme of Basic Education, he planned for an education suitable to present-day Indian society. He pondered over the difficulties of the present-day Indian society and tried to find out their solution through education. His educational philosophy is based upon ancient Indian idealism. While he did not restrict the scope of physical education his attention was mainly directed towards spiritual growth.

EDUCATION FOR SARVODAYA

Gandhiji was very much aware of the needs of the country and considered Basic Education as the only type of education which may lead to success. His chief aim in planning for education in India was to fulfil the needs of the country. India is a country of villages. Most of the villagers in India cannot afford to pay for their children's education. In addition to it they require their children's assistance in their occupations. Therefore, Gandhiji planned for Basic Education which may not be a burden upon the parents and through which the children may be able to earn to meet the expenses of education themselves, laid stress upon the importance of dignity of labour and manual skill. He was convinced that an education which prepares the young men for white-collar jobs can hardly be suitable for an agriculture community. It is hence that he so much emphasized the learning of craft in his plan of Basic Education. In spite of all this idealism Gandhiji's approach everywhere was pragmatic. He was an experimenter in every field of life. Before devising his plan of Basic Education he experimented upon its different aspects. For him all human truths were relative. God was the only absolute. Therefore he tested every thing before suggesting it for the education of the child. He postulated that the child should himself gather knowledge from the environment and put it in actual use in life. Like the pragmatists and instrumentalists Gandhiji stressed the importance of interest and activity and the need for variety in the subjects taught to the educand.

Sarvodaya Society

The social philosophy of M. K. Gandhi may be termed as 'Sarvodaya'. This was the foundation of his philosophy of education. Sarvodaya aims at all round development of all, without distinction of caste, creed, sex and nationality. Gandhiji wanted to establish a welfare state in India which he called 'Ram Rajya'. The ideal of Sarvodaya does not aim at the maximum number but maximum good of all without exceptions. While Marx aimed at the welfare of the proletariat, Gandhiji aimed even at the welfare of the capitalist. According to Vinoba Bhave the important characteristics of the Sarvodaya Society are the abolition of all monopoly, emphasis on social welfare and equal, moral, social and economic importance of honest work. There is no place for any type of exploitation in Sarvodaya Society. No one may be forced to do a certain type of work, so much so that even the wealth of the capitalist cannot be forcibly snatched away. Centralization, according to Gandhiji, is the chief source of social evils. Sarvodaya requires decentralization. Gandhiji aimed at political, economic, social and all other types of decentralization. In the political field decentralization requires establishment of village panchayats. In the economic field it requires that wealth and money should not be allowed to be concentrated in few hands but should be distributed among all the people. Social decentralization means the abolition of all types of untouchability and social distinctions.

Nai Talim

In order to achieve the above mentioned aims of Sarvodaya in India, Gandhiji presented his plan of Basic Education. He called it Nai Talim (New education) because it sought to build up a new society in the country. He realized that what the country needs today is not so much higher education as the education of the masses. Therefore, he did not lay so much emphasis upon higher education.

The Basic Education sought to fulfil the needs of the educands in a Sarvodaya Society. It is hence that Gandhiji planned for craft centred education with mother tongue as the medium. Literacy, according to him, is not an end but only a mean of education. Education ultimately aims at the development of both mind and body and the capacity of earning one's livelihood. The syllabi for the new education were framed in such a way so as to eliminate narrow nationalism and emphasize the ideal of Sarvodaya. World history was taught along with Indian history. Similarly, the syllabus included the study of fundamental universal ethics. The cost of education was brought down by compulsory manual labour and education was tried to be made self-sufficient as far as possible.

Social Revolution

Pointing out the value of basic education for bringing about a silent social revolution in the country, Gandhiji said, "It will provide a healthy and moral basis of relationship between the city and the village and thus go a long way towards eradicating some of the worst evils of the present social insecurity and poisoned relationship between the classes. It will check the progressive decay of our villages and lay the foundation of a just social order in which there is no unnatural division between the 'haves' and the 'have-nots' and everybody is assured of a living wage and the right of freedom. And all this would be accomplished without the horrors of a bloody class war or a social capital expenditure such as would be involved in the mechanisation of a vast continent like India. Nor would it entail a helpless dependence on foreign imported machinery or technical skill. Lastly, by obviating the necessity for highly specialized talent, it would place the destiny of the masses, as it were in their own hands.

Non-violent Education

As has been already pointed out, Gandhiji emphasized the principle of non-violence in every field of life. He considered non-violence as the characteristic human quality. He said, "Non-violence is the law of our species as violence is the law of brutes". Even truth was subordinate to non-violence. Gandhiji said, "One had better not speak it (truth) if one cannot do so in a gentle way". To those who doubted the value of non-violence to be the principle of human social organisation, Gandhiji pointed out, "The fact that there are so many men still alive in the world shows that it is based not on force of arms but on the force of truth and love". This principle of non-violence, Gandhiji used in every aspect of education, so much so that his theory of education may be called non-violent education. Explaining his idea he wrote, "If India has resolved to eschew violence, this system of education becomes an integral part of the discipline she has to go through. We are told that English spend millions on education. America also does so. But we forget that all wealth is obtained through exploitation. They have reduced the art of exploitation to a science, and might well give their boys the costly education they do. We cannot, will not think in terms of exploitation, and we have no alternative but this plan of education which is based on non-violence". Thus, according to Gandhiji, India can play her role in the community of nations only by adopting the gospel of non-violence. To quote Gandhiji again, "Good brought about through force destroyed individuality. Only when the change was effected through the persuasive power of non-violent non-cooperation (*i.e.,* love), could the foundation of individuality be preserved and real, abiding progress be assured for the world".

WARDHA SCHEME

This principle of non-violence was the basis of Gandhiji's scheme of Basic Education. Through this scheme he wanted to develop those qualities in future citizens of India which he considered necessary for building a non-violent society. His system of education wanted to root out exploitation and centralization in society and create a non-violent social order. In 1937, Gandhiji evolved a scheme popularly known as the Wardha Scheme of Basic National Education. This Wardha scheme was based on same principles of education which were listed by Gandhiji in a paper in 1932 in Yervada Jail. These postulates were as follows:

(1) Boys and girls should be taught together.

(2) Their time should be mostly spent on manual work under the supervision of the teacher. Manual work should be considered as part of education.

(3) Work should be entrusted to each boy and girl after ascertaining his or her inclinations.

(4) The child should know the why and the wherefore of every process.

(5) General knowledge should be imparted to the child as soon as it is able to understand things. This knowledge should precede literary education.

(6) The hand of the child be trained to draw geometrical figures before he learns to write, that is good handwriting should be taught from the beginning.

(7) The child should learn to read before he is able to write, *i.e.*, he should learn to recognize letters as if they were pictures and then draw their figures.

(8) By this method and by word of mouth, the child should acquire much knowledge before he is eight years old.

(9) Children should not be compelled to learn anything.

(10) The child should be interested in whatever he learns.

(11) The process of teaching should be conducted in a play-way, for play is an essential part of education.

(12) All education should be imparted through the mother-tongue of the child.

(13) Every Indian child should learn Hindi-Urdu, *i.e.*, Hindustani as a national language before his literary training commences.

(14) The second stage of the child's education begins when he is eleven and lasts up to sixteen.

(15) Manual labour has a place in education during this period also. The time for literary training should be increased according to need.

(16) The child should learn some vocation as preparation for his future life.

(17) He should acquire a general knowledge of World History, Geography, Botany, Astronomy, Arithmetic, Geometry and Algebra.

(18) A boy or a girl of sixteen years should know sewing and cooking.

(19) In the third stage which begins at sixteen and ends at twenty-five, a young man or woman should receive education according to his or her desires and circumstances.

(20) The education commencing at the age of nine should be self-supporting. The student, while he is learning, should be engaged in such a vocation that its produce may meet the expense of the school.

(21) Production should, no doubt, begin right from the start. But it may not be enough to meet the expenses during the initial years.

(22) Teachers cannot possibly have big salaries, but they must get enough to maintain themselves. They should be animated by a spirit of service. They must have a good character.

(23) Huge and costly buildings are not necessary for education.

(24) English can and should have a place in the syllabus only as a language. Just as Hindi is our *lingua franca* English is a language of international intercourse and commerce.

On 23rd October, 1937, a conference was organised at Wardha to finalise the basic system of education. This conference resolved that the children should be provided free education for seven years. Mother tongue should be the medium of education. Every educand must be taught some basic craft. The expenses of education should be met by the sale of the production in the school. In order to implement these recommendations a committee was formed under the chairmanship of Dr. Zakir Hussain. This committee highlighted the basic principles, aims and organisation of Basic Education in its first report on 2nd December, 1937. In its second report in 1940 this committee reviewed the curriculum of Basic Education. Its recommendations were accepted by Indian National Congress in its Session at Haripura. After Zakir Hussain Committee, another committee was formed under the chairmanship of B.G. Kher to review basic education. This committee connected it to Sargeant scheme. In the final form, the basic principles of Gandhiji's scheme of primary education were: compulsory free education, education through craft, education through mother tongue, self-reliance, education connected with the life of the educand and finally inculcation of the ideals of democratic citizenship. A booklet was published by Government of India to popularise Gandhijian system of education entitled *Understanding of Basic Education*. This booklet thus summarised the scheme of basic education, "Activities involving personal and community cleanliness are the foremost in a basic school. Education for the young is not stuffing impractical idea into the minds of children. It is essentially training them in good habits, the daily experiences that every child has to undergo as regular morning evacuation, cleaning the teeth, nose and eyes, bathing, physical exercise, washing clothes and other daily activities can be exploited for teaching as well as the inculcation of good habits".

MEANS OF EDUCATION

The scheme of Basic Education clarifies the means of education according to M. K. Gandhi. The most important means of education in basic scheme was craft. About this means of education Gandhiji said, "The principal idea is to impart the whole education of body and the mind and the soul through the handicraft that is taught to the children. You have to draw out all that is in the child through teaching all the processes of the handicraft, and all your lessons in History, Geography, Arithmetic will be related to the craft". Thus some handicraft was necessary to be the centre of the child's education. Besides, other crafts recommended were: weaving, carpentry, agriculture, gardening and other handicrafts and rural crafts. It was pointed out that the following criteria should be followed in deciding about the basic craft:

(1) Craft fulfilling individual and social means.
(2) Craft based upon local requirements.
(3) Craft in tune with the local conditions.
(4) Craft favourable to the interest, aptitude and ability of the child.
(5) Less expensive and simple craft.
(6) Craft leading to all round development of personality.

At the back of craft as the means of education were the psychological principles of education through activity as is visible in the Western playway of education, project methods, etc. Besides, this means of education was economically useful as the basic craft could be utilized by the educand to earn his livelihood. It was also supposed to create a tendency for physical labour in the educands. According to Gandhiji, "Labour is the source of all wealth. All higher castes live on the exploitation of the lower castes. Wealth is inevitably reduced and large scale poverty occasioned". Thus, craft was means to inculcate the lesson of physical labour.

Another important element in the means of education in basic scheme was synthesis between the actual problems of life and education, between different subjects of the curriculum and finally between theoretical education and practical ability. In order to implement the principle of synthesis in basic education it was insisted that the teachers and educands should together formulate yearly projects divided into quarterly, monthly, weekly and daily projects. After this planning, the means such as raw material and necessary tools should be gathered. Efforts should be made to fulfil the schedule of the projects. Each project must be evaluated monthly or quarterly as the case may be. In the end the teachers should note their experiences in order to profit by them in future.

TYPES OF EDUCATION

Our discussion of the Gandhian scheme of education so far shows his emphasis upon primary education and the education of the child. He, however, equally devoted his thought to the adult education also known as social education. He realized that in order to bring about a Sarvodaya Society in India, the views of the adults should be changed. Therefore, he made adult education programme a vital element of his political movement. Thousands of volunteers were trained in adult education at Sabarmati and Sevagram Ashrams. They spread in thousands of villages and hundreds of urban centres to educate the adult males and females in night schools. The help of thousands of regular teachers in so many educational institutions was also utilized for this purpose.

An important characteristic of Gandhian philosophy is the aim of Sarvodaya. Therefore, he planned different types of education for the country. Besides basic education and social education he thought seriously over rural education and education for women.

MEDIUM OF EDUCATION

A staunch votary of mother tongue as the medium of education, Gandhiji said, "I must cling to my mother tongue as to my mother's breast, in spite of its shortcomings. It alone can give me the life giving milk". He was vehemently against English as the medium of education in this country. He said, "To inflict English on children is to stunt their natural growth and perhaps to kill originality in them". He pointed out to many modern western countries including U.S.S.R. who have made tremendous scientific progress without any help of English language. He maintained that our insistence on English is a remnant of our long slavery to the British. He was never prepared to accept this submission to foreign yoke. He maintained that the national language alone can be the vehicle of creating a common culture and rich literature. He was very much conversant with the language problem in India. He wanted to keep the country united particularly from the point of view of language. Therefore, he devised a common national language Hindustani which may be written in both Devanagari and Persian script. According to him there is no difference in Hindi and Urdu.

CHARACTERISTICS OF GANDHIAN EDUCATIONAL PLAN

M. K. Gandhi viewed the process of education from many different angles and saw that it must achieve something more than one objective. That is why he ascribed to it many different aims. At times a superficial study of these aims may give the impression that they are mutually contradictory or self-defeating, but a deeper examination will show that they complement each other. Even a cursory glancing through the history of education will show abundantly that different educationists have ascribed different aims to education. For some it is training for livelihood and sustenance, for others it is self-realization, for yet others the individual aims take precedence over the social objectives of education while some educationists favour the social aspects. Most educationists, however, have felt that education must strive for human perfection. Cultural development is another aim that has been ascribed to education. Idealists emphasize the idealistic aspect more than the realistic while naturalists and realists stress the realistic forms of education. Gandhiji's philosophy of education aims at harmonizing all these contradictory viewpoints. His Wardha plan of education laid great stress upon training in self-reliance, because he felt that the highest criterion of an educational system was its ability in putting an end to unemployment. For him both character formation and manual skill were important. Education should also be accompanied by earning money, and that is why he felt that the educator's salary should be paid out of goods produced by the educands. He believed that character building was as important as, if not more than, collecting information. The criterion of an individual's cultural development is not the extent of his knowledge but the qualities he manifests. In the cultural aspect of education, he placed emphasis upon the behaviour and thinking of educands. Culture, according to him, is not an adjunct of the mind but a quality of the soul, and cultural development an important objective of education. Education is the means to the child's physical, mental and spiritual development. His plan of education gave importance to physical, moral, aesthethic and religious education along with the teaching of mathematics and literary skills. In addition to this he stressed that handwriting should be neat and clean.

Gandhiji 's educational plan exhibits all the major qualities found in the Western educational patterns. For this reason, the following points must be kept in mind in attempting an evaluation of his plan:

1. Naturalism: Gandhiji's educational philosophy gives due recognition to biological naturalism because it lays stress on man's complete development. Like Rousseau, Gandhiji revolted against the existing pattern of education and suggested the establishment of a new system of education. He laid more stress on the child's environment than on books. He wanted to give an indigenous touch to education, and make it capable of achieving independence and naturalness. But, at the same time, he did not neglect discipline. His education is centered around the child, not around textbooks.

2. Idealism: On the one hand one finds a strong element of realism in Gandhiji' sphilosophy of education, but on the other it also exhibits some signs of idealism. There is no denying that he was always an idealist because he always was a religious individual. He felt that the aim of man's life was realization of God, and that is why he stressed the importance of moral and religious education. He preached that one must indulge in service, sacrifice and contemplation in order to achieve self-realization. Gandhiji's educational philosophy shows all the finest elements of idealism, and while he does not restrict the scope of physical education, his attention is mainly given to spiritual training. He wanted to use education as a means of developing a harmonized personality in the child. Like Pestalozzi, he wanted to make the child the centre of educational progress and like Herbart he felt that the aim of education was building up a moral character. He attached the greatest importance to the childs interests and inclinations. He agreed with Froebel that the child, at birth, is Mi of many undeveloped abilities and it is for education to develop these.

3. Pragmatism: Despite his inclination towards idealism, Gandhiji always attended to the practical and pragmatic aspect of education. That is why he entitled his autobiography *My Experiments with Truth*. He was an experimenter in every sphere of his life. Before arriving at a settled opinion about education he preferred to experiment in all its spheres. He accepted no truth as absolute. For him God was the only absolute entity. In keeping with the pragmatic tradition, he also believed that the child should gather for himself all the knowledge from the environment and select from it that which he could put to use in later life. The pattern of education suggested by him compares in many respects with that suggested by the pragmatists. Both stress the importance of interests and activity, and the need for variety in the subjects taught to the educand. Like Dewey, Gandhiji also felt that the child should learn through actual work. Besides, he also agreed with Dewey that education should seek to establish the democratic values in life. In short, he wanted to relate education to life as far as possible.

4. Educational system is based on psychological facts: Although Gandhiji was not a professional psychologist, he had gained remarkable insight into human psychology through his acute observation of life around him. By virtue of this qualification, he could attempt to make his educational system completely psychological. He, too, objected to the attempts at stuffing the child's mind with too many facts. He felt that education should aim at arousing curiosity and providing motivation to the child so that he should himself achieve his own physical, mental and spiritual development. He insisted on the importance of acquiring manual skills, but he felt that this training should be supplemented by knowledge of other objects so as to achieve physical, mental, moral, psychological and spiritual development also. He was very much in favour of the eduands' indulging in games and sports and gymnastic activity, because he felt that physical development is an essential prerequisite of mental development.

In his own Ashram children were given opportunities of physical development by participating in the work done there. He also felt that education should not be allowed to become mechanical but should be acquired through play.

5. Importance of impressions and actions: Gandhiji's opinion that impressions of early childhood have a tremendous impact on later development is in agreement with the modern psychologists. He was aware that the impressions once imprinted on the child's flexible mind are difficult to wipe out later on. In his infancy and childhood, the child learns a very great deal by imitating his parents, and for this reason it is desirable that the impressions made on his mind should be beneficial.

Phyhologists also agree with Gandhiji's theory that there should be learning through doing. Most educationists agree that learning through doing helps in the complete development of the child and that this also enables him to earn his livelihood later on in life.

6. Sociological importance of Gandhiji's plan: Gandhiji's plan of education is not only psychologically valid but it has sociological significance also. While thinking of his plan of education, Gandhiji was not concerned with one or two individuals, but with the vast multitude of illiterate men and women who make up the country's population. He wanted to use education as the medium of establishing in the country a non-violent social system from which exploitation of all kinds would be absent. He was a vigorous opponent of exploitation and he realized that it could not be eradicated without education. He advocated discipline as an essential part of freedom and liberty. He wanted that education should help the individual to become an ideal democratic citizen. He opposed the teaching of all those subjects in schools which had no real link with life. He stressed the importance of social service, labour, agriculture, handicrafts, hygiene, collective living, etc., and pointed out that they were more important than any curriculum. Sarvodaya was as much his guiding principle in education as it was in the field of politics. This concept of a Sarvodaya Society was based on traditional Indian and modern democratic values.

From the economic standpoint also, Gandhiji's educational plan appears to be appropriate for India's economy. Gandhiji felt that the principles of truth and non-violence could be as effective in the field of economic activity as they were elsewhere. He opposed exploitation in all its various forms and pointed out that exploitation had its origin in the individual's desire to get his work done by someone else instead of doing it himself and the desire to take charge of fruits of another's labour and effort. Gandhiji advised that the only way of putting an end to exploitation is for every individual to do his own work. He suggested that the educand should himself do his own work and all work connected with the school. He should learn to respect labour and should not feel that manual labour is in any way worse than or inferior to mental labour. India being an agricultural country in which the villagers have small pieces of land to cultivate, it would be better if these people developed various kinds of cottage industries. Only then can the villagers become self-sufficient.

7. Education conforming to the country's needs: Whatever the arguments one may advance against Gandhiji's plan of education, one cannot question his sincerity, because it is only too obvious that in presenting it, he was perfectly aware of the needs of his countrymen. He considered this the only kind of education which can be successful in this country. Most villagers cannot afford to pay for their children's education and in addition most of them require their children's assistance in their own occupations. Hence, their children should receive an education which can enable them to share their parent's burden. And this is possible only when the system of education lays stress on the importance of labour and manual skills. There can be no arguing the fact that the existing pattern of education in the country only prepares the young men for white-collar jobs. But this type of education can hardly suit the needs of an agricultural community. In the second place, Gandhiji wanted the educand to be engaged in gainful work the product of which could be sold to pay for his education. This may appear to be impractical on the face of it, but it is inspired by the idea that the child's education should not add to the parents' burden. The only other alternative is free education, and this is hindered by the psychological fact that anything gained free has little value for the recipient. Besides, free education does harm to the educand's character. Gandhiji favoured the idea that education as well as the educand should be independent of everyone else. There are definitely many difficulties in tanslating this plan into action. But on the theoretical level, one cannot question the justice of his thesis that education should be independent and self-reliant. There is no doubt that it is difficult to turn manual skill and physical labour into a game, and that it almost necessarily becomes monotonous and mechanical, but this does not prove that the idea itself is wrong. Gandhiji considered not only what the child studied but also what he would do later on. The existing problem of educated unemployed has been created only because the present system of education has no aim and purpose. Besides, Gandhiji wanted that the individual should become independent during his education, or at least that he should learn some skill which would enable him to find employment immediately after completing his education.

8. Teaching methods: The teaching methods in the Gandhian scheme of education can be deduced from his Basic Education. As has been pointed out, Gandhiji pleaded that the child should be educated through a basic craft. He should first be tought a basic craft from among the different types of it and other subjects such as Arithmetic, Language, Geography, History and Civics should be taught in association with the basic craft. In his educational institutions children were busy in craft activities for hours. There was no provision of rigid time-table or ringing of the bell after every hour. There was no compulsion to work in the class-room. The child was left free to select a craft according to his natural interests, abilities and according to his learning. This method of teaching has been justified by Western educationists Rousseau insisted upon the value of total freedom in teaching methods. Herbart admitted the value of synthesis in education.

As has already been pointed out, an important characteristic of the teaching method in Gandhian scheme was synthesis. Projects were drawn for the year, quarter, month, week and the day. They were carried on according to schedule and reviewed periodically. The teacher profited by this review. He gathered experiences to make better projects and implement them more successfully. This method was natural, saved time, was interesting, synthesized knowledge and action, helped in transfer of learning and led to the development of high moral character. It was based upon the educational principle of proceeding from gross to subtle. It required experienced and able teachers who could synthesize the educand and his environment and the different parts of the curriculum. They should be trained for this purpose.

This teaching method of Gandhiji's scheme of education has its advantages as well as disadvantages, It was pointed out that it converted schools into mini-factories and prolonged hours of engagement in crafts hardly left any leisure to the children for recreation and extra-curricular activities. Gandhi thought that the sale proceeds of the products of basic crafts in an educational institution will be sufficient to meet the salaries of the teachers. This, however, could never be realized. It was based on false expectations. However, no body can doubt Gandhiji's intensive insight into the teaching methods of the children and adults so much clear in his plans of basic education and adult education.

EDUCATION FOR, DIFFERENT SECTIONS OF SOCIETY

We have already pointed out Gandhian scheme for education of different sections of society according to age. He planned equally well for the education of children, as well as the adults. On the basis of sex, society is divided into two broad sections, male and female. Gandhiji planned for the education of both these sections. Regeneration of Indian women was a part of the political movement of M. K. Gandhi. Therefore, he had to speak and write about the education of women of India. In the basic scheme of education and in his plans of adult education Gandhiji did not make any distinction on the basis of sex. He recommended same primary and adult education both for the male and female. He was, however, not very much in favour of co-education. He allowed co-education up to the age of 8 years and then after 16 years of age. He, however, pleaded for separate educational institutions for boys and girls in adolescent age. The selection of co-educational or otherwise institutions was finally left to the discretion of the parents. Gandhiji maintained that family alone can create suitable tendencies for the success of co-education in educational institutions. He strongly supported all types of education both for male and female.

Society is again divided into progressive and backward sections both socially as well economically. As a champion of the uplift of backward classes in the country Gandhiji devised elaborate plans for the education of scheduled tribes and scheduled castes in India. These plans were mainly based upon local circumstances. They aimed at the unity of the nation without distinction of caste, language, religion, region or community, etc. Thus, Gandhiji planned for education suitable for all the sections of society. This was a necessary corollary to his social ideal of Sarvodaya. His scheme of education not only aimed at character building but also social, political and economic uplift of all the sections of the society.

17

Rabindra Nath Tagore

EDUCATION AS SELF-REALIZATION

Rabindra Nath Tagore believed that the aim of education is self-realization. He was a poet and a saint, who had, through his imagination and insight, realized the universal soul in himself and in nature. He believed that this realization was the goal of education. Because the universal soul is the root of our own soul, man's aim in life is to reach that universal soul of which all human beings are parts. The evolution of nature is consciously or unconsciously driving us towards this universal soul, a process which can be assisted by education. Even if it is not assisted the progress towards the universal soul will continue, but then individuals will be deprived of self-realization. It is thus evident that Rabindra Nath's educational philosophy is an adjunct of his general philosophy of life. In fact, he did not find any dichotomy between thought, life and philosophy. Besides, he believed that every human being is one who has potentialities of progressing towards the Super human being, the universal soul. His conception of the universal soul bore clear imprint of the Gita and Upanishadic philosophies. Although Rabindra Nath was clearly aware of the ideas of Western thinkers on education, he based his own ideas on the ancient Indian thought. Indian tradition believes that man's soul and the universal soul are one, and that self-realization amounts to realization of integration with God.

Principles of Self-Education

Self-education is based on self-realization, and the process of self-realization is as permanent as that of education. What is most important in this is that the educand must have faith in himself and in the universal self, underlying his own individual soul. All those actions which provide a natural sense of satisfaction and contentment will promote the educative process. This contentment is the reaction of the soul, and hence not the same as mere satisfaction and pleasure. In following Rabindra Nath's concept of self-education, the educand had to follow the three following principles:

1. Independence: Rabindra Nath believed in complete freedom of every kind for the educand—the freedom of intellect, decision, heart, knowledge, action and worship. But in order to attain this freedom the educand had to practise equanimity, harmony and balance. Through this practice' the educand can learn to distinguish between the true and the false, the natural and the artificial, the relevant and the irrelevant, permanent and temporary, universal and individual, liberal and narrow, etc. Consequently, after making this distinction the educand can bring about a harmony and synthesis in the true, natural, relevant, permanent and real elements that he has acquired. Once the educand has acquired this ability he can turn to self-guidance, for which he is now competent. He can himself distinguish between the elements likely to impede his progress and those which may help him. Rabindra Nath interprets independence as normalcy or the fact of being natural. In other words, when intelligence, feeling and determination are naturally distributed, it can be said to be a state of freedom. This independence is not to be confused with the absence of control, because it is self-control, it implies acting according to one's own rational impulse. Once this level of freedom has been achieved, there is no danger of the individual straying from his path, because his senses, intelligence, emotional feelings and all other powers are directed by his ego.

2. Perfection: The second active principle underlying self-education is that of perfection. Perfection here implies that the educand must try to develop every aspect of his personality and all the abilities and powers with which he has been endowedby Nature. Hence, the aim of education is not merely passing examinations, acquiring degrees and certificates of merit and ultimately achieving economic self-sufficiency through pursuing some profession. The sole aim of education is development of the child's personality which is possible only when every aspect of the personality is given equal importance, when no part of the personality is neglected and no part is exclusively stressed.

3. Universality: Development of the individual remains imperfect and incomplete until he acquires an abiding faith in the universal soul, apart of which exists inside himself. And for this, it is necessary to identify one's own soul with the universal soul. Thus, education exists not in simple development but it inheres in literally a rebirth in which the individual rises above the limitations of his individual personality and loses this individuality in the universality of the universal soul. One can search for this universal soul not only within oneself, but in every element of Nature and of one's environment. This search is assisted by knowledge, worship and action. Once this realization of the universal soul is achieved, it becomes easier to progress further.

It is evident from the foregoing account that the aim of Rabindra Nath's pattern of education is independence, perfection and universality. In the process of education, the educator creates an environment in which the child's personality undergoes a free, perfect and unrestricted development.

AIMS OF EDUCATIONS

According to Rabindra Nath, the aim of education is self-realization. He is a poet and a saint who through his imagination and insight, realized the universal soul within himself and in Nature. According to him this realization by everyone is the goal of education. Self-realization, according to Rabindra Nath, means the realization of the universal soul in one's self. Man's aim of life is to achieve this status. It is a process which cannot be realized without education. In the absence of education the individual will be deprived of self-realization. Rabindra Nath does not find any dichotomy between thought and life, philosophy and education. He believes that every one is potentially divine and every one can realize his potentiality. His philosophy is very much influenced by the 'Gita' and the 'Upanishads'. He is, however, well aware of the educational ideas prevalent in the West. Therefore, like Vivekananda, he synthesizes the ancient Vedantic traditions with the modern Western scientific attitude in formulating the goal of education.

1. Integral development: Defining the aim of education, Rabindra Nath says, "The fundamental purpose of education is not merely to enrich ourselves through the fullness of knowledge, but also to establish the bond of love and friendship between man and man".

This is the humanistic aim of education in Tagore's philosophy. His approach to ultimate reality is integral. He believes in an inner harmony between man and Nature and God. In man, again, the physical, the mental and the spiritual aspects are equally important and internally related. Therefore, like Sri Aurobindo, Rabindra Nath believes in a multisided education with physical, intellectual, moral and religious aims.

2. Physical development: Like Vivekananda, Rabindra Nath condemned the prevalent system of education which partially exercised the intellect only to the entire neglect of the body. According to Rabindra Nath, "Education of the body in the real sense, does not exist in play and exercise but in applying the body systematically to some useful work". Thus, one of the aims of education according to Rabindra Nath, is physical development. It is hence that he so much emphasizes games in school education. Pointing out the value of physical activities in the child's education he says, "Even if they learnt nothing, they would have had ample time for play, climbing trees, diving into ponds, plucking and tearing flowers, perpetrating thousand and one mischiefs on Mother Nature, they would have obtained the nourishment of the body, happiness of mind and the satisfaction of the natural impulses of childhood". Thus physical fitness is the first cardinal principle in the child's development. This is realized through his intimate contact with Nature. As a poet Tagore very well realizes the life giving values of Nature's contact with man. About the child's contact with the Nature he says, "I speak in very moderate terms: Seven years—till then let child has nothing to do with clothes and shame. Till then let Nature alone conduct the indispensable education of the savage". This is particularly important for the educational institutions in our society. Almost all contemporary Indian philosophers of education, including Gandhiji, Vivekananda, Dayananda and Sri Aurobindo, besides Tagore, lay emphasis upon the importance of setting educational institutions in natural environment so that the educand may learn by their touch with Nature.

3. Mental development: Besides the physical aim of education, Tagore equally lays emphasis upon the mental aim of education. Like Vivekananda, he is critical of the prevalent system of education which laid sole emphasis upon bookish learning. Presenting this attitude he says, "We touch the world not with our mind, but with our books. This is deplorable. Intellectualism takes us away from Nature and creates a gulf between man and man." To quote Rabindra Nath, 'We know' the people of books, not those of the world, the former are interesting to us, but the latter tiresome". In fact, the intellectual aim of education, according to Rabindra Nath, is the development of the intellectual faculties which should be developed through education. These are the power of thinking and the power of imagination. Both these are necessary for real manhood. Rabindra Nath criticizes the prevalent system of education which puts too much stress on memory and two little on imagination and thinking. He suggests, "Ever since childhood, instead of putting all the burden on the memory, the power of thinking and the power of imagination should also be given opportunities for free exercise".

4. Harmony with environment: In the end, the aim of education according to Rabindra Nath, is the harmony of the educand with the environment. The educand should know his environment and create harmony with it. To quote Rabindra Nath, "True education consists in knowing the use of any useful material that has been collected, to know its real nature and to build along with life a real shelter for life". This is particularly true about the rural education. Education should facilitate the educand's assimilation of his national culture. Through education, the educand should imbibe his cultural heritage and should be able to use it in his interaction with the environment. Explaining this aim of education, Rabindra Nath says, "If we believe that the chief aim of education in India is to be initiated into this unique pursuit of India, then we must constantly remember that neither the education of the senses, nor the education of the intellect, but the education of the feeling receive the place of honour in our schools.... Our true education is possible only in the forest, through intimate contact with nature and purifying austere pursuits".

5. Earning livelihood: Thus, about the aim of education, Tagore's approach is realistic. He, however, does not favour the utilitarian aim of education. This is his objection against the imposition of British system of education upon India. He says, "Knowledge has two departments: one pure knowledge, the other utilitarian knowledge. Whatever is worth knowing is knowledge. It should be known equally by men and women, not for practical utility, but for the sake of knowing.... The desire to know is the law of human nature". But Rabindra Nath does not ignore the earning of livelihood aim of education. He appreciates the practical bias in Western system of education. Though he does not want to make education an instrument for earning bread alone but he admits that bread earning is a necessary part of any sound goal of education. Therefore, he says, "From the very beginning, such education should be imparted to them (village folks) that they may know well what mass welfare means and may become practically efficient in all respects for earning their livelihood". While he is critical of the British system of education which wanted to create clerks out of the Indian educated people, he emphasized that the real aim of education is to develop men and women who may be able to fulfil the needs of the country. In his own words, "One of the main aims of education is to prepare the individual for the service of the country".

6. Multisided aim: The above discussion concerning the means of education according to Rabindra Nath, make it clear that his is a multisided attack on this problem. He is against any one sided aim of education. He is humanist. A humanistic aim of education requires a multisided approach.

CRITICAL EVALUATION

1. Education for human re-generation: Thus, Rabindra Nath's philosophy of education aims at developing a system of education for human re-generation. Man is in the centre of all his thinking, his philosophy, religion, literature, poetry, social activities and educational programmes. He is a humanist in the real sense of the term, not a naturalistic humanist but an integral humanist in the Indian tradition. He is not rationalist but believes in something higher than reasons in man. He does not think science alone to be capable of delivering the human goods but wants to synthesize it with Vedanta. He is a nationalist and at the same time an internationalist. To him the ultimate God is the universal man and only aim of all the man's activities was the realization of this God. Human regeneration is his sole aim and only ideal. His educational system is a means to achieve this aim. He, therefore, bases his educational system on essential human virtues such as freedom, purity, sympathy, perfection and world brotherhood.

2. Corrective to prevalent defects: Like other contemporary Indian thinkers of his time Tagore objected to the prevalent system of education due to its origination in a foreign country. He protested against emphasis on foreign language resulting in the alienation of the educated people from the general society. He tried to build up educational centres where these defects may be removed. He deliberated on different problems of Indian society particularly that of the rural people and tried to remove them through education. His educational system was a synthesis of East and West, Ancient and Modern, Science and Vedanta. It is hence that man like Jawaharlal Nehru considered Vishva-Bharati as the true representative of India.

18

Swami Vivekananda

In the Neo-Vedanta humanistic tradition of contemporary Indian thought, Vivekananda presented a philosophy of education for man-making. Among the contemporary Indian philosophers of education he is one of those who revolted against the imposition of British system of education in India. He was severely critical of the pattern of education introduced by the British in India. He felt that the current system of education did not confirm to India's culture. He pointed out that such an education only brings about an external change without any profound inner force.

CRITICISM OF PREVALENT EDUCATIONAL SYSTEM

Against the contemporary educational system the chief objection raised by Vivekananda was that it turned men into slaves, capable of slavery and nothing else. About the prevailing university education, he remarked that it was not better than an efficient machine for rapidly turning out clerks. It deprived people of their faith and belief. The English educated people believed that *Gita* was false and the *Vedas* were no more significant than rural folk lore. Criticising this system of education Vivekananda compared it to the person who wanted to turn his ass into a horse, was advised to thrash the ass in order to achieve this transformation and killed his ass in this process. Vivekananda also criticised the contemporary system of education from the humanistic viewpoint. He was a humanist and pleaded for education for manmaking. Such was not the education propounded by the British. Therefore, Vivekananda condemned it. He remarked, "It is not a man-making education, it is merely and entirely a negative education. A negative education or any training that is based on negation, is worse than death. The child is taken to school, and the first thing he learns is that his father is a fool, the second thing that his grandfather is lunatic, the third thing that all his teachers are hypocrites, the fourth, that all the sacred books are lies. By the time he is sixteen he is a mass of negation, lifeless and boneless. And the result is that fifty years of such education has not produced one original man in the three presidencies. Every man of originality that has been produced has been educated elsewhere, and not in this country, or they have gone to the old universities once more to cleanse themselves of superstitions".

AIMS OF EDUCATION

1. Self-development: In contrast to the contemporary system of education Vivekananda advocated education for self-development. He said, "By education I do not mean the present system, but something in the line of positive teaching. Mere book learning won't do. We want that education by which character is formed, strength of mind is increased, the intellect is expanded and by which one can stand on one's own feet. What we want are Western science coupled with Vedanta, *'Brahmachary's* as the guiding motto, and also *'Shraddha'* and faith in one's own self". These words by Vivekananda represent the characteristic Indian definition of education. Education according to most of the Western educationists aims at man's adjustment with the environment. According to the Indian philosophical tradition, on the other hand, education is the realization of the knowledge inherent in man. True knowledge does not come from outside, it is discovered with the individual, in the self which is the source of all knowledge. To quote Vivekananda again, "All knowledge that the world has ever received comes from the mind; the infinite library of the universe is in your mind. The external world is only the suggestion, the occasion, which sets you to study your mind. The falling of the apple gave suggestion to Newton, and he studied his own mind. He rearranged all the precious links of thought in his mind and discovered a new link among them which we call the Law of Gravitation". Thus, according to Vivekananda, the function of education is the uncovering of the knowledge hidden in our mind. Education is the process of self-development. In the words of Vivekananda, "You cannot teach a child any more than you can grow a plant. The plant develops its own nature".

A person's education is not judged by the number of books he has read but by the thickness of the cover of ignorance on his mind. The thicker is this cover, the greater is the ignorance. As the light of knowledge dawns this cover of ignorance gradually shatters. The teacher's job is to uncover knowledge by his guidance. His guidance makes the mind active and the educand himself unveils the knowledge lying within him.

2. Fulfilment of Swadharma: Vivekananda supported the idea of Swadharma in education. Every one has to grow like himself. No one has to copy others. It is hence that he condemned the imposition of foreign education. He asked, "Getting by heart the thoughts of others in a foreign language and stuffing your brain with them and taking some university degree, you can pride yourself as educated. Is this education"? True improvement is self-inspired. There should be no external pressure of any type on the child. External pressure only creates destructive reactions leading to obstinacy and indiscipline. In an atmosphere of freedom, love and sympathy alone, the child will develop courage and self-reliance. He should not be unnecessarily checked in his activities. The educator should not constantly tell him to do this or that. Such negative directions tend to blunt his intelligence and mental development. He should be talked to stand on his own, to be himself. This is so since as Vivekananda suggests, "If you do not allow once to become a lion, he will become a fox". Therefore, education should be modified to suit the individual child. Each child should be given opportunities to develop according to his own inner nature.

3. Freedom of growth: Thus Vivekananda is against any type of external pressure upon the child. He is a staunch champion of freedom in education. Freedom is the first requirement for self-development. The child should be given freedom to grow according to his own nature. In the words of Vivekananda, "You cannot teach a child any more than you can grow a plant. All you can do is on the negative side—you can only help. You can take away the obstacles, but knowledge comes out of its own nature. Loosen the soil a little, so that it may come out easily. Put a hedge around it, see that it is not killed by anything, and there your work stops. You cannot do anything else. The rest is a manifestation from within its own nature". The teacher should not exert any type of pressure on the child. The child should be helped in solving his problems himself. The teachers should have an attitude of service and worship. Education ultimately aims at realization. It is a means to the establishment of a fraternity of mankind.

4. Character formation: Character is the solid foundation for self-development. The aim of education as self-development, therefore, leads to the aim of education for character. Defining character, Vivekananda said, "The character of any man is but the aggregate of his tendencies, the sum total of the bent of his mind. As pleasure and pain pass before his soul, they leave upon it different pictures and the result of these combined impressions is what is called a man's character". The aim of education is character building. This depends upon the ideals cherished by the individual. The educator should present high ideals before the educands. The best way to develop a character is the personal example of high character set by the teacher. Laying emphasis upon this point Vivekananda said, "Without the personal life of the teacher there would be no education. One would live from his very boyhood with one whose character is like a blazing fire, and should have before him a living example of the highest teaching.... The charge of imparting knowledge should again fall upon the shoulders of 'tyagis'. In ancient Indian system of education the teachers used to present high ideals", before the pupils, who in their turn imitated these ideals according to their capacities. Following things are required for character formation:

(*i*) *Hard Work*: Character formation, according to Vivekananda, requires hard work. This is not possible by those who have a wish for all types of enjoyments. Struggle is the best teacher in character building. Activity and *purushartha* are the signs of life. Inactivity shows absence of vitality. While living in all types of comforts and escaping from all types of labour, no one can build up high character.

(*ii*) *Moral and Spiritual Values*: Besides hard work, character formation requires traits such as purity, thirst for knowledge, perseverance, faith, humility, submission and veneration, etc. These qualities may be developed by the teacher's example and the pupil 's efforts. According to Vivekananda, "Without faith, humility; submission and veneration in our hearts towards the teacher, there cannot be any growth in us. In those countries which have neglected to keep up this kind of relation, the teacher has become a mere lecturer, the teacher expecting his five dollars and the person taught expecting his brain to be filled with the teacher's words and each going his own way after this much is done. The true teacher is he who can immediately come down to the level of the student, and transfer his soul to the student's soul and see through and understand through his mind.

(*iii*) *Gurukula System*: Such a relationship between the teacher and the taught is possible only in a Gurukula system of education. Therefore, Vivekananda favoured the ancient Indian Gurukula system of education. In these Gurukulas the pupils served the teacher, who in his turn, helped the pupils everywhere to achieve knowledge. There was hardly any economic relationship between the teacher and the taught, which is the curse of the present system of education.

(*iv*) *Formation of Good Habits*: Character is intimately connected with habits. Habits express character. Good habits make for good character. While the contemporary psychologists admit the value of habits in one's life, Vivekananda has pointed out the value of habits not only in this life but in lives to come. A bad habit may be broken by developing the opposite good habit. If a man constantly thinks that he will be courageous and progressive, he may develop confidence for breaking bad habits. It is not the teacher nor the guardian who may reform the habit of a person but only he himself Man is caught in the net of his own *karmas* from which he alone can get out, no one else can directly help him. Our own self in us is our best guide in the struggle that is life.

(*v*) *Learning Through Mistakes*: The child should be allowed to commit mistakes in the process of character formation. He will learn much by his mistakes. Errors are the stepping stones to our progress in character. This progress requires courage and strong will. Strong will is the sign of great character. Will makes men great. Therefore, there is no occasion to be discouraged or to weep, one should exercise his will and he will see that things which he considered to be impossible become easy and possible. Vivekananda himself was an ideal teacher. His words worked like magic upon men and women. This is possible only in the case of a teacher who has himself risen high. Presenting his own example,

Vivekananda asked the people to build up their character and manifest their real nature which is the Effulgent, the Resplendent, the Ever Pure.

MEANS OF EDUCATION

1. Love: The best means of education, according to Vivekananda is love. Education should be based upon love. Love is best inspiration in character building. The child should be taught through love. This is love for men, for human beings. The only motive in imparting education should be love for the educand, for the man in him. That is why Vivekananda's philosophy of education is known as education for man-making. The teacher's aim should be neither money making nor attainment of fame but only bestowing human love. The spiritual force works through love. This love within the educator is the real source of his influence upon the educand. This may be amply clear by the example of the relationship of Vivekananda with his Guru Ram Krishna. It was the force of spiritual love in Ram Krishna which helped Vivekananda in God realization. It is this which makes the educator to take the educand from untruth to truth, darkness to light, death to immortality.

2. Help: The task of the educator is to help the educand in manifesting and expressing his abilities and capacities. Educator should help the individual to recognize his cultural heritage and to use it in his struggle of life. The educator can guide the educand because he himself has the experience of treading on this path and knows how to face its difficulties. Vivekananda has not only presented high ideals of education but also developed a sound system by which these ideals may be achieved.

3. Guidance: Education is not a bed of roses. Every educand has to face problems peculiarly his own. He solves them by his own efforts and with the guidance of the teacher. The skilled teacher guides the pupil through these difficulties and takes him forward. This requires a sufficient knowledge of human psychology because most of our problems are psychological in nature. The teacher should teach the educand to concentrate his attention, only then can the problems be solved. The greater the attention, the more is the effort effective.

4. Concentration: Concentration, according to ancient Indian thought, is the key to true knowledge. Therefore, Vivekananda has placed much emphasis upon focusing of attention. It is only after years of concentration that a man becomes a scholar and a great scientist. The educands should be distinguished according to their abilities, every one of them has to develop concentration. Again, while teaching concentration the educator should keep in mind the varying abilities of concentration is spontaneous and easy, for others it is difficult and requires long training. Hence, the educator must organise his teaching in such a way that he may be helpful to each educand separately. He should attend to every one's difficulties and try to solve them as much as possible. Thus, Vivekananda supported the ancient Indian means of achieving concentration.

5. Brahmacharya: Again, according to ancient Indian thinkers, Brahmacharya or abstinence is the first means of achieving concentration. It gives mental and spiritual powers of the highest kind. It transforms sex drive into a spiritual force. *Brahmacharya* implies purity of thought, deed and action. It helps to improve and sharpen various psychological processes such as learning, remembering, thinking, etc. It helps in achieving power of memory and improve the powers of the mind. Vivekananda therefore strongly emphasized the need for the students to observe *Brahmacharya.* This leads to both mental and physical advantages. Firstly, it takes effective care of all distractions. Secondly, it improves the body and the mind so that they may become effective means of knowledge.

6. Discussion and contemplation: In addition to concentration the other means of education are discussion and contemplation. It is only through these that the educand may remove his difficulties. Discussion should be carried out in an informal atmosphere. Contemplation should be practised in a calm and quiet atmosphere with the mind fully alive. In the end the educational process requires faith and reverence of the educand in the teacher and his teachings. Without faith and reverence no true knowledge can be achieved. It is faith and reverence which are sound foundation for all character development and self-education. The faith and reverence, however, depend not only upon the educand but also upon the high examples presented by the teacher. In the educational process, therefore, the teacher also occupies a very high place.

MEDIUM OF EDUCATION

1. Mother tongue: In teaching languages Vivekananda laid particular stress upon teaching through the mother tongue. Here he is supported by all other contemporary Indian philosophers of education.

2. Common language: Besides mother tongue, there should be a common language which is necessary to keep the country united. This may be taught in addition to the regional languages.

3. Sanskrit: The teaching of Sanskrit forms an important part of the curriculum envisaged by Vivekananda. Sanskrit is the source of all Indian languages and a repository of all inherited knowledge. It is, therefore, absolutely necessary that every Indian should know Sanskrit. Vivekananda appreciated the greatness of Sanskrit in eloquent words when he said that this language granted power, ability and prestige to the nation and that our awareness of our cultural heritage and past greatness depends very much upon our knowledge of this language. He felt that in the absence of this knowledge, it will be impossible to understand Indian culture. If the society has to develop and progress it is necessary that men and women should know this language which is the store house of ancient heritage, besides the knowledge of the mother tongue.

TYPES OF EDUCATION

Vivekananda elaborately discussed the teaching methods in physical, moral and religious education. This discussion gives an idea, of types of education as well as methods of teaching.

1. Physical education: Vivekananda laid particular stress on the value of physical education in curriculum. He said, "You will be nearer to Heaven through football than through the study of *Gita.* You will understand *Gita* better by your biceps, your muscles a little stronger. You will understand the *Upanishads* better and the glory of the Atman, when your body stands firm on your feet and you feel yourself as man". Self-realization or character building is impossible in the absence of physical education. One must know the secret of making the body strong through physical education, for a complete education it is necessary to develop both mind and the body. Vivekananda himself took physical exercise every day. He glorified power and opposed weakness in any form. Power was happiness and weakness a never ending burden. It is hence that he so such emphasized the importance of physical education particularly for young men and women.

2. Moral and religious education: Laying emphasis upon religious education Vivekananda said, "Religion is the innermost core of education. I do not mean my own or any one else's opinion about religion. Religion is as the rice and everything else, like the curries. Taking only curries causes indigestion, and so is the case with taking rice alone". Therefore, religious education is a vital part of a sound curriculum. This religious education is necessary in order to counter effect the evil influence of modern materialism. It is only by synthesis of religion and science that men may reap the advantages of both. As has been already pointed out, religious education in itself is never sufficient. It should not be the whole of curriculum but only a part of it. This religion, again, is not any particular dogma or sectarian philosophy, in fact, it is what Tailor called religion of man. It is hence that Vivekananda did not distinguish between secular and religious education. He thought that the former may be given by the latter. He said, "We have to give them secular education. We have to follow the plan laid down by our ancestors, that is, to bring all the ideals slowly down among the masses. Raise them slowly up, raise them to equality. Impart... secular knowledge through religion".

(*i*) *High Ideals*: The best way of imparting religious education is to present the high ideals of saints and religious men before the students. They should be taught to worship saints to follow their ideals. Among the great souls, Vivekananda pointed out to Ram Chandra, Krishna, Mahavir and Ram Krishna. In the ideal of Shri Krishna he laid more emphasis on his personality as the author of *Gita.* He said, "Keep aside for the present the Vrindavan aspect of Shri Krishna, and spread far and wide the worship of Shri Krishna roaring out the *Gita* with the voice of a lion; and bring into daily use the worship of *Shakti* the Divine Mother, the source of all power. We now mostly need the ideal of the hero with the tremendous spirit of *rajas* thrilling through his veins from head to foot, the hero who will dare and die to know the truth, the hero whose armour is renunciation, whose sword is wisdom; we want the spirit of the brave warrior in the battle field".

(*ii*) *Courage*: Thus, Vivekananda wanted men and women to develop qualities according to their particular sex and their role in society. He asked young men to develop manly qualities. Even in religious practices he considered courage to be a higher quality. Religion is not mere ritualism. It is a progress towards high ideals in the face of extreme difficulties.

(*iii*) *Service and Devotion*: Besides courage, Vivekananda prescribed service and devotion in religious education. For this purpose he eulogised the ideal of Hanuman who was a living example of service, devotion and courage. He deplores the dramatic imitation of *Ras Lila* because it is against the interest of the country at present. Purity is the real basis of the country at present. Even in music Vivekananda advised young men to adopt manly music so that it may infuse bravery and courage. This, however, does not mean that Vivekananda rejected any particular type of religious practice. He only wanted to adopt religious practices according to the needs of the times. India, according to him, today needs a religion which should be harmonious with science and teach patriotism, service and sacrifice. Then alone religious education may be useful to the nation. Religion influences total man. It encourages all types of qualities, soft as well as virile. Vivekananda emphasized the inculcation of the latter type of virtues. He exhorted young men by saying, "Never allow weakness to overtake your mind. Remember Mahavir, remember the Divine Mother, and you will see that all weakness, all cowardice will vanish at once".

(*iv*) *Self-confidence*: It goes without saying that such a moral and religious education will develop self-confidence among young men and women. Self-confidence, according to Vivekananda, is the real religion. It includes world brotherhood and love of humanity, because a person having self-confidence means having confidence in humanity. Thus, Vivekananda's religion was humanistic. Religion is the source of all powers. It is again, the source of all good. Thus, for Vivekananda, ethics and religion are one and the same. God is always on the side of goodness. To fight for goodness is therefore service to God. Weakness is the source of all evils. It is at the root of all violence, hatred and enmity. If a man sees his own self everywhere he need not fear any one. Fearlessness and power are eternal truths, the real nature of the self.

(*v*) *Realisation of Truth*: Thus, Vivekananda pleaded for realization of truth through religious practices. Long before Gandhiji identified truth with God. Vivekananda called truth God. The seeker after truth should search for it in every aspect of life. Truth is power, untruth is weakness. Knowledge is truth, ignorance is untruth. Thus, truth increases power, courage and energy. It is light giving. It is, therefore, necessary for the individual as well as collective welfare.

(*vi*) *Achievement of Power*: Thus Vivekananda worshipped power. This power, however, was not physical or biological as that of Nietzche. It was spiritual power. Rising high in the tradition of Vedanta, Vivekananda never allowed his feet to leave the solid ground. His teachings influenced the West where materialism was rampant. This was due to the reason that his teachings were based upon universal truths. Modern man is not prepared to leave the world. He wants to enjoy it. Vivekananda, therefore, gave a practical garb to his religion. India in his time was groaning under slavery. Vivekananda, therefore, asked Indian men and women to shed all types of weakness and to march forward courageously. According to him we have to speak less and work more, achieve power first than anything else. To quote Vivekananda,

"First of all our young men must be strong. Religion will come afterwards".

(*vii*) *Study of Scriptures*: In the curriculum for religious education, Vivekananda considered *Gita, Upanishads* and the *Vedas* as the most important. The study of these scriptures will fill young men and women with courage. These are the eternal sources of the life force of Indian culture. These are the bases of our spiritual education. Vivekananda, however, was not in favour of preaching any particular religious dogmas. Religion for him was self-realization. Temples, mosques, churches and synegogues do not make religion. Religion is divinization. It is not intellectual development but transformation of total man. It is nothing if it does not teach us service and sacrifice. It is the basis for character formation. It should lead to man-making. In tune with his Guru Ram Krishna, Vivekananda pleaded for unity of world religions. He considered all religions to be equal. A true religion cannot be limited to a particular place or time. The religious books, teachers and institutions are eternal. Their ancient forms are worshipped and their modern forms are respected. Thus, in his moral and religious education Vivekananda pleaded for the education of unity of world religions.

3. Education for weaker section of society: Vivekananda respected human individuality everywhere and pleaded for freedom for everyone. "Each soul", according to him, "is potentially divine. The goal is to manifest external and internal. Do this, either by work, or worship, or psychic centre or philosophy by one or more or all of these—and before. This is the whole of religion. Doctrines or dogmas, or rituals or books, temples or forms are secondary details". It was due to his devotion for the poor and backward people that Vivekananda wanted to make education an instrument for the uplift of the masses. Like Gandhiji after him, Vivekananda, throughout his life, worked for the uplift of backward classes. He pleaded for universal education so that these backward people may fall in line with others. He said, "A nation is advanced in proportion as education and intelligence is spread among the masses. The chief causes of India's ruin have been the monopolizing of the whole education and intelligence of the land among the handful of men. If we are to rise again, we shall have to do it by spreading education among masses". Thus, education should spread to every household in the country, to factories, playing grounds and agricultural fields. If the children do not come to the school the teacher should reach them. Two or three educated men should team up, collect all the paraphernalia of education and should go to the village to impart education to the children. Thus, Vivekananda favoured education for different sections of society, rich and poor, young and old, male and female.

4. Education for women: In the education for women Vivekananda laid particular stress on chastity and fearlessness. He conceived an ideal institution for women known as Math where literature and religion may be taught. Pointing out to the curricula in this institution he said, "Other matters such as sewing, culinary art, rules of domestic work and upbringing of children will also be taught while '*Japa*' worship and meditation, etc., shall form an indispensable part of the teaching. The duty of the teaching in school ought to devolve in every respect on educated widows and '*Brahmacharinis*'. It is good to avoid in this country any association of men with women's schools". Thus, he presented a comprehensive curricula for women so that they may develop high character, courage and confidence. He presented the ideal of Sita and lamented that modern Indian women are imitating Western ideals which had led to all round degeneration. Like males he advised females also to observe *Brahmacharya* which is a solid foundation for any type of education. He was extremely sorry for the lowly condition of Indian women. He considered women to be the incarnation of power and asked men to respect them in every way. He pointed out that unless Indian women secure a respectable place in this country, the nation can never march forward. The regeneration of Indian women, according to him, depends upon proper education. Women's education should be in the hands of women. Clarifying his scheme in this connection he said, "After five or six years' training in this 'Math', the guardians of the girls may marry them. If deemed fit for 'Yoga' and religious life, with the permission of their guardians they will be allowed to stay in this Math, taking the vow of celibacy. These celibate nuns will in time be the teachers and preachers of the Math. In villages and towns they will open centres and strive for the spread of female education. Through such devout preachers of character there will be the real spread of female education in this country.... Spirituality, sacrifice and self-control will be the motto of the pupils of this Math, and service or 'Seva Dharma' the vow of their life.... If the life of the women of this country be moulded in such fashion, then only will there be the re-appearance of such ideal characters of Sita, Savitri and Gargi".

CRITICAL EVALUATION

Our discussion about Vivekananda's concept of the aims and ideals of education, its process and curriculum has made it amply clear that he was a humanist in the true sense of the term. He said, "Look upon every man, woman and every one as God. Blessed you are that this privilege was given to you when other had it not. Do it only as a worship. The only God to worship is the human soul in the human body. Of course, all animals are temples too, but man is the highest, the Taj Mahal of temples. If I cannot worship in that, no other temple will be of any advantage". Vivekananda's humanism, however, was different from naturalistic humanism. It is in this background that his education for man-making should be understood. Man, according to him, is the highest of all living beings so much so that according to Vivekananda even the angels will have to come down again and again for salvation through a human body.

The educational ideals advocated by Vivekananda have been supported by most of the modern Western educationists. Education today is defined as the process of all round development of the child. Such a development can take place only from within while the external environment provides occasion for such development. The teacher has to provide the environment so that the child may become aware of the treasure of knowledge lying buried in his mind. Modern psychologists point out that in every individual there are certain dormant powers which have to be developed through education The teacher's real job is to see that there should be no impediments in the child's path to self-development. He is like a gardener who prepares grounds for the growth of his plants, protects them and nourishes them so that the plant may grow properly. Similarly, the teacher takes care of the child, provides him a suitable environment and looks after his proper growth. Thus, though education comes from within the teacher is an indispensable part of it. While the motivation comes from within the teacher activates it. He encourages the child to use his mind, body and sense organs. Thus, Vivekananda presented a positive system of education. He wrote, "Education is the manifestation of the perfection already in man. I look upon religion as the innermost core of education". In his philosophy of education Vivekananda synthesized spiritual and material values. He felt that India needed a system of education based on the ancient Vedanta but at the same time worthy of making individual earn his livelihood so that the country may progress. He maintained that no profession is bad provided it is done with a sense of service and self-sacrifice. It is the absence of this dignity of labour which is responsible for the degraded condition of this country. Long before M. K. Gandhi, Vivekananda pleaded for the worship of God in poor. He said, "So long as the millions lie in hunger and ignorance, I hold every man a traitor who having been educated at their expense pays not the least heed, to them". He asked young men to change the situation. He pleaded for universal, compulsory and free education. He asked the educator to reach every village and every hutment so that the country may awake from ignorance.

19

Sri Aurobindo

OBJECTIVES OF EDUCATION

Defining the objectives of education Sri Aurobindo said, "It must be an education that for the individual will make its one central object the growth of the soul and its powers and possibilities, for the nation will keep first in view the preservation, strengthening and enrichment of the nation-soul and its dharma and raise both into powers of the life and ascending mind and soul of humanity. And at no time will it lose sight of man's highest object, the awakening and development of this spiritual being".[1]

Sri Aurobindo was not only one of the greatest philosopher and yogi of his time but also one of the greatest political leader, social reformer and educationist of his era. He was a great patriot whose first concern was always the good of motherland. Therefore, he presented a national system of education which may be adopted for the educational reconstruction in India and at the same time develop the Indians as world citizens and the fore-runners of the advent of the supramental race upon earth. Sri Aurobindo's philosophy not only gives an important place to individual and nation but also to humanity. In these three principles, the higher determines the lower. Therefore, the national scheme of education will be not only from the point of view of the needs of the country but also from the standpoint of the needs of humanity. It is so since the highest principle governing the life of individual and nation is the humanity itself. It is as a human being first and last that the individual has to grow. It is as a member of a community of nations that a nation has to grow

1. Sri Aurobindo, *Sri Aurobindo and The Mother on Education*, Part I, p. 3.

and develop. It is the forgetting of this central truth in the life of the individual and nation that has been the source of all evil and error. Again, Sri Aurobindo everywhere considers fulfilment of Swadharma as the law of life. Each individual in a nation has to fulfil his Swadharma. The purpose of education in a nation is to prepare the individual to serve their roles according to their status in society. Individual differences are the basis of modern system of education. Nature has bestowed different human beings with different capacities and powers. Therefore, the educationist has to develop in the child whatever has been already endowed to him by God. The child is, "A soul with a lean, a nature and capacities of his own, who must be helped to find them, to find himself, to grow into their maturity, into a fullness of physical and vital energy and utmost breadth, depth and height of his emotional his intellectual and his spiritual being".[1] Thus, each human being is a self-developing soul.[2] Parents and teachers have to help him in this development. In the words of N.C. Dowsett, the concept of education in Sri Aurobindo's[3] philosophy is summarised thus, "The meaning of the word education is to educe the inner, hidden, latent, dormant, potential secret within every human being, secret because it is not of the senses but of the inner truth of being and because it is that most unknown pan of the being which has yet to evolve to its full stature".[4]

THE TRUE EDUCATION

Defining true education, Sri Aurobindo wrote, "There are three things which have to be taken into account in true and living education, the man, the individual in his commonness and in his uniqueness, the nation or people and universal humanity. It follows that that alone will be true and living education which helps to bring out to full advantage, makes ready for the full purpose and scope of human life all that is in the individual man, and which at the same time helps him to enter into his right relation with the life, mind and soul of the people to which he belongs and with that great total life, mind and soul of humanity

1. Sri Aurobindo, B.C.L., 1971, Volume 15, p. 605.
2. *Ibid.*, pp. 27-28.
3. Dowsett, N.C., *Psychology for Future Education*, Aurobindo Ashram Pondicherry (1977), p. 9.
4. *Sri Aurobindo and The Mother on Education*, Part I, p. 1.

of which he himself is a unit and his people or nation a living, a separate and yet inseparable member".[1]

Besides Swadharma, ttye role of a nation is determined by Swabhava. Swadeshi, was the avowed principle in Sri Aurobindo's political philosophy. Each nation, according to him, has to grow and develop in tune with its peculiar Swabhav and Swadharma. This principle has been advocated by Indian thinkers since ancient times. Indian philosophy always considered everything as an instrument of spiritual growth. It may be called *spiritual instrumentalism* in contrast to the biological instrumentalism of John Dewey. Thus, the nation has to develop its mental, ethical and aesthetic being to make it a fit instrument for the growth of the soul. This is the highest purushartha. India, according to Sri Aurobindo, is a nation which has to fulfil a spiritual role in the community of nations. Its ideal for the humanity also is spiritual. Therefore, Sri Aurobindo has everywhere called for the spiritual growth of humanity.

Rational Education

This, however, does not mean that Sri Aurobindo finds no place for reason in education. In his philosophy everywhere Sri Aurobindo has supported reason like any staunch rationalist and lauded its role as the law giver to the irrational elements, the passions, the sensibilities and the sense organs. A true and living education is also a rational education though it goes beyond reason for the spiritual growth of man. A rational education, according to Sri Aurobindo, includes the following three things:

1. To teach men how to observe and know rightly the facts on which they have to form a judgment.
2. To train them to think fruitfully and soundly.
3. To fit them to use their knowledge and their thought effectively for their own and the common good.[2]

Meeting of East and West

Brought up in the West Sri Aurobindo had the first hand knowledge of the Western system of education. Like Vivekananda and Tagore he was also conversant with the advantages of European

1. Sri Aurobindo, B.C.L. 1972, Volume 17, p. 198.
2. Sri Aurobindo, B.C.L., 1971, Vol. 15, p. 186.

system of education. Though one of the greatest admirers of ancient Indian thoughts, Sri Aurobindo was a votary of the synthesis of whatever is good in East and West. This synthesis is visible everywhere in his thought. Therefore, while presenting a scheme for Indian education, he advocated synthesis of ancient Indian educational ideals along with the Western methods and techniques. As he said, "The first problem in a national system of education is to give an education as comprehensive as the European and more thorough, without the evils of strain and cramming. This can only be done by studying the instruments of knowledge and finding a system of teaching which shall be natural; easy and effective. It is only by strengthening and sharpening these instruments of their utmost capacity that they can be made effective for the increased work which modern conditions require. The muscles of the mind must be thoroughly trained by simple and easy means; then, and not till then, great feasts of intellectual strength can be required of them".[1]

Integral Education

True education, according to Sri Aurobindo, is not only spiritual but also rational, vital and physical. In other words, it is an integral education. This integral education has been explained by Sri Aurobindo's closest collaborator the Mother, in these words, "Education to be complete must have five principal aspects relating to the five principal activities of the human being: the physical, the vital, the mental, the psychic and the spiritual Usually these phases of education succeed each other in a chronological order following the growth of the individual. This, however, does not mean that one should replace another but that all must continue, completing each other, till the end of life".[2] Sri Aurobindo's scheme of education is integral in two senses. Firstly, it is integral in the sense of including all the aspects of the individual being, physical, vital, mental, psychic and spiritual. Secondly, it is integral in the sense of being an education not only for the evolution of the individual alone but also of the nation and finally of the humanity. In his *Essays On Gita* Sri Aurobindo initially presented the concept of integral education as outbringing all the facets of an individual personality. The ultimate aim of education is the evolution of

1. *Sri Aurobindo and The Mother on Education,* Part I. p. 7.
2. *Sri Aurobindo and The Mother on Education,* Part I. p. 8.

total humanity which includes the evolution of the nation which in its turn depends upon the evolution of the individual In this scheme of evolution the principle of growth is unity in diversity. This unity again, maintains and helps the evolution of diversity. Thus each individual in nation and each nation in humanity has to develop a system of education according to its own Swabhav and fulfilling its Swadharma.

Supramental Education

The education again, is ultimately supramental education, that which leads to our evolution towards the supramental. This supramental evolution, however, will necessarily pass through and only after the evolution of the physical, the vital, the mental and the psychic. Physical education is the education of the body. It includes the order, discipline, plasticity and receptivity of the body. Its principal aspects are: 1. Control and discipline of functions, 2. A total, methodical and harmonious development of all the parts and movements of the body, and 3. Rectification of defects and deformities, if there are any.[1] The vital education is indispensible, though difficult. It is so since the nature of vital has been often misunderstood. In the words of The Mother, the vital education involves two principal aspects, "The first is to develop and utilise the sense organs, the second is to become conscious and gradually master of one's character and in the end to achieve its transformation".[2] Thus vital education includes sense training and the development of character. This character again will be developed according to individual differences. It requires redirection and transformation of the instincts and emotions, drives and propensities. Describing the mental education the mother has laid down the following five phases:

1. Development of the power of concentration, the capacity of attention.
2. Development of the capacities of expansion, wideness, complexity and richness.
3. Organisation of ideas around a central idea or a higher ideal or a supremely luminous idea that will serve as a guide in life.
4. Thought control, rejection of undesirable thoughts so that one may, in the end, think only what one wants and when one wants.

---

1. *Ibid.*, p. 10.
2. *Ibid.*, p. 11.

5. Development of mental silence, perfect calm and a more and more total receptivity to inspirations coming from the higher regions of the being.

While the physical, vital and mental education are the means to develop the personality, the psychic education alone leads to the future evolution of man. Sri Aurobindo's system of education does not aim only at the adjustment and normal development of the human personality but its total growth and transformation. The idea of psychic education has not been developed in any existing philosophy of education. It is so since psychic element was never considered and understood by the Western educationists. In India also in spite of the importance of psychic element found in Yoga, its nature has been seldom understood. The core of the psychic education is the achievement of our identification with the psychic principles in us. This may be reached by psychological, religious or mechanical methods. Every one will have to find out the method best suitable to him and his aspiration. The psychic education requires sincere and steady aspiration, a persistent and dynamic will, concentration, revelation and experience. In the words of The Mother "Only one thing is absolutely indispensable: the will to discover and realise".[1] This is in fact the field of occult and yoga.

Thus the supramental education requires the above steps as a prelude to its realisation. It is only after one gets through the physical, vital, mental and psychic education and realises a certain transformation that one can enter into supramental education. To quote The Mother again, "Then will begin also a new education which can be called the supramental education; it will, by its all-powerful action, work not only upon the consciousness of individual being, but upon the very substance of which they are built and upon the environment in which they live".[2] The idea of supramental education like that of the psychic education is Aurobindo's significant contribution to the field of education. This is more important at the present juncture when most of the educationists are realising the need for an educational system aiming at man-making. According to Sri Aurobindo, humanity today has already reached what has been called by him a subjective stage. The future evolution has to be above the mental

1. *Sri Aurobindo and The Mother on Education,* Part I. p. 14.
2. *Sri Aurobindo and The Mother on'Education,* Part I. p. 16.

level. This will require a great insight and persistent efforts. The different types of education already discussed should not be given successively but simultaneously. The focus should be all the time on the inner growth. As the educand advances he should be taught to identify his real self and to find out the law of his being. The principles of this new type of education have been explained by Sri Aurobindo and the Mother in their different works.

AIMS OF EDUCATION

The aims of education in the educational philosophy of Sri Aurobindo are as follows:

I. Perfection: Sri Aurobindo was a perfectionist. He was never satisfied with partial remedies. It is hence that he left the political arena to pursue a more perfect method of realisation of perfection of human race. It is hence that he presents his integral yoga as a solution not only of the individual needs but also of the social and political problems facing nations and humanity. This perfectionism is the strength and this again is the weakness of Sri Aurobindo's philosophy of education. In tune with the Indian concept of human nature Sri Aurobindo considered the individual as, "A growing soul with a being, a nature and capacities of his own".[1] The aim of education therefore was to realise these capacities and grow, "into a fullness of physical and vital energy and utmost breadth, depth and height of his emotional, his intellectual and his spiritual being".[2]

2. Harmony: Harmony is the key to understand Sri Aurobindo's thought everywhere. Those who complain about the difficulty in understanding his writings lack this inherent urge to harmony. On the other hand, those who seek harmony easily understand Sri Aurobindo's works. In his philosophy of education, as in his metaphysics, epistemology, political philosophy and social philosophy, Sri Aurobindo searches after the principle of harmony in the individual, community and humanity and aims at its realisation. He seeks to achieve harmony of the individual by the growth and evolution of his different aspects such as physical, vital, mental and psychic, etc. For this he proposes a scheme of physical, vital, mental, moral, religious and spiritual education. He also seeks harmony of different individuals in

1. Sri Aurobindo, B.C.L. 1970, Volume 13, pp. 499-500.
2. Sri Aurobindo, B.C.L. 1971, Volume 13, pp. 605

a community. Compatibility and not uniformity is the law of collective harmony. The roles of the male and female, the different types of individuals in a community are not identical but diverse and therefore complementary. Thus Sri Aurobindo proposes an educational system in which details must be planned according to individual differences. This is particularly true about the women's education, education of backward classes and the education of below normal, abnormal and supernormal children.

3. Evolution: The edifice of Sri Aurobindo's philosophy is based upon his theory of evolution. It stands and falls with the truth of evolution. Evolution, however, has been felt and realised by almost all the thinkers of our age. Therefore, Sri Aurobindo aims at the evolution of the individual, nation and humanity through education. This evolution will be continued as spiral. It is hence that Sri Aurobindo aims at nothing less than supramental education. Evolution involves not only growth but also transformation, not only adjustment but a more intimate harmony. In the words of N.C. Dowsett, Sri Aurobindo's education aims, "To educate the true individual potential within each student, to help him to manifest that within him which is uniquely his, so he may find that as a perfection to be offered to life as his individual contribution to a collective perfection which is the evolving spirit of man and the true heritage to which he aspires".[1] This evolution can be achieved by man's opening and uniting with the universal divine. In other words this requires divine perfection.

4. Humanisation: Education, according to Sri Aurobindo, as according to Vivekananda, aims at man-making. The individual and the nation have to grow as members of one humanity Sri Aurobindo's system of national education ultimately aims at evolution of humanity. Describing the aim of Sri Aurobindo's international university at Pondicherry. The Mother declared, "It is in answer to this pressing need that Sri Aurobindo conceived the scheme of his international university, so that the elite of humanity may be made ready who would be able to work for the progressive unification of the race and who at the same time would be prepared to embody the new force descending upon earth to transform it".[2]

---

1. Dowsett, N.C., *Psychology for Future Education*, Aurobindo Ashram Pondicherry (1977), p. 9.
2. *Ibid.*, pp. 25-26.

5. Harmony of the individual and collectivity: While most of the thinkers in social-political field have either laid emphasis upon the individual or the collectivity, Sri Aurobindo aims at realisation of harmony between individuals and also between nations. His scheme of education therefore is truly international. It is not only for India but also for the world. Explaining this ideal of Sri Aurobindo's scheme, The Mother said, "For all world organisation, to be real and to be able to live, must be based upon mutual respect and understanding between nation and nation as well as between individual and individual. It is only in the collective order and organisation, in a collaboration based upon mutual goodwill that lies the possibility of man being lifted out of the painful chaos where he is now. It is with this aim and in this spirit that all human problems will be studied at the university centre; and their solution will be given in the light of the supramental knowledge which Sri Aurobindo has revealed in his waitings".[1]

6. Building the innate powers: The central aim of education according to Sri Aurobindo is, "The building of the powers of the human mind and spirit—the evoking of knowledge and will and of the power to use knowledge, character, culture that at least if not more".[2] The child is born with certain innate powers of the body, the vital, the mind and the spirit. The aim of the school and the teacher is to develop these powers to their perfection. For this a programme of sense training, body building, character formation, development of logical and other mental faculties, religious education and finally a training in integral yoga is necessary. Moral development and aesthetic development should go side by side.

7. Cultivation of values: The present crisis of man is due to the chaos of values. Old values have been challenged while new values have not firmly taken their place. In his social philosophy Sri Aurobindo has particulary discussed this problem.[3] The values to be cultivated should be physical, mental as well as spiritual. Character formation very much depends on value The supreme value in Sri Aurobindo's thought is harmony. Other values are:

1. *Ibid.*, p. 28.
2. Sri Aurobindo, B.C.L., 1972, Volume, 17, p. 194.
3. Sharma, R.N., *Social Philosophy of Sri Aurobindo*, 1981, Vineet Publications, Meerut, Chapt. I.

spirituality, divinity, evolution, ascent, transformation, etc. All these must be cherished and developed. But the most important value required for all growth is sincerity. Once that is developed, the rest follows. Right emotions and Sanskars, Swabhav and nature are the foundation of Sri Aurobindo's scheme of education. Sri Aurobindo not only aims at moral status but also going beyond it, rising above virtue and vice. This is the supramental status aimed at both by the individual and collectivity in Sri Aurobindo's thought.

The Educational Model

While Sri Aurobindo outlined a national system of education, a model to realise his scheme was developed by The Mother in the form of Sri Aurobindo international university at Pondicherry.[1] It was developed as a new centre of education to experiment for the realisation of the aims outlined by Sri Aurobindo. The curriculum, the teaching methods, the system of education and all the other details were formed with this central aim. The fundamental principle underlying the model was freedom since freedom is the only essential spiritual principle working any where. As has been already pointed out, this ideal control of education not only aimed at revelation of Sri Aurobindo's aim in India but also in humanity. All the aims of education outlined earlier were practised here. Children were admitted from a very early age. They gathered from all the parts of the country as well as from different countries in the world to make it a true representative of world cultures. The natural scenery, dress, games, sports, industries, food, art, etc., were developed on the principle of unity and diversity. An effort was made to realise a cultural synthesis. Students of different nations were placed at different places with their own groups so that while they may develop international culture, no rigid time-table, classes, curriculum, teaching method or system of evaluation and examination was insisted. This was left upon individual choice of the educand himself.

The idea was to give full freedom to the individual growth of the educand. The experiment fared very well but did not grow elsewhere due to obvious difficulties in such experiments. However, it is undoubtedly a model for a new system of education

1. Sri Aurobindo, B.C.L., 1972, Volume, 17.

which may be hoped to develop in India and also in parts of the world.[1]

THE SCHOOL

The ultimate ideal of the school is man-making. It prepares the educand to work first as a human being and then as a member of a nation and finally as an individual. The circles of moral responsibility and loyalties proceed from wider to narrower and not vice-versa. The man has to develop first as a human being then as a citizen and finally as an individual. Most of the present confusion of values is due to an inversion of this order.[2]

Sri Aurobindo believes in three ultimate principles, individuality, commonality and essentiality. These, in other words, are the educand, the society and the humanity. Integral evolution, according to him, must include evolution of all these three elements. Thus the individuality and commonality should develop together. This is the purpose of the school. The school should treat all children as equal and provide sufficient scope for the development of their individual variations without insisting upon similarities. In his lecture at Baroda College Sri Aurobindo observed that the colleges and universities should educate through their academic as well as social activities.[3]Thus the college should have its bearing upon the community around it.[4] The school cannot be isolated from society. It cannot give total education in isolation. Its teachings have to be practised in the society outside it. The university merely gives some materials to the educand which he may use.

In the integral school four types of rooms are required to carry on various activities: 1. Rooms of silence, 2. Rooms of collaboration, 3. Rooms of consultation, 4. Lecture rooms. Thus the school will develop different types of activities such as silence, collaboration, consultation and lectures. It will provide play, activity, discovery, innovation and finally development of the powers of the body, mind and spirit of the educand. In brief, the integral school will provide opportunities for integral development.

---

1. Sri Aurobindo, B.C.L., 1972, Volume III, p. 131.
2. Ibid., p. 132.
3. Joshi, Kirit, *Nav Chetana*, Mothers International School (1977), pp. 5-7.
4. *Sri Aurobindo and The Mother On Education*, Part II, pp. 4-5.

THE TEACHER

Like the ancient Indian system of education, Sri Aurobindo has assigned a very important place to the teacher. He has however not made him central as in the ancient Indian scheme. The central place, as in the Western systems of education, has been occupied by the educand. His philosophy of education, therefore, is paidocentric. However, the teacher remains the philosopher and the guide. The Guru does not have absolute authority. He aims at turning the disciple's eye towards the beacon light of his own Godhead. In fact, the real teacher is within the educand. He is the God. He is the ultimate guide and yet the teacher plays an important role in arousing the educand towards God within. He has not to impose his opinions or demand passive surrender from the educand. He has to create an atmosphere so that the educand may grow freely. Sri Aurobindo accepts the role of a gardener in the teacher as maintained by many Western educational philosophers. The teacher acts as an aid, a means and a channel. His relationship with the educand is very close. In the ancient Indian tradition, Sri Aurobindo emphasises an inner relationship between the educator and the educand. For this the teacher should develop certain innate qualities.

Describing as to who is a teacher, The Mother has laid down the following qualifications, "Teachers who do not possess a perfect calm, an unfailing endurance, an unshakeable quietness who are full of self-conceit will reach nowhere.

One must be a saint and a hero to become a good teacher.

One must be a great yogi to become a good teacher.

One must have the perfect attitude in order to be able to exact from one's pupils a perfect attitude.

You cannot ask of a person what you do not do yourself. It is a rule.

You must then look within you at the difference between what is and what should be, and this difference will give you the measure of your failure in the class.[1]

In brief, the teacher should be an integral yogi. He should be able to eliminate his ego, master his mind, develop an insight into human nature and to progress in impersonalisation. He should be absolutely disciplined and having an integrated personality.

1. *Ibid.*, p. 7.

The most important thing in a teacher is not the knowledge but the attitude. An intellectual excellence is not sufficient without a development of other aspects of personality. The teacher should have the capacity to project himself to the educand so that he may have an understanding of the needs of the educand. The schools aim not only on the progress of the educand but also of the educator. In the words of the Mother, "The school must be an occasion of progress for the teacher as well as for the student. Each must have the freedom to develop himself freely. One never applies a method well unless one has discovered it oneself."[1] In practice the central trait of the teacher is the inner calm. He should exercise influence not by scolding but by moral control. In the words of the Mother, "I must tell you that if a professor wants to be respected, he must be respectable."[2]

Personality Traits of the Teacher

In order to fulfil his role, the teacher should take it seriously and honestly. He should develop his personality more than the ordinary man so that he may be able to influence others. He should be a representative of divine on earth. He should be in close touch with the divine consciousness. He should be a representative of the supreme knowledge, the supreme truth and the supreme law. Then alone his influence will work. The Mother has prescribed the following personality traits for a true teacher:

1. Complete self-control not only to the extent of not showing any anger, but remaining absolutely quiet and undisturbed under all circumstances.
2. In the matter of self-confidence, he must also have the sense of the relativity of his importance.

Above all, he must have the knowledge that the teacher himself must always progress if he wants his students to progress, must not remain satisfied either with what he is or with what he knows.

3. Must not have any sense of essential superiority over his students nor preference of attachment whatsoever for one or another.

1. *Ibid.*, p. 8-9.
2. *Ibid.*, p. 8.

4. Must know that all are equal spiritually and instead of mere tolerance must have a global comprehension or understanding.
5. "The business of both parent and teacher is to enable and to help the child to educate himself to develop his own intellectual, moral, aesthetic and practical capacities and to grow freely as an organic being, not to be kneaded and pressured into form like an inert plastic material."[1]

THE CURRICULUM

As has been already pointed out, the essential principle of Sri Aurobindo's philosophy of education is freedom. Unity is never demanded at the cost of diversity. On the other hand, diversity creates a rich unity. Therefore, no rigid scheme of curriculum has been prescribed. However, hints are scattered in Sri Aurobindo's works about different criteria of curriculum. The earliest permissible age for starting regular study according to Sri Aurobindo is seven or eight years. At this age the child is sufficiently grown up to take up regular study. The proper medium for early education of the child is the mother tongue. It is only after the mother tongue that the child can learn other languages. As has been already pointed out, the following criteria for planning curriculum are found in Sri Aurobindo's writings:

1. Human nature: The curriculum should aim at developing whatever is already given in seed form in the child. Education can only lead to the perfection of the instruments which are already present in the educand. Nothing can be taught or imposed from outside. In the words of The Mother, "Fundamentally the only thing you must do assiduously is to teach them to know themselves, and to choose their own destiny, the way they want to follow". [2]

2. Individual differences: The curriculum should be planned according to individual differences. The mind has to be consulted in its own growth. The aim of the teacher is to help the growing soul in drawing out his best and to make it perfect for a noble use.[3]

---

1. *Ibid.*, p. 8.
2. *Ibid.*, p. 1.
3. Sri Aurobindo, B.C.L., 1972, Volume, 17, p. 205.

3. From near to the far: Another principle governing the planning of curriculum is to proceed from near to the far, from that which is to that which shall be.[1]

4. Modern and uptodate: Sri Aurobindo was not a reactionary or a conservative. He was a modern thinker with a love for modernity and uptodate knowledge. Therefore, he prescribed that the education must be uptodate in form and substance and modern in life and spirit.[2]

5. Universal knowledge: The curriculum should include whatever is universally true. That is the basis of all scientific knowledge and philosophy. Truth and knowledge are one and not confined to any country Therefore, according to Sri Aurobindo, education should be universal without any nationality or borders.[3]

6. Successive teaching: Sri Aurobindo disagrees with some educationists who wish to introduce every subject simultaneously to the child. He prescribes that the subjects should be taught successively. New subjects should be introduced after the earlier are mastered. Thus few subjects should be taught at a time.

7. Co-curricular activities: The school should provide not only academic but also co-curricular activities.

8. Five-fold curriculum: As has been already pointed out, integral education is five-fold. It includes the physical, the vital, the mental, the psychic and the spiritual education. Therefore, the curriculum must be five-fold according to these five types of education. Of these the education of the mind involves the most detailed curriculum. It requires different, curriculum for the development of the different powers of the mind such as observation, memory, judgment, comparison, contrast, analogy, reasoning and imagination, etc. Sense training requires curriculum involving all the five senses.

9. Multisidedness: Integral education is multisided. It aims at allround growth. Therefore its curriculum involves music, poetry, art, painting and sculpture, besides the academic subjects. These are necessary for the aesthetic development of the child. These aim at contemplation and understanding of beauty and just arrangement of the tastes, habits and character

---

1. *Ibid.*
2. *Ibid.*, p. 194.
3. *Ibid.*, p. 193.

of the educand. According to Sri Aurobindo, in contrast to many other educationists music, art and poetry purity, control, deepen and harmonise the movements of the soul.[1] In his work entitled *The National Value of Art*, Sri Aurobindo points out three uses of art. Firstly, it is purely aesthetic, secondly, it is intellectual and educative and thirdly, it is spiritual. The aesthetic development purifies conduct and disciplines the animal instincts and lower feelings of the heart. The artistic sense helps in the formation of morals and purification of the emotion.[2] Thus art has both intellectual and spiritual value. It is subtle and delicate and makes the mind subtle and delicate.[3]

10. Provision for the genius: The curriculum must provide for the genius. According to Sri Aurobindo, "What we call genius is part of the development of the human range of being and its achievements especially in things of the mind and their will can cany us half way to the divine".[4] The curriculum should cater for the perfection of the different powers of the genius.

11. Moral and religious education: Curriculum for moral education should aim at refining the emotions and forming the proper habits and associations. Religious teaching like moral teaching does not involve so much of curriculum as teaching by example and provision of right atmosphere. In the words of Sri Aurobindo, "Whether distinct teaching in any form of religion is imparted or not the essence of religion, to live for God, for humanity, for country, for others and for oneself must be made the ideal in every school".[5]

Thus the aim of the curriculum according to Sri Aurobindo, is the actualisation of the potentialities of the educand. The material is the basis and spiritual is the summit of education. The cuniculum gradually becomes more and more abstract leading to the realisation of higher experiences. Same curriculum may be followed by male and female. The schools may be co-educational. Sufficient emphasis should be laid upon aesthetic, moral and religious teaching. The curriculum should not be fixed but flexible and evolutionary. A variety of choice and opportunities must be

---

1. Sri Aurobindo, B.C.L., 1972, Volume 17, pp. 244-46.
2. *Ibid.*, pp. 24-42.
3. *Ibid.*, p. 245.
4. *Ibid.*, pp. 207-8.
5. Sri Aurobindo, 1972, Volume 17, p. 212.

prescribed for maintaining the freedom of growth. The integral curriculum should find a due place for every subject and every discipline.

A TENTATIVE EDUCATIONAL PLAN

Norman C. Dowsett has presented the following tentative educational plan developed by International Centre of Education, Pondicherry, based upon educational philosophy of Sri Aurobindo.[1]

1. The Play school (1-3 years)
   Provision of love, security, wonder, discovery and adventure.
2. Pre-School discipline of the physical mind (3-5 years)
   a. order
   b. activities, physical exercises and games.
3. Prime-School of fulfilment of the vital mind (5-7½ yrs)
   a. body awareness—discipline of the physical mind to continue.
   b. fulfilment of vital energies—The vital should be fulfilled through art, drawing, painting, sculpture dance, drama, music, etc.
4. High school of the freedom of the mental mind I phase (7½-10½ years) use of the instruments of knowledge.
5. High school of the freedom of the mental mind II phase (10½-14 years) integration of the progressive series of creative energies.
6. Graduation school of psychic education (14-17): years appreciation of individuality, progressive understanding of his inner potential and his contribution to the group, society, nation and the world.
7. College of spiritual education (17-21 years) spiritual realisation, integration of all that has been achieved.

THE IDEAL CHILD

Sri Aurobindo's system of education is paidocentric. It aims at the creation of ideal children. The ideal children are absolutely sincere and constantly progressive. They are forbidden fighting

1. Dowsett, N.C., *Psychology for Future Education*, Aurobindo Ashram, Pondicherry (1977), pp. 218-29.

any where. They are always truthful. The Mother has given the following description of an ideal child.[1]

1. Good-tempered: He does not become angry when things seem to go against him or decisions are not in his favour.

2. Game: Whatever he does it to the best of his capacity and keeps on doing in the face of almost certain failure. He always thinks straight and acts straight.

3. Truthful: He never fears to say the truth whatever may be the consequences.

4. Patient: He does not get disheartened if he has to wait a long time to see the results of his effort.

5. Enduring: He never slackens his effort however long it has to last.

6. Poised: He keeps equanimity in success as well as in failure.

7. Courageous: He always goes on fighting for the final victory though he may meet with many defeats.

8. Cheerful: He knows how to smile and keep a happy heart in all circumstances.

9. Modest: He does not become conceited over his success, neither does he feel himself superior to his comrades.

10. Generous: He appreciates the merits of others and is always ready to help another to succeed.

11. Courteous: On the field he does not jeer at errors, he does not cheer at the opponent's defeat; he treates them as guests, not enemies. In school he is considerate to the authorities, the fellow students, and the teachers. In life he is respectful to others; he treats them as he would be treated.

12. Obedient: On the field he observes the regulations. In life he respects the rules which help to promote harmony.

13. Fair: On the field he competes in a clean, hardfought but friendly way; he helps an injured opponent. In school he does not waste his time nor that of the teachers. He is always honest. In life he sees impartially both sides of a question.

Thus Sri Aurobindo's integral education gives highest place to the children. They are considered as divine force, the leaders of the future gnostic race on the earth. All the hopes for man's future

1. *Sri Aurobindo and The Mother on Education,* Part II, pp. 28-29.

lie upon the proper development of the younger generation. There is no gap between the teacher, the Guru and the children. Integral education considers the inner relationship and rapport as the first condition of all education. It is in this spirit that the Mother said to the children of the Ashram, "My children, we are united towards the same goal and the same accomplishment for a work unique and new, that the divine Grace has given us to accomplish. I hope that more and more you will understand the exceptional importance of this work and that you will sense in yourself the sublime joy that the accomplishment will give you. The divine force is with you, feel its presence more and more and be very careful never to betray it. Feel, wish, act, that you may be new beings for the realisation of a new world and for this my blessings shall be always with you".[1]

Thus the children are highly respected. The job of the teacher is not utilitarian or for earning his bread but for man-making. It is in the spirit of offering of one's action to God that the teachers can create the spirit of sacrifice in the children. Sri Aurobindo's integral education is based upon faith in human nature. As against the explanation of human nature offered by most of the Western thinkers including Hobbes, Sri Aurobindo, like many other religious savants, considers man as divine. It was in this spirit that the Mother said to the children of the Ashram, "Be courageous, enduring, vigilant; above all be sincere, with perfect honesty. Then you will be able to face all difficulties. And victory will be yours" [2]

TEACHING METHODS

Thus the teaching methods in integral education of Sri Aurobindo are based on the one hand on faith in the inner goodness and evolutionary nature of the educand and on the other hand on the psychological principles involved in teaching. Sri Aurobindo's explanations and suggestions are everywhere psychological. Without going into the details he has always kept his eye focussed on the tendencies working within him. Therefore his suggestions are very valuable.

1. *Ibid.*, Part III, p. 22.
2. *Ibid.*, p. 23.

Teaching Children

Sri Aurobindo and The Mother gave particular attention to the methods of teaching children. In this connection the following suggestions are offered:[1]

1. The teachers should have sufficient documentation of what they know. They should be able to answer all questions.
2. They should have at least the knowledge if not the experience of true intellectual and intuitive attitude. This knowledge can be attained through mental silence.
3. He is the best teacher who has the capacity and not only knowledge of the different fields of evolution.
4. Thus the professors must be sincere in discipline and experience. They should not be propagandists.
5. To start with, "The children, as soon as they have the capacity to think (it begins at 7 years but towards 14 years it is very clear) should be given small indications at 7 and a complete explanation at 14, of how to do it, and that it is the unique method to enter into relation with the profounds, that all the rest is a mental approximation, more or less inapt of something that can be known directly".[2]

Teaching very Small Children

About the teaching of very small children, The Mother has laid down the following principles for the teachers:[3]

Never to deceive oneself.

Never to be angry.

Always to be understanding.

Never try to impose on them.

Never scold but always try to understand. With Rousseau Sri Aurobindo believes that the child is naturally good but gradually corrupted by bad environment. In an adverse environment the child looses all contact with the self in him. Therefore, the Mother has insisted that the most necessary thing to be taught to the child is to follow the inner psychic consciousness. As she said, "That is why I insist on that and I say that from the very earliest age children must be taught that there is a reality within themselves,

1. *Ibid.*, pp. 19-21.
2. *Ibid.*, p. 20.
3. *Ibid.*, p. 21.

within the earth, within the universe and that he himself, the earth and the universe, exist only as a function of this truth and if it did not exist, he would not last, even the short time he lasts and that everything would dissolve as soon as it is created.[1]

This, however, does not require philosophical explanations. The child is not prepared for mental understanding of the self. He should be made to realise the inner consciousness. His education, therefore, should be by projects and playway methods. The child responds to the psychic vibrations. He is most impressed by affection and feelings. Therefore, integral education rules out all harsh treatment, scolding or being angry towards the children. One must have sufficient patience with them. The habits for cleanliness and hygiene should start very early. This, however, does not require creating fear of illness in the child. The Mother has warned, "Fear is the worst incentive to education and the surest way of attracting what is feared".[2]- This warning is timely not only for early education but for secondary and university education in our country.

How to Teach

Sri Aurobindo, in his exposition of teaching methods, keeps his eye focussed on the truth alone. He is neither prejudiced in favour nor against the ancient Indian teaching methods or the Western ways of teaching. As he said, "The past hangs about our necks with all its prejudices and errors and will not leave us; it enters into our most radical attempts to return to the guidance of the all-wise Mother. We must have the courage to take up clearer knowledge and apply it fearlessly in the interests of posterity".[3]

Successive Teaching

Accepting that every child has multiple tendencies and abilities requiring teaching of various subjects, Sri Aurobindo favours successive teaching as against simultaneous introduction of so many subjects in early education. Among the different subjects to be taught to the child, the basic subjects should be introduced first so that a sound foundation for education is made. As Sri Aurobindo points out, "The old system was to teach one or two subjects well

1. *Ibid.*, p. 23.
2. *Ibid.*, p. 26.
3. *Ibid.*, p. 11.

and thoroughly and then proceed to others and certainly it was a more rational system than the modern. If it did not impart so much varied information, it built up a deeper, nobler and more real culture".[1] Thus different subjects should be studied one by one. The same principle is applicable to the teaching of text-books. Each chapter should be studied thoroughly and in succession. In the words of The Mother, "One should leave a chapter when it has been fully grasped then only take up the next one and so on. If a chapter is finished, it is finished: and if it is not finished it is not finished".[2] The child's education should start at the age of 7 or 8 for, according to Sri Aurobindo, "That is the earliest permissible age for the commencement of any regular kind of study".[3] At this age the child is capable of concentration and interest. Therefore, the first thing to be created in the child is interest in the subject.

Education Through Practical Experience

Thus, like all other modern educators, Sri Aurobindo pleads for introduction of different subjects to the child through practical experience. First of all he should acquire mastery of the mother tongue as the medium of the education, because that is the required sound basis for regular instruction. Elaborating the needs of practical foundation of child's education, Sri Aurobindo gives valuable suggestions for the teaching of different subjects appealing to the imagination, the dramatic faculty, love for the narrative, hero worship, urge to enquiry and other natural characteristics of the child. To quote his advise, "Almost every child has an imagination, an instinct for words, a dramatic faculty, a wealth of idea and fancy. These should be interested in the literature and history of the nation. Instead of stupid and dry spelling and reading books, looked on as a dreary and ungrateful task, he should be introduced by rapidly progressive stages to the most interesting parts of his own literature and the life around him and behind him, and they should be put before him in such a way as to attract and appeal to the qualities of which I have spoken. All other study at this period should be devoted to the perfection of the mental functions and the moral character. A foundation should be laid at this time for the study of history, science, philosophy,

1. Sri Aurobindo, B.C.L., 1972, Volume 17, p. 213.
2. *Sri Aurobindo and The Mother on Education*, Part II p. 17.
3. *Ibid.*

but not in an obtrusive and formal manner. Every child is a lover of interesting narrative, a hero-worshipper and a patriot. Appeal to these qualities in him and through them let him master without knowing it the living and human parts of his nations's history. Every child is an inquirer, an investigator, analyser, a merciless anatomist. Appeal to those qualities in him and let him acquire without knowing it, the necessary fundamental knowledge of the scientist. Every child has an insatiable intellectual curiosity and turn for metaphysical inquiry. Use it to draw him on slowly to an understanding of the world and himself. Every child has the gift of imitation and a touch of imaginative power. Use it to give him the ground work of the faculty of the artist".[1]

Three Principles of Teaching

Now, before trying to understand methods of teaching of different instruments of the educand one should remember the following three principles of teaching laid down by Sri Aurobindo:

1. The first principle is that nothing can be taught.
2. The second principle is that the mind should be constantly consulted in its growth.
3. The third principle is to work from the near to the far, from that which is to that which shall be.[2]

Integral Teaching

Integral teaching involves training of all the aspects of the educand's mind and personality. Starting with sense training it develops the memory and judgement, the observation and comparison, analogy, reasoning, imagination, language, grammar and meaning of the logical faculty, etc. All these characteristics are present in every child. In the words of Sri Aurobindo, "Every child is an inquirer, an investigator, analyser, a merciless anatomist".[3] The first thing to do is to arouse the curiosity, imagination and natural interest of the child so that he may spontaneously enquire, understand and learn. As Sri Aurobindo advises the teachers, "The first work is to interest the child in life, work and knowledge, to develop his instruments of knowledge with the utmost thoroughness, to give him mastery of the medium he must

1. *Ibid.*, pp. 11-12.
2. Sri Aurobindo, B.C.L., 1972, Volume, 17, p. 204.
3. *Ibid.*, p. 215.

use. Afterwards the rapidity with which he will learn will make up for any delay in taking up regular studies and it will be found that... he will learn many things thoroughly well".[1]

Observation

Sense training starts with observation. The child has a natural urge to observe the nature around. It is hence that most of the educationists have advised that early education should start with child's observation of nature under the guidance of the teacher. Explaining this method of teaching Sri Aurobindo said, "We may take the instance of a flower. Instead of looking casually at it and getting a casual impression of scent, form and colour, he should be encouraged to know the flower to fix in his mind the exact shade, the precise intensity of the scent, the beauty of curve and design in the form. His touch should assure itself of the texture and its peculiarities. Next, the flower should be taken to pieces and its structure examined with the same carefulness of observation. All this should be done not as a task, but as an object by skillfully arranged questions suited to the learner which will draw him on to observe and investigate one thing after the other until he has almost unconsciously mastered the whole".[2]

The observation is not confined to the flowers and leaves. The child will also learn by the observation of stars, earth, stones, insects, animals and things made by human beings. The example of observation given above is particularly useful in the teaching of botany. To quote Sri Aurobindo, "The observation and comparison of flowers, leaves, plants, trees will lay the foundations of botanical knowledge without loading the mind with names and that dry set acquisition of information which is the beginning of cramming and detested by the healthy human mind when it is fresh from nature and unspoiled by unnatural habits".[3] Elaborating further use of observation method of teaching other subjects, Sri Aurobindo said, "In the same way by the observation of the stars, astronomy, by the observation of earth, stones, etc., geology, by the observation of insects and animals, entomology and zoology may be founded. A little later chemistry may be started by interesting observation of experiments without any

1. *Ibid.*
2. *Sri Aurobindo and The Mother on Education*, Part II, p. 13.
3. *Ibid.*, p. 14.

formal teaching or heaping on the mind of formulas and book knowledge" [1]

Training of Memory and Judgement

As in the case of sense training so also in the case of training of the mind Sri Aurobindo wants to make them spontaneous and unconscious. He is against all mechanical, burdensome and unintelligent way of memory training. He is against any use of rote memory. Memory training should involve nothing of similarities and differences in things observed. According to Sri Aurobindo, "A similar but different flower should be put in the hands and he should be encouraged to note it with the same care, but with the avowed object of noting the similarities and differences. By this practice daily repeated the memory will naturally be trained"[2]. This in its turn will train the faculty of judgement. To quote Sri Aurobindo again, "At every step the boy will have to decide what is the right idea, measurement, appreciation of colour, sound, scent, etc., and what is the wrong. Often the judgments and distinctions made will have to be exceedingly subtle and delicate. At first many errors will be made, but the learner should be taught to trust his judgement without being attached to its results. It will be found that the judgment will soon begin to respond to the calls made on it, clear itself of all errors and begin to judge correctly and minutely. The best way is to accustom the boy to compare his judgments with those of others. When he is wrong, it should at first be pointed out to him how far he was right and why he went wrong; afterwards he should be encouraged to note these things for himself. Every time he is right, his attention should be prominently and encouragingly called to it so that he may get confidence".[3] The training of memory and judgement is the basis of every scientific teaching. In the opinion of Sri Aurobindo, "There is no scientific subject the perfect and natural mastery of which cannot be prepared in early childhood by this training of the faculties to observe, compare, remember and judge various classes".[4] Judgement gives the ability to choose between right and wrong. It is therefore a prelude to every decision about values.

1. *Ibid.*, p.
2. *Ibid.*, p. 14.
3. *Ibid.*, p. 15.
4. Sri Aurobindo. B.C.L., 1972, Volume, XVII, p. 223.

Training of Logical Faculty

Training of judgement very much depends upon the training of logical faculty. According to Sri Aurobindo, training of logical reasoning requires the following three elements:[1]

1. the correctness of the facts,
2. the completeness as well the accuracy of the data,
3. the elimination of other possible or impossible conclusions from the same facts.

The young child should be trained to take interest in drawing inferences from the facts. For this purpose he should proceed, "From the example to the rule and from the accumulating harmony of rules to the formal science of the subject"[2] The reasoning should proceed from concrete to abstract, since this is the law of training of mental faculties, the sound should be acknowledged before the sense. Explaining his principle in this connection Sri Aurobindo has remarked, "The true knowledge takes its base on things, arthas, and only when it has mastered the thing, proceeds to formalise its information".[3]

Training of Imagination

Several subjects including literature, particularly, require a training of imagination. This is the first requirement of any excellence in any creative art. As Sri Aurobindo has given an important place to art and literature in his plan of education, he insists upon the child's training in imagination. According to him, "This is a most important and indispensable instrument".[4] For the training of imagination Sri Aurobindo recommends, "It may be divided into three functions, the forming of mental images, the power of creating thoughts, images and imitations or new combinations of existing thoughts and images, the appreciation of the soul in things, beauty, charm, greatness, hidden suggestiveness, the emotion and spiritual life that pervades the world".[5]

Training of Language

Explaining his principle for training of language, Sri Aurobindo finds out that first the child should know the things and then the

---

1. *Ibid.*, p. 226
2. *Ibid.*, pp. 226-21.
3. *Sri Aurobindo and The Mother on Education,* Part II, p, 16.
4. *Ibid.*
5. *Ibid.*

ideas. He laments that most of the dealings with language show an absence of fine sense of words. He suggests, "The mind should be accustomed first to notice the word thoroughly, its form, sound and sense; then to compare the form with other similar forms in the points of similarity and difference, thus forming the foundation of the grammatical sense; then to distinguish between the fine shades of sense of similar words and the formation and rhythm of different sentences, thus forming the foundation of the literary and the syntactical faculties".[1] All this should be done informally. One should avoid set rules of teaching and memorising. Sri Aurobindo is everywhere against mechanical processes. The teaching should first arouse the interest of the child and then depend upon spontaneous use of his abilities. The child should be allowed absolute freedom in his progress.

Free Progress System

The followers of Sri Aurobindo have developed a free progress system of education, whose salient features are as follows:[2]

1. The structure is oriented towards individual needs, interests and abilities.
2. The aspiration, experience of freedom, self-education and experimentation relating inner needs with the curricular provisions, discovering the higher lines of life and the art to encompass.
3. Each student is free to study any subject he chooses at any given time under a sympathetic guidance.
4. Promotion of individual endeavour.
5. Weekly announcement of time-table and lectures to be delivered.
6. Promotion of discussion between teachers and taught and between taught and taught.
7. Projects are announced in each subject and the students select according to their choice.

No Set Distinction

In his system of education, Sri Aurobindo does not make any distinction on the basis of sex. The education for man and woman

---

1. *Ibid.*
2. Joshi Kirit, *Nav Chetna,* Mothers International School, New Delhi (1977), pp. 5-7.

should be similar in all respect. Clarifying this rejection of sex distinctions in education, The Mother said, "What we claim is this, that in similar conditions, with the same education and the same possibilities, there is no reason to make a categorical distinction, final and imperative between what we call men and women. For us human beings are the expression of a single soul".[1] In his interpretation of his Indian social system Sri Aurobindo laid emphasis upon equality of sexes. He lamented that later on the women were subjugated to men leading to degeneration of society. He proposes that the women should be everywhere treated as equals to men. He is against Indian psychological dictum that male and female should avoid each other's company. He, on the other hand, maintains,"There is no impossibility of friendship between man and woman pure of this element (sex), such friendships can exist and have always existed. All that is needed is that the lower vital should not look in it through the back door or be permitted to enter".[2] Therefore, no distinctions are made between boys and girls in Mother's International School or Sri Aurobindo International University at Pondicherry. The most unique feature of the education at these two institutions is the prescription of physical exercises both for boys and girls. Clarifying this policy the Mother said, "In all cases, as well as for boys as for girls, the exercises must be graded according to the strength and capacity of each one. If a weak student tries at once to do hard and heavy exercises, he may suffer for his foolishness. But with a wise and progressive training girls as well as boys can participate in all kinds of sports, increase their strength and health".[3] According to Sri Aurobindo both men and women are equally capable to evolve toward perfection to reach gnostic age.

DISCIPLINE AND FREEDOM

The Mother has rightly said, "No big creation is possible without discipline".[4] Defining discipline in terms of the highest principle Sri Aurobindo maintained that it is "to act according to a standard of truth or a rule or law of action or in obedience to a superior authority or the highest principle discovered by the reason or

1. *Sri Aurobindo and The Mother on Women*, 1978, p. 17.
2. Sri Aurobindo, B.C.L., 1970, Volume 23, p. 817.
3. *On Women*, 1978, p. 58.
4. *Sri Aurobindo and The Mother on Education*, Part II, p. 26.

intelligent will".[1] Thus discipline is a controlled life. The physical, the vital and the mental sources are guided by spirituality. It is against unbridled indulgence in fancies, impulses and desires. It is obedience of the inner sense. Partly, it is also obedience of authority.

Kinds of Discipline

Discipline, according to Sri Aurobindo,as: Individual discipline, Group discipline and finally Discipline towards the Divine. These distinctions have been made on the basis of the authority functioning in imposition of discipline. Individual discipline is imposed by the individual himself. Group discipline is imposed by the group or the majority or the leader in it. Discipline towards the Divine means, rigorous perusal of the dictates of the Divine. However, these three types of discipline are essentially the same since underlying the individual, group and the universe there is only one Divine principle. Sri Aurobindo maintains that the three aspects of reality, *viz.*, individuality, commonality and essentiality are in fact one.

Disciplinary Measures

The best way to impose discipline, according to Sri Aurobindo is the atmosphere and the example by the teacher. The following measures have been recommended by Sri Aurobindo and the Mother to inculcate discipline among the students:

1. Generally speaking, the discipline should start at the age of twelve.
2. The most important measure is the example of the teacher. The teacher should be punctual, properly dressed, calm, methodical, orderly, sympathetic and courteous. He should himself present high examples of sincerity, honesty, straightforwardness, courage, distinterestedness, unselfishness, patience, endurance, perseverance, peace and self control. He should first of all train his own emotions and morals. He should have a respect of the child. Nothing should be imposed from outside but suggested by examples. Examples are the best for the personal guidance and to exercise influence upon the educands. In the words of the Mother, "It is through example that education becomes

1. Sri Aurobindo, B.C.L., 1970. Volume 23, p. 862.

effective. To say good words, give wise advice to a child has very little effect, if one does not show by one's living example the truth of what one teaches".[1]

The vibrations between the teacher and the taught should be favourable, there should be no use of force in discipline. According to The Mother, before the age of seven years the child is not conscious of himself and does not know why and how to do things. During this period he should be trained to acquire traits of a human being. From the age of seven years to fourteen years of age, the child should be taught to choose what he wishes to be. At 14, he should be clear at what he wants to do. After 14 years of age he should be left independent to pursue his course. He may be only advised now and then.

There can be no definite rules for the guidance of the students in the process of discipline. Sri Aurobindo recommends emphasis upon individual difference without any hammering of the child. He believes that, "Every one has in him something divine, something his own, a chance of perfection and strength in however small a sphere which God offers him to take or refuse. The task is to find it, develop it and use it".[2]

Finally, discipline is ultimately spiritual This requires psychic realisation. Sri Aurobindo suggests the following two ways for converting mental seeking into living spiritual experience".[3]

1. The concentration of the conciousness within especially in the main centres—in the heart (the cardiac centre in the middle of the chest) and the head.
2. To accord the nature—physical, vital and mental with the inner realisation so that one may not be divided into two discordant parts.

Among the several ways to accord the nature with the inner realisation, the following two have been particularly emphasised by Sri Aurobindo:

1. To offer all the activities to the divine and call for the inner guidance—the inward soul is being opened, the psychic being comes for help, gradually the imperfections are being removed and the physical consciousness is being reshaped.

---

1. *Sri Aurobindo and the Mother on Education*, Part II, p. 27.
2. Sri Aurobindo, B.C.L., 1972, Volume, 17, p. 204.
3. *Ibid.*, Volume 23, pp. 517-19.

2. To stand back detached from the movements of the physical, vital and mental being—becoming aware of the inner opening of body, life and mind in the psychic entity.

Discipline and Freedom

From the above discussion, it is clear that according to Sri Aurobindo, freedom is the real discipline. This, however, is only spiritual freedom. In the realm of Spirit there is no chasm between discipline and freedom. Each one has to grow and expand according to his own principle. The inner voice in every educand is in fact the divine principle in him. Thus realisation of freedom is God realisation. As order is the prelude to liberty, similarly discipline is a precondition for realisation of freedom.

Code of Conduct

This, however, does not mean that there is no code of conduct at The Mother's International School or at Sri Aurobindo's International University. As the principal guide of both these institutions the Mother has laid down code of conduct for the educands. She is against any outward limitation of the child's liberty but she insists that once the choice for joining the above mentioned institutions has been made, there is no turning aside. She is against any use of compulsion or obligation. She however insists upon taking judgement and following them. She advises the educands to arrive at rational decisions and to follow them. She maintains that the class discipline must be followed. In her own words, "But if a student has decided to follow a class, it is an absolutely elementary discipline for him to follow it, he must go to the class regularly and behave decently there: otherwise he is quite unfit to go to school".[1] She was against any illusions about the abilities of the educands. She warned, "Do not mistake liberty for licence and freedom for bad manners. The thought must be pure and the aspiration ardent".[2] She laid down the following code of behaviour for the students:

1. The good manners should be always observed.
2. Everyone should always speak the truth.
3. Truth in speech demands truth in acts too.

---

1. *Sri Aurobindo and The Mother on Education,* Part III, p. 20.
2. *Ibid.,* p. 22.

4. It is forbidden for children to fight at school, in the street, in the playground and at home. "Always and everywhere it is forbidden for children to fight among themselves, for each time one gives a blow to someone, it is to one's own soul that one gives it."[1]
5. The child should always remember:
   The necessity of an absolute sincerity.
   The certitude of Truth's final victory.
   The possibility of constant progress with the will to achieve.[2]

EVALUATION AND EXAMINATION

Rejecting the so-called mental tests, the Mother said, "I find tests an obsolete and ineffective way of knowing if the students are intelligent, willing and attentive. A silly, mechanical mind can very well answer a test if the memory is good and these are certainly not the qualities required for a man of the future".[3] She not only rejects the mental test but also suggests alternatives. "To know if a student is good, needs, if the tests are abolished, a little more inner contact and psychological knowledge for the teacher. But our teachers are expected to do yoga, so this ought not to be difficult for them."[4]

Spontaneous Evaluation

In two words, the method of evaluation in Sri Aurobindo's system of education, may be called spontaneous evaluation. This depends upon the inner contact, keen observation and impartial outlook of the evaluator. The tests of progress are not the essay type examinations. In the words of Sri Aurobindo, "We must direct our school and university examinations to the testing of these active faculties and not of the memory".[5] Criticising the prevalent system of education conducted by the British in India, Sri Aurobindo pointed out that in it the students do not achieve the real purpose of education. He was against education only for earning livelihood. According to him the students are, "To learn in order to know, to study in order to have the knowledge of the secrets of nature and of life, to educate oneself in order to increase

1. *Ibid.;* p. 27.
2. *Sri Aurobindo and the Mother on Education,* Part II, p. 22.
3. *Ibid.,* Part II, p. 30.
4. *Ibid.,* p. 31.
5. *Ibid.*

one's consciousness, to discipline oneself in order to be master of oneself, to overcome one's weakness, one's incapacity and ignorance, to prepare oneself in order to progress in life towards a goal that is nobler and vaster, more generous and more true...".[1]

To meet the above purpose, Sri Aurobindo's International Centre of Education, Pondicherry, has evolved "Free Progress System," based upon subjective evaluation by the teachers. Progress records ware to be-filled by the students while the teacher has to note their comments. Clarifying this system of evaluation, the Mother told the teachers, "At the end of the year you will give notes to the students, not based on written test-papers, but on their behaviour, their concentration, their regularity, their promptness to understand and their openness of intelligence".[2]

Our discussion of the philosophy of education, as given by Sri Aurobindo, clearly points out that this is a new experiment in education. Its philosophical foundations and psychological credibility is sound. Its success, however, requires a large band of devoted, sincere and spiritual teachers, prepared to carry on the burden of education against all odds. So long as such a band is not available it is just an experiment.

1. *Ibid.*
2. *Ibid.*

20

Concluding Remarks

In concluding our discussion of Western and Indian philosophies of education. We are summarising important identical trends with in East and West. This will help in arriving at a synthesis of Eastern and Western approaches in the field of philosophy of education.

IDEALISM

According to Adams, "Idealism in one form or other permeates the whole of the history of philosophy."[1] This is particularly true in the case of Indian philosophy of education. Explaining the idealist philosophy of education, Rusk said, "It bestows dignity and grandeur upon human life by emphasising the distinctiveness of man's nature, attributing to him powers, not possessed by animals, which issue in ideal-logical and aesthetic; it admits the existence of a Supreme Being; by its respect for human personality it provides the basis for democracy."[2]

All the notable Indian philosophers of education followed Neo-Vedanta philosophy, a contemporary version ot ancient Indian idealism. Therefore they presented a teleological explanation of the world with harmony between man and Nature. They provided central place to man in the universe and presented axiological explanation of the world enigma. According to them, ideas and ideals are the acme of education. This idealist trend however, was not opposed to realism, positivism and pragmatism. Therefore a synthesis between all these is possible.

1. Adams J., *The Evolution of Educational Theory*, p. 28.
2. Rusk, R.R., *The Philosophical Bases of Education*, p. 154.

REALISM

The philosophy of realism in almost opposed to that of idealism. According to the realists the world is material in nature. The object and its qualities exist outside the mind and without any necessary relation with it. Thus realist metaphysics is materialism. Its epistemology is positivism and axiology pragmatism. In contemporary Indian philosophy of education one finds a meeting of the extremes of idealism and realism, due to their eclectic and integral approach to thought and life. This meeting of extremes may be found in the educational philosophy of Vivekananda, Dayananda, Sri Aurobindo, Rabindranath Tagore, Gandhi and Radhakrishanan. In the aims and ideals of education they were idealists while their detailed plans of education were based upon realism and pragmatism.

PRAGMATISM

Pragmatism believes that man's first concern is to make this world worthy of human life. Pragmatism is this-worldly. It is against all other-worldly goals. It is pluralistic. It is utilitarian. It lays emphasis upon change as a necessary element of life. It is individualist though emphasising the social aspect of man. It is humanist and experimentalist. In the field of education, the pragmatist trend has led emphasis upon economic, cultural and ethical progress of the individuals so that they may develop characters of world-critizens. This is a sound basis for the creation of a better world in future. Programmes and schemes for social service at different stages of education find an important place in educational institutions today. From time to time, the boys and girls, render social service to the community outside the educational institutions so that they may develop a habit of genuine altruism and social service based upon the value of equality of all human beings.

Contemporary Indian philosophy of education had to be pragmatist since its avowed aim was to present a national system of education suitable for a free country. Contemporary Indian philosophers were very much conversant with the socio-economic problems of Indian masses, their poverty and illiteracy. Therefore, while drawing the details of their schemes of education they everywhere paid attention to making education a means of livelihood while being a means of integral development of human personality. The pragmatic approach is explicit in the advice of Vivekananda to the students to care more for body building than even spiritual development. M. K. Gandhi's scheme of basic education was everywhere guided by pragmatic spirit.

ECLECTICISM

Indian philosophers of education have looked to human personality from an eclectic perspective to discover the inner kernal which is often missed by social sciences. They emphasise the spiritual aspect of man as an integrating principle which alone can boost his future evolution. It is because of an eclectic theory of human nature that Sri Aurobindo, Radhakrishnan, Tagore, and Gandhi advocated an eclectic scheme of education including physical, moral and religious education. "The aim and principles of a true national education." said Sri Aurobindo," "is not certainly to ignore modern truth and knowledge but to take our foundations on our belief, our mind, our own spirit."[1]

Thus contemporary Indian philosophy of education has been characterised by eclecticism. This is because most of its spokesmen, including Aurobindo, Radhakrishnan, Vivekananda, Gandhi and Tagore had a wide and deep knowledge of western science, art, literature and culture and a first hand contact with the West. It is hence that they could compare Eastern thought with Western and reach at an eclectic viewpoint. Thus one finds a meeting of idealism and realism, ancient Indian ideals and modern western principles, nationalism and internationalism, individualism and socialism in their writings. They drew their inspiration from ancient scriptures, Upanishads and Gita.

NATIONALISM

The most powerful expression of the nationalist tendency in education among contemporary Indian thinkers may be found in the educational theory of Swami Vivekananda and Sri Aurobindo. Both these thinkers called patriotism the highest religion. They almost worshiped their motherland. Their reformist schemes in education were inspired by love of the fellow countrymen. They asked the students to work hard and live for the country.

This nationalism however, was spiritual nationalism and therefore was in tune with internationalism. It is what

1. Sri Aurobindo, *The Life Divine*, Vol. II, p. 726

Sri Aurobindo called 'Subjective Nationalism'. Therefore it was free from all the defects of aggressive nationalism seen in the West. In fact it was based upon the ancient Indian ideal of *Swadharma.* According to this ideal, everywhere, in man, nation and humanity the ideal is to follow the *Swadharma.* The humanity itself has a *Swadharma* according to its nature. The idea of *Swadharma* includes respect for the other's *dharma* and the understanding that for everyone his own *dharma* is the best.

HUMANISM

The most important trend incontemporary philosophy of education is humanism. The English word 'humanism' has been derived from the Latin term 'Homo' which means human being. Thus literally speaking, humanism is the philosophy in which man occupies a central place. In historical evolution, whatever has been found to be useful for human welfare has been attached to the concept of humanism such as the idea of social welfare, scientific attitude, progress of democratic institutions, etc. Like the West, humanism was born in India in ancient thought of the Upanishads. These Upanishads show humanistic trends. The metaphysical postulates in Bhagwad Gita are the same as found in the Upanishads. Indian philosophy after the Upanishads and the Gita had been a re-interpretation of the ancient philosophy according to changed circumstances and with difference of emphasis. Not only these orthodox systems but also the heterodox systems as well had their origin in the Upanishads. The contemporary Indian thinkers have developed their thinking on the basis of ancient Upanishadic thought. Thus Sri Aurobindo, Vivekananda, Rabindranath, Gandhi and Dayananda have presented Neo-Vedanta Philosophy according to contemporary conditions in India and in the context of development of thought in the West and East. All these philosophers, with minor differences among them, have maintained what can be called integral humanism, the philosophy of our age which alone supplies the philosophical framework for understanding the problems of education.

The humanist trend in contemporary Indian philosophy of education may be seen in Vivekananda's interpretation of the aim of education as man making. It is clear in Sri Aurobindo's ideal of superman as the aim of future education. It is explicit in Rabindranath Tagore's emphasis upon cosmopolitanism in education. Dayananda considered human welfare as the only ideal of the truth seeker, the teacher and the taught. Similar tendencies may be seen in the educational philosophy of other Indian thinkers.

SYNTHESIS OF RATIONALISM AND INTUITION

Dayananda, Sri Aurobindo, Vivekananda, Rabindranath Tagore and Radhakrishnan follow the ancient tradition according to which aims and ideals, goals and values are intuitive the means are supplied by reason. Swami Dayananda, the great revivalist thinker proposed and adhered to the rationalist principle in the propounding of his famous work *Satyartha Prakash.* He promised that he will not accept anything which is not supported by reason. In Indian, the fields of intuition and reason have been clearly defined and none of the two has been allowed to transgress another's field. Thus, in the field of educational values, for example, intuition is the primary means while reason has to follow the dictates of intuition. Contrary to the western rationalism which makes reason a slave of passions, the Indian thinkers make it subordinate to intuition and always superior to passions. The primary function of reason has been to control the infra-rational passions and tendencies. Upto the mental level reason is the highest law but as one rises above mind reason has to bow its head and acquiesce. Thus the rationalist trend in contemporary Indian philosophy of education is a part of the fundamental integral approach. In the educational philosophy of J.L. Nehru and M.N. Roy, of course, one finds a tendency towards western type of rationalism, but at places they have also agreed about the value of intuition and other sources of human knowledge.

INTEGRALISM

Contemporary Indian philosophers of education Sir Aurobindo, Vivekananda, Rabindranath, Gandhi and Dayananda depict an integral approach in philosophy. "The work of philosophy," says Sri Aurobindo, "is to arrange the data given by the various means of knowledge, excluding none, and put them into a synthetic relation to one truth, the one supreme and universal reality."[1] Thus, these philosophers believe in a monistic, idealistic and integral philosophy. There is one spirit underlying matter, life and

1. Aurobindo, S., *The Renaissance in India*, p. 72.

mind in the world. This spirit is the reality while man, nature and God are its triple manifestation. In the words of Radhakrishnan, "It is the basis and background of our being, the universality that cannot be reduced to this or that formula."[1] This spirit evolves in the form of the universe. This evolution is not linear, dialectical or emergent but spiral. To quote Bhagwan Das, "The words 'evolution' and 'involution' embody, with instinctive correctness, the idea that these processes are forth and back, circling and cycling in a spiral."[2]

To realise this spirit Indian philosophers have utilised intuitive method. This is spiritual intuition, distinct from physical, mental or vital intuitions. According to Bhagwan Das, "It is the immediate condition or rather awareness of the self by the self, eternal self-consciousness."[3] In the words of Radhakrishnan, "The deepest things of life are known only through intuitive apprehension."[4] Thus contemporary Indian philosophers have advocated the use of intuitive method in order to arrive at an integral philosophy of education.

Contemporary Indian philosophers have looked to human personality from an integral perspective. They have maintained an integral theory of human nature. It is because of this that Sri Aurobindo, Vivekananda, Rabindranath, Gandhi and Dayananda have advocated a multisided scheme of education including education for physical mental, social, moral and religious development of the male and female. To formulate such a scheme of education, these philosophers borrowed both from ancient Indian wisdom and modern western scientific knowledge. This was the basis of the international universities founded by Rabindranath and Sri Aurobindo. In the words of Sri Aurobindo. "The aim and principles of a true national education are not certainly to ignore modern truth and knowledge but to take our foundations on our own belief, our own mind, our own spirit."[5]

1. Radhakrishnan, S., *An Idealist View of Life*, p. 205.
2. Bhagwan Das, *The science of the self* p. 44.
3. *Ibid*, p. 137 footnote.
4. Radhakrishnan, S., *An Idealsit View of Life.*, p. 142.
5. Aurobindo, S., *Integral Education*, compiled by Dr. Indrasen, p. 4.

Question Bank

PHILOSOPHY OF EDUCATION

Q. 1. Why should a teacher study educational philosophy? Would not educational psychology do?

Or

Discuss whether there is a need for a philosophy of education over and above a science of education.

Q. 2. Discuss and elucidate, "All educational questions are ultimately questions of philosophy"—Ross.

Or

"Education is the dynamic side of philosophy." Discuss.

Or

"Education may be regarded as the practical side of philosophy and philosophy as the intellectual aspect of education." How far do you agree with this statement? Give reasons.

Or

"Both philosophy and education go hand in hand. Education depends on philosophy for its guidance and philosophy depends on education for its own formulation". Discuss.

Q. 3. What is Philosophy of Education? Discuss its scope and nature.

Q. 4. Point out the fields of Education in which a teacher needs philosophy.

Q. 5. Discuss the Methodology of Philosophy of Education.

Q. 6. Explain the need of Philosophy of Education in Modern Times.

Q. 7. "Idealism in one form or another permeates the history of education the world over." Discuss and explain important characteristics of idealism.

Q. 8. Discuss idealist aims and ideals in education.

Q. 9. Write short note on Idealist Curriculum.

Q. 10. What is the role of an educator according to idealism? Explain idealist educational methods.

Q. 11. Write short note on Idealist Concept of Discipline.

Q. 12. Point out the influence of Idealism in the contemporary field of education. Show the disadvantages of Idealism.

Q. 13. Trace the history of Naturalism in education. Point out its philosophical presuppositions and philosophical forms.

Q. 14. Write short note on Naturalist Educational Methods.

Q. 15. What is the role of a teacher according to Naturalism? Discuss its concept of discipline and school organisation.

Q 16. Analyze the contribution of Naturalism to education. What criticisms have been levelled against it?

Q. 17. Explain the fundamental principles and forms of Pragmatism.

Q. 18. Evaluate the contribution of Pragmatism to education.

Q. 19. Explain the aim of education and principle of curriculum according to Pragmatism.

Q. 20. What is the role of education according to Pragmatism? Explain pragmatic educational methods and discipline.

Q. 21. Write a short note on Criticism against Pragmatism.

Q. 22. Discuss Realist Philosophy of Education.

Q. 23. Discuss educational implication of Logical positivism. Assess its contribution to philosophy of education.

Q. 24. What is Existentialism? What are its chief characteristics? Explain Existential philosophy of education.

Q. 25. What is Humanism? What are its essentials? Discuss its contribution to education.

Q. 26. Discuss Rousseau's contribution to Naturalist philosophy of education.

Q. 27. Write an essay on John Dewey's philosophy of education.

Q. 28. What criticisms have been levelled against Dewey's philosophy of education? Discuss his influence on modern education.

Q. 29. Discuss Bertrand Russell's philosophy of education.

Q. 30. Write short note on Vedic philosophy of education.

Q. 31. Explain the role and influence of teacher in Vedic philosophy of education.

Q. 32. How has Buddhism continued Brahmanical tradition in education? How does Buddhist philosophy of education differ from it? Summarize Buddhist contribution to education.

Q. 33. Discuss the condition of education under Muslim Rulers.

Q. 34. Discuss Dayananda's contribution to education.

Q. 35. Explain Annie Besant's philosophy of education and assess her contribution in education.

Q. 36. Critically discuss the Aims and Ideals of Gandhi's philosophy of education.

Q. 37. Write an essay on M. K. Gandhi's Education for Sarvodaya.

Q. 38. Discuss the characteristics of Gandhiji' s educational plan. Give a critical evaluation.

Q 39. Examine Rahindra Nath Tagore's philosophy of education and its influence on Indian education.

Or

Explain the philosophical thinking behind Tagore's scheme of education in Shanti Niketan. How has its character changed now? Why?

Q. 40. Discuss the aims of education according to R.N. Tagore.

Q. 41. How has Vivekananda criticised prevalent system of education? Discuss aims of education according to him.

Q. 42. Discuss the means, types and medium of education according to Vivekananda.

Q. 43. Discuss teaching methods in various types of education according to Vivekananda.

Q. 44. Discuss the nature of education envisaged by Aurobindo.

Q. 45. Write a short note on Principles of Sri Aurobindo's New Education.

Q. 46. Explain Sri Aurobindo's concept of the School and the Teacher.

Q. 47. Discuss Sri. Aurobindo's criteria, for planning curricula. Give a tentative educational plan.

Q 48. Describe Sri Aurobindo's methods and principles of

teaching.

Q. 49. Elaborate the various elements of Integral Teaching according to Sri Aurobindo.

Q. 50. What are the characteristics of Socialism? Give, the outline of an educational programme for realizing the objectives of Socialism.

Q. 51. What is Fascism? Explain how political ideologies influence educational aims, curriculum and methods with reference to Fascist approach.

Q. 52. What is Marxism? How has it influenced educational theory and practice?

Q. 53. Explain Secularism. Does it go against religious ideas in schools? Justify your answer.

Or

"Secularism acquaints the child with the basic principles of human values." Explain this statement.

Or

Define Secularism. Identify the characteristics of secular education. Give plan, for secular education in India pointing out the difficulties in it.